# Melancolia Poetica

# Melancolia Poetica

A Dual Language Anthology of Italian Poetry 1160-1560

Marc A. Cirigliano

*t*

*Published by*
Troubador Publishing Ltd
9 De Montfort Mews
Leicester LE1 7FW, UK
Tel: (+44) 116 255 9311
Email: books@troubador.co.uk
Web: www.troubador.co.uk

**Series Editor**
Professor George Ferzoco
University of Leicester, UK

**ISBN: 978-1905886-821**

Typesetting: Troubador Publishing Ltd, Leicester, UK

*For my family*

# Table of Contents

# Forward

This volume, which embraces some of the poetry of the late Middle Ages and Renaissance in Italy, is a broad based dual language anthology intended for use either in Italian language and literature classes, or for self-study and enjoyment by the interested general reader. The theme of this anthology, *melancolia poetica*, is meant to stimulate free spirited face-to-face or online discussions about the nature of late medieval and Renaissance Italian poetry, authorial intentionality and any reader's considered response, the significance of the poems themselves or, perhaps most essentially, poetry itself. As with all anthologies, specialists in the field will find some poets and poems omitted that they would have included. Any shortcomings, limitations, errors or omissions are due to me and me alone.

A number of friends and colleagues advised, admonished and encouraged me during the long but fruitful winter of preparing this tome. My dear friend and mentor, Sidney Thomas, offered suggestions and encouragement all along my way through *i più deserti campi*. I am very thankful to Julia Koberlein for casting her fine editor's eye over much of the manuscript. Tim Shaw and Brian Koberlein offered encouragement and even threats when my enthusiasm started to flag. Bob Milton, Seth Oppenheimer, Irene Rivera de Royston, Jackie Eddy and Frank Macomber also encouraged my work. Above all, my dear wife Lindy and two sons Dan and Matt were at my side the entire time.

Two quick bits of advice for the student of literature in general and of poetry in particular: keep, what Karl Popper described so well, an open mind, and use as your foundation Coleridge's positive notion of genial criticism – i.e., exploring as one who loves literature – when you read, analyze and re-read. As well, remember the central quality that Leonardo said was the key to success in any endeavor: diligence.

**Marc A. Cirigliano**

# Preface

## Francesca Santuzzi
*Bergamo*


They have the tone of fairy-tales those so-called 'Dark Ages,' those medieval ones, because they speak of dark castles, of fortresses descended from imperial lineage, of gigantic walls, of dark secrets, of foreboding drawbridges, or hostile enemies, of belligerent sovereigns, of heroic knights, of plaintive princesses, of sad minstrels with winged words—thus Italy, from north to south, is covered with castles.

And there is a region in the deep south of Italy, Basilicata, land of peasants, rough, with melancholy rivers, romantic rocky villages on jagged mountains…Those are the most savage and saddest places of that province; the beauty of the horrible is there fused in depth; Basilicata portends Calabria, however without having neither all the sublime majesty of her, nor all the calm and varied beauty of the other provinces…so commented the illustrious traveler of the Ottocento, the Piedmontese writer Iginio Ugo Tarchetti in his book One in Love with the Mountains. A country that boasts ancient origins, existing before the time of the Romans, with a castle possessing an evocative tower, this land calls itself Cirigliano, presumably from Caerellius, the name of Roman centurion on whose property it rose. And it is here that one finds the roots of the family of Marc Cirigliano, art historian, passionate scholar of early Italian literature and art, who, in his latest book, Melancolia poetica, proposes to enlighten us with his poetic journey.

> Canzonetta novella,
> va' canta nova cosa;
> lèvati da maitino
> davanti a la più bella…
> *Giacomo da Lentini*

The Middle Ages, depicted in history books as the time beginning with the fall of Rome to the discovery of America, has been tinged as a dark age, sprinkled with violence, barbarism and superstition.

It was in the Trecento, with the scholarly detachment of their age, that the humanists called it 'Gothic' and 'barbarous.' And so, we began to speak of the Middle Ages in negative terms, with Petrarch defining the period as 'dark,' with the only way out being a return to classical Latin and canons of classical art. Today, of course, we have superceded these preconceptions that held for so long the idea that the Middle Ages were only the theater for battles, sacks and wars, an infinite succession of popes, kings and emperors, and constant diplomatic negotiations. Modern criticism agrees in establishing, underscoring and reevaluating all that was spiritual, linguistic, literary, artistic, political, economic and social produced with great vitality, giving life, between ferment and contradictions, to a complex civilization that enabled the growth of humanity. For these reasons, the Middle Ages, often seen as a disjointed era preparing for the splendors of the Renaissance, is one of the most interesting and controversial periods in Italian and European history.

Artistically expressed, through Gothic Art, aesthetic values and ethics of the highest understanding, it arrived philosophically at incredible speculative summits. From an economic point of view, it spurred a recovery that broadly improved the standard of living. Because they were so essential to commerce, travel and trade increased.

It was a time that gave birth to our national languages we still use today. Universities arose that were, both then and now, essential centers of learning, where law and jurisprudence were amplified and extended the idea of the city. The greatest masterpieces of art were realized that served as the foundation for Italy and all subsequent nations of Europe. With political institutions, as well as economic and cultural dominion, the age granted an engagement of city and countryside, and of the Classical Antiquity and the barbarians who lived on its borders, but ended by burning and then integrating themselves in it.

And in many other minor ways can we find a continuity with those times, as in the use of certain herbs to cure disease, or the way we celebrate holidays or express certain feelings. We can, then, discover, to our surprise, that that 'dark' past continues to shine today and that its antique heart pulses now more strongly than ever.

★   ★   ★

Literature is the entire universe in which we observe the complexity of human life, a document of the conscience of a people or the individuals who make a people. It consists of messages that we dare not lose, that transmit through the centuries, that are collected by its heirs whose individual and communal sensibilities have been conditioned by it, nourished by layers of literary suggestions across the centuries. Therefore …*the visions of Dante or the dreams of Quixote, the torment and redemption of Faust, the night of love between Romeo and Juliet, the palpitations of Tristan and Isolde on the enchanted boat, the hallucinations of Raskolnikov or the languid troubles of Madame Bovary, all determine, in some way, our daily lives, ideally and personally, even if we never have a direct knowledge of those texts.*[1]

And in the course of the 12th and 13th centuries we can find the beginning of some of the principles of European literature, that do not rise suddenly from the rough and primitive, but which rise from many centuries of culture in they were nourished by noble philosophical, spiritual and literary experiences. At the beginning of the Duecento began the flowering of our literature in *lingua volgare* as in French and Provencal, both of which influenced the birth and growth of our first literary texts. It was at the court of Frederick II, German Emperor who lived almost exclusively in Palermo, where, for the first time our literary idiom appeared. Not just spoken, but actually written, the Italian language, *il volgare*, was the presupposition of our linguistic unity and national language, which, until that moment, had been Latin, the language of the learned.[2]

At his court, the poets of the so-called Sicilian School, among whom were Giacomo da Lentini, Rinaldo d'Aquino, Pier delle Vigne and Frederck II himself, inspiring themselves with the themes and forms of Provencal poetry, solidify love poetry, elaborating metric models and styles that they developed quickly, like the sonnet, that they gradually enrich linguistically and thematically.

Next, Tuscany becomes the center of poetry. Here, courtly love, sung by the Sicilians, altered by the Provencal poets, rounds itself out with political, moral and philosophical implications. Dante, Petrarca and Boccaccio, the three crowns of the Trecento, give *il volgare* a very finished literary mantle and a decidedly national character. Above all, the great Florentine, Dante, a name that no one in Italy can ignore, a colossus of world literature, father of our language and greatest of the poets, who, at the distance of centuries, is still worthy of scholars and lovers of poetry. With his masterpiece, *La Commedia*, renamed "Divine" by Boccaccio, Dante traces philosophical and existential travails, as well as impassioned politics of his Florence and his Italy.

On Dante, another great Italian poet, Carducci expressed: *he reunited the doctrine of art … he sung of the oldest things in life, the highest thoughts of humanity, the loftiest secrets of the soul. The name of our people flies and extends centuries into the future like the glories of the Campidoglio and the name of Rome.*[3]

Not influenced by ultramontane literature, religious poetry, with its cornerstone, St. Francis' Canticle, produced hymns for common use, often anonymous, but also praiseful ones for personal use, with a high level of expression, as with Jacopone di Todi. It was also here in the late Middle Ages, where they continued the concept of life that was founded in the early Middle Ages: on religion, theology and morality. It was at this point, where art teaches the truth under the guise of allegory, that we begin to value the earthly aspects of humanity: politics, economic interests, etc.

Then, the greater part of poets felt the need to write on both religious and earthly themes, torn between what was ascetic and what was human. The early Middle Ages were now superceded, past the impoverishment into which it had fallen, when education and culture had declined, with the only cultivated people being monks, who reaffirmed the passionate love of knowing, the respect for Latin and Greek culture and its classics. It was now to Humanism, at the beginning of the Renaissance, a luminous period in which Italy, escaping from medieval distress, shone brightly, learned, with cultured and literate leaders in comparison to other countries of the Quattrocento.

★　★　★

With a fascinating voyage rendered in agile and gliding form, Marc Cirigliano, in his bilingual poetic anthology, *Melancolia poetica*, has prepared an exploratory voyage through our most significant and richest period of Italian poetry, between 1160 and 1560, between the late Middle Ages, Humanism and the Renaissance. Privileging the theme that titles this book, Melancholy,[4] we have a term well explained by the author in his introduction that does not have the meaning then that it has in the 20th century: a sentimental and pessimistic abandonment to sadness, but a word typical of the 'comic' style, which indicated, like in its original Greek etymology, black bile, the dark and despiteful humor, a state of ire derived from the impossibility of enjoying sensual and earthly pleasures. With an elegant style, the author succeeds in an alluring but equally accessible rendering for the non-specialist, a poetic dictation of the *volgare italiano*.

Beginning with the *Ritmo laurenziano*, across religious and comic poetry, the Sicilian School, Dante and the *Stil nuovo*, Petrarchism, Humanism, into the mature Renaissance, the *Certame coronario*, Lorenzo il Magnifico, Pico, Raphael, Michelangelo and Ludovico Ariosto. Women's poetry was a genre that decisively stopped under the patriarchal Romans and during the early Middle Ages, ages that both denied women a literary identity. When women reappear in the 12th century with the Trobaritzes in Provence, we begin to see the rise of a feminist consciousness and significant contributions to poetry. Marc Cirigliano includes many substantial presences such as the Anonima poetessa, La Compiuta Donzella, Lucrezia Tornabuoni de' Medici, Barbara Torelli, Veronica Gambara, and Vittoria Colonna, about whom Michelangelo wrote *Un uomo in una donna, anzi uno dio*.

Of great value and noble intent, the learned work here is not only for students, with research and documentation to nurture them, but also for the accurate translations themselves of these significant poets. Here we have the most beautiful verses of Italian poetry in a collection that will disseminate the enormous riches of the early centuries of Italian poetry, our national patrimony, a testimony to the evolution of the human spirit. Faced with their grandeur, we, like Vasari before us, must exclaim: *Truly the heavens have sent us those who do not represent humanity alone, but divinity itself.*[6]

# Notes

1. L. Santucci, *Letteratura italiana*, "Le origini," Edizione Fabbri.

2. It is right to point out to an other hypothesis. According to the interesting studies of Abbot Vincenzo Galiani, in his book *On the Neapolitan dialect*, written with Gian Vincenzo Meola and published anonymously in 1799, the first poetry in *il volgare* was called 'Sicilian,' because it originated from the court of the king of Sicily, Federico II. In truth, the dialect they used was the Neapolitan, then named Pugliese because, at that time, the most important state of southern Italy was Puglia.

3. Galiani's thesis is supported by the large number of Neapolitan words, descending directly from Latin, found again in many places from the origins of *il volgare* and in the Dante himself. For historical and political causes the supremacy of the Neapolitan dialect then lost, but is sure that *poesia volgare* was born Neapolitan, was called Sicilian and then developed Tuscan.

4. From the lecture "L'opera di Dante", given by Carducci in Rome on January 8, 1888.

5. In the *Ottocento*, the writer Ugo Tarchetti still used the term "melancholy" in its late medieval and Renaissance sense in his poetry "Retrospettive": Oggi di negro umor mi son svegliato/esco di casa, e lunghesso la via/due demoni cavalcanmi allato: /il mal d'amore e la malinconia.

6. A Vittoria Colonna, *dalle Rime di Michelangelo*.

7. *Vite dei pittori, scultori ed architetti celebri*, G. Vasari.

# Introduction: A Poem in the Making

People have always loved the poetic word. The symbiotic impulses of creating and experiencing verse are universal human urges. No matter the language, no matter the age, no matter the subject – there has always been poetry. The apt assemblage of words, the sonorous sound of their utterance, the influence they exercise over creator and audience – these are the stuff of poetry, one of the great achievements of the human mind spurred on by the human soul.

No such less an achievement was the poetry created on the Italian peninsula during the rise of the great cities from the 12th through the 16th centuries, from the origins of Italian as a vernacular language through the Duecento, Trecento, Quattrocento and Cinquecento. Sometimes part of music, sometimes composed for a letter or on a folio leaf in a manuscript, sometimes printed on a page in a book – later ages would find in the Italian poetry of the late Middle Ages and Renaissance an unending source of inspiration for their own art, music, literature, poetry and ideas.

## With Quill in Hand

The writing instrument from 700 AD to 1700 in the West was the quill pen. The best were made from one of the five outer feathers of a left wing of a living bird in springtime. Left wing feathers were preferred because they curved to fit the right hand – the correct hand to use since the left hand was seen as a sign of evil – hence the adjective from the Latin root for left, sinister. Ink was improved in the 9th century when tannic acid and an iron salt, usually ferrous sulfate, were mixed. Gum arabic was added to improve the consistency of the ink and hold it in place once stroked on either parchment or, later, paper.

The writing medium of choice for the Middle Ages was either parchment or vellum. Parchment was made from the skin of cows or sheep, vellum from young calves. Taken from a slaughtered animal – all parts of which were used for everything from food, textiles, and leather, to glue – the skin was soaked in a solution of lime. It was then stretched, dried in the sun and scraped to remove the hair and flesh so that it was very thin. If necessary, they might dye it – purple, for instance – then cut it into rectangles. The skin was then polished with pumice and treated with chalk to prevent the ink from running. Assembled into a codex, sheets were then lined for writing by pricking holes in them and making lines. Writing, by the way, was often not done on the lines, but hung from them.

The writing and printing medium that gradually displaces parchment and vellum beginning in the 12th century was paper. By 105 AD the Chinese developed paper to substitute for writing on either bark and bamboo strips or silk. The Chinese used a mixture of plant bark, discarded cotton and old fishnets overlaid on a screen. When dry, the product was a solid, light and flexible sheet that was a wonderful new medium for ink and paint. The Arabs learned the recipe for paper in the 8th century, with its use spreading to Moorish Spain by the 11th century. In the Duecento, Italians built paper mills near Naples. By the late Duecento, the Fabriano paper mills in Tuscany invented the watermark that would become a sign of high quality paper. By the mid-14th century, paper was abundant not only in Italy, but in much of Europe, helping to transform not only the written word with its availability for personal correspondence and incunabula – early printed books – but the art of drawing, with, for the first time, the practice of doing preparatory sketches for painting and sculpture.

The combination of affordable rag paper and increasing literacy met the growing need for increased documentation as trade, commerce, manufacturing and civic government developed apace. These new secular needs meant that now the Church scriptoria no longer had a virtual monopoly on literacy and the written word. By 1454, Joannes Gutenberg, a goldsmith and business man from Mainz in south Germany, saw the financial and expressive possibilities the new age afforded and invented the printing press with movable type, one of the defining moments of the Renaissance. He accomplished this revolution in human communication by transforming what he knew of the printing of patterns on textiles, wine presses and the new medium of paper into the new medium of printing on paper with movable type.

## Into Deep Contemplation

The poet is in him or herself. With human life seen as an on-going flux between the *vita activa*, or life of acting in the world, and the *vita contemplativa*, or life of contemplation, deep thought was linked to the contemplative life and its accompanying state of the human soul: *melancholia,* or as we translate it into English, melancholy. In the 20th century, melancholy has come to mean a state of sadness or even depression. In the late Middle Ages and Renaissance, it had a different meaning. The people of the late Middle Ages and Renaissance believed that human beings consisted of four possible temperaments, each of which was caused by one of the four humors: the sanguine, the airy springtime humor characterized cheerfulness and strength caused by the presence of much blood in the system; the phlegmatic, the watery winter temperament typified by slowness and apathy caused by excess mucous; the choleric, the fiery summertime disposition producing an angry, violent personality caused by too much yellow bile; and, the melancholic, the earthy autumnal type embodying the solitary, contemplative individual associated with black bile.

Melancolia was used not only to describe a certain type of personality, it was seen as the root cause of aesthetic creation. Petrarch described himself with the qualities associated with melancholy, even though he might have used the term acedia in its place. Saxl, Panofsky and Kilbansky write: "That Petrarch should have felt melancholy before he called himself so....shows most plainly that for the Renaissance the connexion (sic) of melancholy with genius was no mere cultural reminiscence, but a reality which was experienced long before its humanistic and literary formulation." Further along this line of thinking, Boccaccio, who wrote the first major biography of Dante, characterized him as "malinconico e pensoso."[1]

In one of his sonnets Dante tells of meeting the personification of Malinconia, a woman dressed in black, accompanied by both Discord and Suffering, who bears the news that his beloved Beatrice is dead. In the context of Dante's narrative about his relationship with Beatrice, it is Melancholy who gives him news that will: (1) Separate him from society and others. (2) Make him ponder his sorrow. (3) Bring him to write poetry in order to deal with the unceasing eruption of emotions predicated on his loss. As a causative effect of the creative act, melancholy does several tangible things. First, since it brought with it contemplation, there was, by extension, a rejection, temporary at least, of worldly goods and pleasures. This is a necessary prelude to focusing on something that deals with the cognitive. Second, there was the idea of being alone, of experiencing solitude, which enables the creative individual to focus on the project at hand instead of socializing. Finally, there was the idea of engaging in profound thought about an intellectual problem. The ideal of the medieval thought process was to think of God. The ideal of the Renaissance was to think for one's self about one's self and one's peers. The former was religious, the latter humanistic. But for both, to be melancholic meant turning away from the world to experience the life of the mind.

## The Well of Ancient Experience

This melancholy, when turned toward aesthetic contemplation and activity, was governed by the two constantly intertwined tensions of *imitazione* and *invenzione*. *Imitazione*, or imitation, meant the practice of imitating or emulating the masterworks of Antiquity. *Invenzione* was the idea of creating something new, something never before conceived. With the former, ancient authority is held as both a standard by which anything new is measured and a model that serves as a point of departure for any new aesthetic endeavor. With the latter, such authority is rejected in favor of coming up with something original, something never before created. Neither *imitazione* nor *invenzione* existed without the influence of the other. The best works of literature always had an inventive quality, while at the same time openly emulated aspects of a particular work (or works) from Antiquity, specifically Italy's ancient Roman heritage. That they focused on the applications of this knowledge for the conduct of human life makes us call it humanism.

The grandeur of Ancient Rome lived on in the minds of the both Italians and other Europeans well after the last Roman Emperor in the West was deposed by a barbarian chieftain in 476. In the 6th century, Justinian attempted to restore the Empire on a politically fractured peninsula. On Christmas day in 800, Charlemagne was crowned Holy Roman Emperor by Pope Leo III in St. Peter's Basilica in another attempt to restore the Empire. In the Duecento, Frederick II, with his strategy of annexing the cities of the *Regnum Italicum*, attempted to restore the Empire on a peninsula that had been politically divided for over seven centuries. In 1347, Cola di Rienzo overthrew the ruling Roman aristocracy and attempted to restore the ancient Roman Republic. His reign lasted only seven months.

Although each of these attempts ended in failure, it is understandable that people would dream of restoring political unity to both the Italian peninsula and former European, African and Middle Eastern provinces that made up the Empire. Simple things the Romans took for granted appeared almost too good to be true to the chaotic world of medieval Italy. Roman roads, even in a deteriorated state, continued in use well after the Empire's collapse. In fact, travel in Europe was never as facile and quick after the Empire until the advent of the railroads in the 19th century. Further, under the Empire, the peninsula did not suffer the numerous foreign invasions it did in the Middle Ages. During the height of the Empire, Italy not only ruled the lands of the area known as the Mediterranean Basin, but dominated the sea as well. Finally, to the eyes of medieval Italians, the ruins of Roman architecture, feats of grandeur in design and engineering, were a daily reminder of a society whose culture seemed far superior to that of their own time.

If the emulation of Rome was in mind, so was the idea of doing something new, the idea of engaging in *invenzione*. Dante speaks of his *vita nuova*, or new life, in his work, *La vita nuova*. His life is new in several senses. He is transformed by his love for Beatrice. Aesthetically, he will relate the effects of this love in the vernacular, the spoken dialect of Florence, rather than in the traditional Latin. Poetically, he expresses himself personally, not anonymously, with both feeling and philosophical reflection. Petrarch, too, though aware of both pagan and Christian ancients in his work, speaks of walking alone, doing something new, avoiding what others have done. He is also alone and thoughtful while doing it – hence, he is both melancholy and innovative, as we see in the opening quatrain of his famous sonnet, Solo et pensoso i più deserti campi:

Alone and pensive the most deserted fields
I go measuring with slow, hesitant steps—
I keep my eyes alert to avoid
any human trace in the sand.

## The Universe as It Was Known

An Italian of the late Middle Ages would have had ideas about the universe and the individual that were very different from our contemporary ones. Today our universe is hypothesized as an infinite universe existing with an infinity of other infinite universes. We have come to view the individual as a personality, a distinct identity grappling for existence and fulfillment in a given social milieu. Not only do we entertain the possibility of an infinity of universes, but we also recognize that there are many different societies, many different personality types and, most importantly for our purposes here, many different value systems. By contrast, Europeans of the late Middle Ages and Renaissance held to the Ptolemaic idea that the earth was the fixed, immovable center of a single universe. They thought that seven heavenly bodies – the Moon, Mercury, Venus, the Sun, Mars, Jupiter and Saturn – orbited around it. At the outer edge of these orbits, they believed the entire universe was surrounded by the fixed stars of the Empyrean and, ultimately, the Primum Mobile. As an extension of this fixity, they believed, more or less, that there was one correct culture, that of Christianity, which provided everything one needed to know about values. Humankind, who had inherited the original sin committed by Adam and Eve, was destined, as a result of this sin, not only to commit more sins, but also suffer pain, work for its livelihood and never reach perfection in any undertaking. Any hope of redemption from sin and a reunion with God in the afterlife was predicated on thinking good thoughts, carrying out good acts and receiving the blessing of the Church – all to be done in this life.

## Imperfection and Mortality

After the collapse of the western Roman Empire in 476 AD, the medieval Church developed into the most powerful, most organized and most temporally consistent institution in Europe. Before the Church was founded, before religion became sanctioned by the Roman Empire in the 4th century, the Early Christian community consisted of small, independent groups usually defined by an urban neighborhood. Membership within these neighborhood groups usually cut across class lines, with upper and lower classes trying to work together in the mutual care of each member of the group. Early Christian practice emphasized the beneficent aspects of Christ's teaching, the idea that we are here to help one another in a peaceful, unselfish way. This does, however, change after the faith became the official state religion in the 4th century. Church doctrine comes to emphasize another set of ideas contained in the Bible – namely, humanity's need for official guidance in understanding Christ's teachings since original sin and the fall from grace had rendered its understanding imperfect. In reinforcing this scriptural interpretation of humanity's imperfection, the Church developed an argument out of Neoplatonic philosophy upon which all subsequent Church doctrine was built. The Church specifically argued that heaven was immutable and unchanging, that it contained all the eternal ideas that God had created of which all things on earth were imperfect copies. Among those perfect ideas was the concept of an ideal human being, a perfect archetype for humanity. Since humanity on earth was an imperfect copy of that perfect idea, it was of one type or form. It stood to reason, then, that an institution, the Church, or even an individual, the Pope, could represent all human beings as one in the face of God. Since humanity essentially had a debt to pay because of original sin, the Church contended that it was authorized both biblically and philosophically to oversee the repayment. In both theory and practice, the Church had the enviable intellectual position of promoting the idea that it had divine charge over the human race.

## Seeing the City Abustle

Yet, much of this was in the process of being supplanted by new social, economic, political and philosophical forces. Change was afoot. In the 8th, 9th and 10th centuries, the economy and culture, or more accurately, the economies and cultures of Europe were rural and local. After 1000, they would gradually become more urban and international, with feudalism gradually giving way to commercialism. Feudal lords, each of who ruled a self-sustaining agricultural territory called a manor, saw their respective authority and power diminish in the face of growing cities ruled by merchants who made, bought and sold goods for money.

This change was begun by something as simple as the invention of a new plow, which was capable of digging a deeper furrow. This plow was, in turn, hooked to a new shoulder harness that allowed horses to be linked together in many numbers to pull strongly without, as the traditional yokes had done, choking. Those who worked the land discovered a three-tier system of farming based on an annual rotation of two crops over three fields, with one field annually left fallow. In addition, the bulk of crops no longer consisted solely of grains, but included protein rich legumes.

More and better food meant more people. It also meant, in many instances, a surplus that could be traded for something you couldn't make for yourself. This gave rise to villages, town and cities. Peasants went to the cities to barter their produce or seek new employment, forsaking the crowded feudal manors with their "lords" who claimed divinely sanctioned superiority. In the cities, merchants traded with each other. Cities traded internationally. The first three Crusades (1095-1192) contributed to this growth, as well. After 1100, Venice, Pisa and Genoa developed trading posts in the newly created European state, the Kingdom of Jerusalem. New merchant classes in Venice, Genoa, Pisa, Florence and Milan traded the goods they bought from Moslems in the Middle East to wool manufacturers in the Flemish towns of Ghent and Bruges. An indication of the newly created wealth at this time is the fact that Pisa constructed a massive cathedral between 1068-1118 and enlarged it in 1158. The Venetians built St. Mark's Basilica between 1063-73. In this new urban environment, a city-state the Italians would call a *comune*, the new workers, new merchants, new artisans and new professionals were in a relatively free environment where they were no longer under the control of either the Church or a feudal lord.

## Free to Write

Between the 12th and 14th centuries, the northern Italian cities, known as the *Regnum Italicum*, developed a new concept by which they justified their own autonomy and method of government: liberty. By the early 12th century, northern Italy contained a number of city-states that de facto denied the authority of the Holy Roman Emperor, even though they recognized *de jure* that he still ruled them. At the root of this new political development was the rejection of the principle of hereditary monarchy. Pisa in 1085, Milan in 1097, Arezzo in 1098, and Lucca, Bologna and Siena by 1125 each elected their own local form of government, a local council that asserted each city's right to *merum Imperium*, or pure and complete sovereignty.[2]

Beginning with the German Emperor Otto I in the 10th century, the *Regnum Italicum* was considered part and parcel of the Holy Roman Empire. By mid-12th century, Emperor Frederick Barbarossa wanted the northern Italian communes in the Imperial fold because they flaunted their independence in his face and, perhaps more to the point, possessed great riches and power. Barbarossa gained against the cities in his first campaign, but was forced at the end of his second, by the newly formed Lombard League with 30 cities as members, to release any claim to them by signing the Peace of Constance in 1183. The next Emperor, Frederick II, won initial military victories against the League, but he, too, had setbacks when he lost his treasure in defeat at Vittoria in 1248, had his son captured by hostile armies at Modena in 1249 and died in 1250.

In the course of this struggle, the communes developed new intellectual weapons against the Emperor's claims. Above all, they developed a new concept of law. At the end of the 11th century, the Roman Code of Justinian became the basis for law in the Holy Roman Empire. The jurists of the universities of Bologna and Ravenna – the so-called Glossators – followed Justinian's Code literally, so that the Emperor's authority over the territory of the Empire was in theory recognized. A northern Italian jurist, Bartolo of Sassoferrato (1314-57), changed all of this. Bartolo argued that the primary assumption of the Glossators was incorrect. The Glossators held that when the law does not correspond to the facts, the facts must be made to accord with the literal interpretation of the law. Bartolo, instead, put forth the revolutionary idea that the law should correspond to the facts. Therefore, regarding the Emperor's claim, since the communes had *de facto* been ruling themselves for quite a while, they could claim their own liberty, with each commune independent of any other authority and with each selecting its own means of government.

The central political ally of the communes in their struggle against the Emperor was the Papacy. Alexander III helped fund the Lombard League when it was begun in 1167. Alexander also led the League's attack against Barbarossa in 1174 and initiated the negotiations that led to the Peace of Constance in 1183. The alliance was used again when Frederick II invaded the *Regnum Italicum* in the 1230s. Gregory IX finalized the anti-Imperial treaty with Venice and Genoa in 1238 and then excommunicated the Emperor the next year. After becoming pope in 1243, Innocent IV attacked the Emperor's troops in Lombardy and also encouraged Tuscan communes to be more anti-Imperialist. The peril of a strategy of using the Papacy as a financial, political and military counterweight to the Emperor soon became obvious. The Popes wanted to rule the *Regnum Italicum* themselves. In fact, by the end of the thirteenth century, the Papacy had used both its promise of military aid against the Emperor and internal schisms within individual communes to place a large area of central Italy under its control and expand its influence over much of the *Regnum*. The papacy bolstered this expansionist policy with an intellectual framework developed by Gratian in the 1140s. Gratian condensced the accumulated Papal Decrees to a system, founding the concept of canon law in the process. At the root of this legal philosophy was the idea that the Pope had the right and duty to exercise political authority in addition to his spiritual authority. Indeed in 1302, Boniface VIII, following the chain of authority developed by his forerunners, issued his Bull *Unam Sanctum*, in which he stated "two swords, the spiritual and temporal" should be unified under the Vicar of Christ, "that the temporal should be subordinate to the spiritual power" because "the spiritual power possesses the authority to institute earthly power and to stand in judgment over it if it should fail to act properly."

Not surprisingly, the communes began to strike back. In 1266, Padua began a dispute with its local churches over their refusal to pay taxes. In 1282, Padua literally deprived its clergy of protection of the law. In 1281, Orvieto had an uprising over the presence of the Curia, and in 1284, had an even larger revolt on its hands. In 1285, Florence denounced Church courts. In 1286, clerical immunities were attacked in Pisa. During this time, the Florentine 'Whites' fought to hold off papal influence, opposing the pro-papal 'Blacks.'

## The Birth of Modern Political Ideas

Such writers as Dino Compagni (c.1255-1324), Dante Alighieri and Marsiglio of Padua (c.1275-1342) intellectually supported the cities' anti-papal claims. In his *Chronicle*, Compagni argued that the Emperor would be 'more just' in his rule than the pope. Dante was more elaborate. In his *De Monarchia*, Dante argued that 'universal peace' was the goal of mankind. This was prevented, in the main, because the legitimacy of the Empire was denied and because the false notion 'that the authority of the Empire depends upon the authority of the Church.' Dante argued that the popes had no real temporal power. The problem with both Compagni's and Dante's arguments was that, politically speaking, it put the cities at the beck and call of the Emperor, something from which Bartolus of Sassoferrato had legally freed them.

In his *The Defender of the Peace*, Marsiglio of Padua solved this problem by making the straightforward observation that the rulers of the Church completely misunderstood the nature of the Church's authority in legal, political or other forms of 'coercive jurisdiction.' He first argues that the Church and clergy are exempt neither from taxation, nor civil laws. Christ did, after all, say, "Render to Caesar what is Ceasar's." Further, Marisglio argued that the Church is not a jurisdictional body, but a congregation of voluntary members, the unity of which is "the whole body of the faithful who believe in and invoke the name of Christ." Therefore, a priest only has the power to "teach and practice," and has "no coercive power over anyone." Marsiglio continues this line of reasoning in attacking the power of the Pope, which he says has no scriptural basis. Rather, the "General Council of all Christians," among who are "non-priests," has authority. He then goes on to reason that the secular realm has authority over the Church. In point of fact, the supreme authority in each city is held by "the faithful human legislator." Therefore, the communes have a complete *de jure* independence from the Papacy, an institution that Marsilio says has "distressed the *Regnun Italicum* and has kept it and still keeps it from tranquillity and peace."

## The New Personality

A new type of personality, more modern, began to emerge in the late Middle Ages and early Renaissance. As the new city dwellers – leather and cloth workers, carpenters, masons, merchants, skilled craftspeople, laborers, bankers and, yes, even lawyers – grappled with living in their new urban environment, they found the spiritually oriented and materially condemning medieval ethos unable to give them any meaningful guidance in the conduct of their politics, business and lives. In the place of the medieval worldview predicated on Christ's utterance in The Gospel of Matthew – "My Kingdom is not of this world" – the progenitors of the Renaissance developed sources of cultural sustenance that would help them further build new societies and cultures. While the medieval soul contemplated the Scriptures, the life of Christ and the rocky road to eternal salvation, the Renaissance mind overlaid or, in some cases, even supplanted these, with the added complexity of trying to find and develop a set of ideas and practices for living in a very materialistic urban environment.

This dichotomy between contemplating Christian spirituality and acting to succeed in the newly developing urban economy is nowhere better exemplified than in the personality of the Anonimo Genovese, an anonymous contemporary of Dante's from Genova. On the one hand, he comments on this 'wretched life, finite and brief...lent by the Lord.' Continuing in this vein, he condemns the wealthy who maintain "a train of lords and knights, courtiers and musicians" which in the end "isn't worth a fig." On the other hand, the Anonimo praises the venture capitalist who bravely sails off to sell his goods in an unknown market: "Now every man is in the market, so aim accordingly to get such merchandise and goods as bring you peace."[3]

## New Languages

If there were new developments in politics, urban culture and personal life, they were, in their day-to-day iterations, expressed in the variety of innumerable local dialects that existed in the Italy of the time. During both the Roman Republic and the Empire, pre-Roman indigenous languages survived and were used by locals even though the official language was Latin. After the collapse of the Roman Empire in the 5th and 6th centuries, Latin was still used by the Church in its official documents, the Bible, in copying and preserving ancient texts, and in producing new tomes of medieval learning. However, the spoken word, one not governed by a written vocabulary and grammar, evolved locally out of Latin into various dialects or vernaculars. Hence, in the full flower of medieval and Renaissance Italy, people in Naples, Rome, Florence, Bologna, Milan and Venice could not understand each other if speaking in their respective local languages.

A form of literary Italian is born in Italy when Dante reads poetry of the Sicilian school and sees enough similarities with his own Florentine Tuscan dialect to conclude that there is a common language underlying these two, and hence, all the other Italian dialects. He then goes on to advocate, in his *De vulgari eloquentia*, that this spoken language, which is used by all people, should supplant Latin, for it, too, is capable of lofty literary expression. Although a wise observation that people should recognize their spoken language as their official one, Dante erred in thinking that he had found a common root of Italian underlying all the other dialects. The manuscripts of Sicilian poetry that he had read were produced by Tuscan amanuenses who had changed some of the original Sicilian into Tuscan, unknown to Dante, in the process of their copying. Dante concluded from these altered poems that there was a common underlying "Italian" when it was simply much of the Tuscan he grew up with in the first place! However, by virtue of his reputation as an accomplished poet, philosopher and political activist, the Tuscan of Dante becomes the language of poetry for Italy, even though the Church continued to use Latin, and in everyday life, people used their own local vernaculars for speaking, writing and commerce.

In Quattrocento Florence, Leon Battista Alberti championed the idea – again! – that the language people actually spoke in their daily lives was just as eloquent as Latin, perhaps even more so, since the vernacular was as alive to them as Latin had been to the Romans. In the *Proemio* to the third book of his vernacular masterpiece, *I libri della famiglia*, a philosophical treatise on family life, Alberti writes:

> ...from this we conclude that the language in which the learned wrote was almost an artificial and scholastic invention rather than something understood by the many....I would say that the ancients would not speak in scholastic and scientific artifice, but of daily and domestic things would they write to their wives, children and servants in only Latin.....because it was common to everyone.

To prove this point, in 1441 the Florentines, spurred by Alberti and underwritten by Piero de' Medici, sponsored a contest, the so-called *Certame Coronario*, in which a group of invited contestants would write poetry in the vernacular on the theme of friendship. Although no one was named a winner, the contest promoted the idea that the vernacular could be as beautiful and efficient as Latin in literary and other lofty matters.

The debate continued apace in the Cinquecento, with numerous writers joining the fray. Pietro Bembo advocated a purified form of archaic Tuscan as used by Petrarch. Giangiorgio Trissino argued for a vernacular constructed from all the dialects of Italy. Niccolò Macchiavelli wanted his own contemporary Florentine as the national language of Italy. Although they all disagreed on the details, they were arguing in favor of a vernacular instead of Latin as the language. They just could not decide on which vernacular. The matter was decided near the end of the century, when the *Accademia della Crusca* was founded, basing its principles on those of Bembo.

## A New Sense of Community

Two popular trends that did not eliminate the wealth and elitism of the Church, but provided genuine spiritual relief to the common Christian of this era by making God more accessible to humanity, were the development of the Cult of the Blessed Virgin and the widespread acceptance of the ideas of Francis of Assisi.

From the 11th to 13th centuries, a major shift occurs in religious attitudes in both Europe and Italy. The authority of the Pope, the bishops and, in general, the Church is called more and more in question by a vocal minority. Critics of the Church point out that the original ideals and teaching of Christianity condemned worldly wealth, yet the ruling caste within the Church seemed dedicated solely to accumulating as many worldly riches as possible. For many individuals, the gulf between the have's and have-not's in society was not to be explained away by the original teachings of Christ on the virtues of poverty. Rather, it was the result of the contemporary attitude of the Church hierarchy toward the acquisition of wealth. This disagreement served to underscore that, in the final judgment of the world the average Christian lived in, the Church served as a mediator between God and humanity, making God much less accessible than the material manifestations of wealth the Church displayed as instances of Christian generosity but did not distribute to alleviate suffering.

Mary was alone of all women. The only human untainted by Original Sin. She is the pure vessel, the Second Eve, a virgin who bore the Christ child whose sole task was to redeem humanity by washing away Original Sin and allowing humanity to once again, as in the Garden of Eden, unify itself with God. Upon her death bed, Mary does not die, but is assumed into heaven, where she becomes Christ's Bride and Queen of Heaven. In addition to her roles as Virgin, mother of Christ and Queen of Heaven, she who mourned her Son's Crucifixion and death is capable of understanding the suffering of any human being and thereby becomes the First Intercessor for human requests for God's mercy and forgiveness. In the early 12th century, St. Bernard of Clairvaux's teachings gave credence to a popular collection of stories about Mary, known as the Miracles of the Virgin, and as a result, stimulated interest in the Cult of the Blessed Virgin that had sprung up to worship her. With the popular advent of the cult, humanity had, in the place of the stern, cold and removed patriarchal leaders of the Church, a loving, warm and forgiving mother figure who could intercede on an individual sinner's behalf to the Almighty Himself. Instead of the rigid and procedurally bound practice of going to the Church to seek God's help, one could pray to Mary. She was, after all, pure and without sin and could give you a more direct spiritual experience than wealth of the Church could ever provide.

St. Francis of Assisi (c.1181-1226), the son of a wealthy Assisi merchant, gave up a frivolous, irresponsible and well-funded lifestyle in his late adolescence in favor of a religious vision based on actively working in society with humility, love and poverty. Francis set the example for his followers of helping the poor and sick, and spreading the word of God's love for humanity. He eschewed detailed regulations in the pursuit of these goals, emphasizing that each day should be lived freely and spontaneously. In the place of the elaborate intellectual framework the Church used to justify its position, Francis preached basic Christian ideas in a simple, understandable way. In the Duecento, his lead caught on like wild fire. In 1210 he secured the verbal affirmation of Innocent III for his newly forming order. By mid-century gray cloaked Franciscans were ministering in every slum in Europe. Although he preached the rejection of material possessions, he also rejoiced, for instance in his "Canticle of the Creatures," in the beauty and goodness inherent in God's creation. If Christians from Augustine in the 5th century on admonished people to reject the world and contemplate the Scriptures and Heaven, St. Francis praised reality in the concrete, a fact which either reinforced or was simply emblematic of the intellectual, emotional and cultural recognition and acceptance of the tangible world that was taking place at the time. Whatever the case, the example of Francis, like the Cult of the Blessed Virgin, indicates popular religious currents were questioning authority and empowering individuals to reach out to God themselves.

Empowerment also had a civic side. The new urban trades and businesses created guilds. These were professional trade organizations that set standards for a specific industry, attempted to regulate and control their markets, participated in communal government in order to receive favorable legislation, provided help for their members who encountered financial troubles, buried members and cared for their widows. In Florence there were many guilds, one for the leather manufacturers, one for the wool industry, and so on.

Another new type of organization was a new sort of religious order. While the medieval monastery continued to exist, in the early Duecento the Franciscan and Dominican orders sprung up, providing a new type of city preacher oriented to working on a day-to-day basis with the masses. Another urban innovation developed when the city dwellers altered existing medieval institutions into something that suited their needs. In the place of full-fledged monkhood, they created religious confraternities, religious organizations created by merchants who wanted to take part in aspects of holy service, but did not want to become full fledged monks or preachers because they did not want to give up their successful business careers. In the 11th and 12th centuries, a number of these organizations developed in the cities of Italy. Many were dedicated to serving the Virgin Mary, with their members calling themselves, appropriately, the *Serviti*. One of the first poetic selections in this volume is one of the *laudes*, a sort of popular hymn to the Virgin sung by confraternity members.

## Our Life in Mid-stride

The creative people of this age transform the aesthetic arts and refocus them on their most proper subject: humanity at its best and worst. Underlying this transformation is the recognition and development of a new way of life based on living, growing and learning in a material, urban world. In economic and social life, religion, politics, law, learning, art and poetry, the Italians gradually replace medieval theory with ideas predicated on the practical, intellectual, emotional and reflective experiences of everyday life. In point of fact, the means of daily, practical life – informed by Roman antiquity – become the tangible substance of each of these activities. In the aesthetic realm, the recognition and subsequent development of the material world enables numerous Italian artists and poets to create both new forms of expression and new subject matter that encapsulates this new life. For some, learning replaces believing as the most important way to guide one's path through a world constantly altered by newer and newer discoveries and achievements.

# Notes

1. Klibansky R. Panofsky E., and Saxl F., *Saturn and Melancholy. Studies in the History of Natural Philosophy, Religion and Art*, London: 1964, 250-54.

2. Much of this section on Italian politics was taken from Quentin Skinner, *The Foundations of Modern Political Thought*, New York: Cambridge University Press, 1978, v.1.

3. Lauro Martines, *Power and Imagination: City-States in Renaissance Italy*, Baltimore, MD: The Johns Hopkins University Press, 1988, 87-93.

# Bibliography

William Anderson, *Dante the Maker*, New York: Crossroad, 1982.

Giulio Carlo Argan, *La storia dell'arte italiana*, Firenze: Sansoni, 1981.

Nella Bisiacco-Henry and Sylvain Trousselard, *Bibliographie de la poesie Commique des XIIIème et XIVème Siecles*, <http://www.univ-paris3.fr/recherche/chroniquesitaliennes/PDF/PoesieXVI/comico.pdf>, 1997.

Friedrich Wilhelm Bautz, "Colonna, Vittoria," *Biographisch-Bibliographischen Kirchenlexikons*, <http://www.bautz.de/bbkl/c/colonna_v.shtml>, 2001.

Jakob Burckhardt, *The Civilization of the Renaissance in Italy*, trans. by S.C.G. Middlemore, rev. and ed. by Irene Gordon, NY: Mentor, 1960.

Giovanni Cavalcanti, Istorie fiorentine scritte da Giovanni Cavalcanti, Firenze: Tipografia all'insegna di Dante, 1838-39.

Emilio Cecchi e Natalino Sapegno, eds., *Storia della letteratura italiana*, vols. 1-6, Milano: Garzanti, 1966.

Vittorio Cian, *I contatti letterari italo-provenzali e la prima rivoluzione poetica della letteratura italiana*, Messina: D'Amico, 1900.

Gianfranco Contini, *Poeti del duecento*, in the series Letterature italiana, storia e testi, v. 2, Milano: R. Ricciardi, 1960.

Benedetto Croce, 'La lirica cinquecentesca,' *Poesia popolare e poesia d'arte*, Bari: Laterza, 1957, 341-441.

Charles Till Davis, 'Education in Dante's Florence,' *Speculum*, Vol. XL, No. 3, 415-35.

Domenico de Robertis, 'L'esperienza poetica del Quattrocento,' from *Il Quattrocento e l'Ariosto*, Volume III of *Storia della letteratura italiana*, Milano: Garzanti, 1966,

Francesco De Sanctis, *Storia della letterature italiana*, Milano: Biblioteca Universale Rizzoli, 1983.

Francesco D'Ovidio, *Versificazione italiana e arte poetica medioevale*, Milano: Hoepli: 1910.

Enrico Galavotti, Homolaicus, *Testi di umanesimo laico e socialismo democratico*, < http://www.homolaicus.com/>.

——————, Ludovico Ariosto, http://www.homolaicus.com/letteratura/ariosto.htm.

Arturo Graf, 'Petrarchismo e antipetrarchismo,' *Attraverso il Cinquecento*, Torino: Loescher, 1888, 3-86.

Charles Hall Grandgent, *Dante*, New York: Duffield and company, 1916.

Denys Hay and John E. Law, *Italy in the Age of the Renaissance, 1380-1530*, London: Longman, 1989.

George Holmes, *Dante*, New York: Hill and Wang, 1980.

Martin Irvine, *The Book, the Page, the Text, and Biblio-Futures or The Once and Future Book* <http://www.georgetown.edu/faculty/irvinem/articles/bookfutures/>, 1999-2000.

John Larner, *Italy in the Age of Dante and Petrarch, 1216-1380*, New York: Longman, 1980.

Mario Marti, *Poeti del Dolce Stil Nuovo*, Firenze: Le Monnier, 1969.

Lauro Martines, *Power and Imagination: City-States in Renaissance Italy*, Baltimore, MD: The Johns Hopkins University Press, 1988.

Karl Marx, "Confession," transcribed by Anthony Blunden, <http://www.marxists.org/archive/marx/works/1865/04/01.htm>, 1865.

Joseph Anthony Mazzeo, *Medieval Cultural Tradition In Dante's Comedy*, New York: Greenwood Press, 1968.

Bruno Migliorini, *Storia della lingua italiana*, Firenze: Sansoni, 1960.

Carlo Muscetta and Daniele Ponchiroli, *Poesia del Quattrocento e del Cinquecento*, Torino: Einaudi, 1959.

Bruno Nardi, *Dante e la cultura medievale*, introduzione di Tullio Gregory, nuova edizione a cura di Paolo Mazzantini, Bari: Laterza, 1985.

Karl Popper, *The Open Society and Its Enemies*, London: Routledge and Kegan Paul, 1943, 5th ed. rev., 1956.

Stephen Reimer, *Manuscript Studies, Medieval and Early Modern*, <http://www.ualberta.ca/~sreimer/ms-course/course.htm>, 1998.

Vittorio Rossi, *Il Quattrocento*, reprint of the 1933 edition, updated by Rossella Bessi with an introduction by Mario Martelli, Padova: Vallardi, 1992.

Francesca Santucci, *Letteratura al Femminile*, <http://www.letteraturaalfemminile.it/>, 2003.

Natalino Sapegno, *Storia letteraria del Trecento*, in the series *Letterature italiana, storia e testi, v. 2,* Milano: R. Ricciardi, 1963.

Timothy W. Seid, *Interpreting Ancient Manuscripts*, <http://www.earlham.edu/~seidti/iam/interp_mss.html>.

Quentin Skinner, *The Foundations of Modern Political Thought*, Cambridge: Cambridge University Press, 1978.

J. N. Stephens, *The Italian Renaissance: the Origins of Intellectual and Artistic Change Before the Reformation,* London: Longman, 1990.

Antonio Viscardi, *Le origini: testi latini, italiani, provenzali e franco-italiani*, in the series *Letterature italiana, storia e testi, v. 1,* Milano: R. Ricciardi,1956.

# Ritmo Laurenziano

One of the oldest examples of literature written in an Italian dialect, the *Ritmo* was probably composed by an anonymous troubadour between 1151 and 1157, the dates that a certain Grimaldesco (l. 13) was Bishop in Osimo, a period of time that was concurrent with the tenures of a certain Villano Gaetani (l.9), Archbishop of Pisa from 1146 to 1175, and one Galgano (l. 11), Archbishop of Volterra from 1150 to 1170. The pun on the term *villano* (villain) indicates the lighthearted nature of the poem, which exploits the tension between an ecclesiastic's celestial goal of pointing the way to heaven and the materially oriented tasks of running a diocese. With a preponderance of dactylic and trochaic feet arranged in verses of the *ottonario* (lines of 8 syllables), the poem has a sing-song rhythm that would have made it easy – especially with its monorhyme – for anyone in the 12th century to memorize after hearing it only a few times. Although not an example of Melancholy, the *Ritmo* helps us establish reference points both for the use of the vernacular in verse and for the relationship of such verse to society in general and social commentary in particular.

## Ritmo Laurenziano

Salva lo vescovo senato,           lo mellior c'umque sia na[to],
[. . .] ora fue sagrato           tutt'allumma 'l cericato.
Ne Fisolaco ne Cato           non fue sl ringratiato,
e 'I pap' ha ll[. . .-ato]           per suo drudo plu privato.
Suo gentile vescovato           ben'e cresciuto e melliorato.

L'apostolico romano           lo [...] Laterano.
San Benedetto e san Germano           'l destinoe d'esser sovrano
de tutto regno cristiano:           peroe venne da lor mano,
del paradis delitiano.           Ca non fue ques[to] villano:
da ce l mondo fue pagano           non ci so tal marchisciano.
Se mi da caval balcano,           monsterroll'al bon G[algano],
a lo vescovo volterrano,           cui bendicente bascio mano.
Lo vescovo Grimaldesco,           cento cavaler' a [desco]
di nun tempo no lli 'ncrescono,           anci placono et abelliscono.
Ne latino ne tedesco           ne lombardo ne fra[ncesco]
suo mellior re no 'nvestisco,           tant'e di bontade fresco.
A llui ne vo [ . . . ]oresco           corridor caval pultre[sco]:
li arcador ne vann'a tresco;           di paura sbaguttisco;
rispos' e disse latinesco           stenetietti nutiaresco.
Di lui bendicer non finisco           mentre 'n questo mondo vesco.

2

## The Laurentian Rhythm

Bless the ancient bishop,
[...] now the clergy was consecrated
Neither Physiologus nor Cato
and the Pope [...ed] him
His noble diocese

the best ever born,
all illuminated.
was so gifted,
for his private cavalier.
has greatly grown and improved.

The Apostolic Roman
St. Benedict and St. Germain
for the entire Christian realm:
they delight in Paradise.
since the world was pagan
If he gives me a dappled horse,
the Volterran Bishop,
Bishop Grimaldesco,
at no time do they weary him,
Neither Latin nor German
invest a king better than he
To him I go for a swift
The archers sport roughly;
He paused and loftily said
I cannot bless him enough

him [...] Laterano.
intended him to be the sovereign
because it came from their power
Never was he a villain:
I never knew such a gentleman.
I will show him to the good G[algano],
whose blessing hand I kiss.
a hundred horses at his seat
rather they please and embellish.
nor Lombard nor French
he is of such on-going goodness.
Moorish colt:
I don't joust in fear;
'unbend your bow and I will educate you.'
while he's a bishop in this life.

# Francesco d'Assisi
## (1181/82–1226)

According to the *Speculum perfectionis* (*The Mirror of Perfection*) of Brother Jacopone da Todi, St. Francis wrote the *Laudes creaturarum* in 1224 in San Damiano after a restless night during which he was harassed in his cell by mice and troubled by a long term illness in his eyes. The son of wealthy cloth merchant of Assisi and a mother of possible noble birth, Francis had a comfortable childhood and adolescence. In 1202 he fought in the war between Assisi and Perugia. A prisoner of war for nearly a year, he was released whereupon he fell seriously ill. After recuperating, he set out to rejoin his hometown forces, but returned to Assisi after having a religious vision. Subsequently engaging in solitude and prayer, he underwent a religious conversion, a process during which he had a vision of Christ, experienced poverty on a pilgrimage to Rome and, at the ruined chapel in San Damiano, heard a celestial voice from the crucifix above the altar tell him to 'repair my house.' In order to do so, Francis sold much of his father's cloth and his horse, an action that ended in an audience before the bishop and his father. Not one to beat around the bush, Francis took off his clothes, renounced his father and said, 'Our Father who art in heaven.' With similar simple fervor, he went to Rome in 1209 with 11 of his followers, obtaining Innocent III's approval for rule for his order.

Attempting to imitate Christ's spiritual renunciation of worldly goods and pleasures, Francis – and many of his followers – lived as he preached, providing a much needed sympathy, understanding and aid for the poor and sick in the face of the rapacious greed generated by the sharply competitive economies of the burgeoning urban centers of his contemporary Italy. The *Laudes,* for all its simplicity, is one of the most profound religious statements of all time, and even if taken merely as poetry, provides a pure and unadorned form that embodies a content in a way that is at once simple, universal, and yet, quite original. From a strictly historical view, we see here the incipient Renaissance spirit in which reality is praised, not in the abstract, medieval sense, but in the concrete. Above all, it demonstrates the applicability of the then nascent Renaissance belief in being creative by using one's vernacular (i.e., in Francis' case, Umbrian) after meditation and solitude.

Please note the Umbrian dialect often has u in place of *o, iorno* instead of *giorno* (l. 7), the addition of *ne* to *è* (l. 4) and the use of the *ano* ending both for *confare* instead of *anno* (l. 3) and the 3rd per. pl. future (lines 25 and 30). This version also retains the original spelling, where *k* was used in the place of the now common ch.

# San Francesco d'Assisi

*Laudes Creaturarum (o Cantico di Frate Sole)*

Altissimu, onnipotente, bon Signore,
tue so' le laude, la gloria e l'honore et onne benedictione.

Ad te solo, Altissimo, se konfano,
et nullu homo ene dignu te mentovare.

Laudato sie, mi' Signore, cum tucte le tue creature,
spetialmente messor lo frate sole,
lo qual'è iorno, et allumini noi per lui.
Et ellu è bellu e radiante cum grande splendore:
de te, Altissimo, porta significatione.

Laudato si', mi' Signore, per sora luna e le stelle:
in celu l'ài formate clarite et pretiose et belle.

Laudato si', mi' Signore, per frate vento
et per aere et nubilo et sereno et onne tempo,
per lo quale a le tue creature dài sustentamento.

Laudato si', mi' Signore, per sor'aqua,
la quale è multo utile et humile et pretiosa et casta.

Laudato si', mi' Signore, per frate focu,
per lo quale ennallumini la nocte:
ed ello è bello et iocundo et robustoso et forte.

Laudato Si', mi' Signore, per sora nostra matre terra,
la quale ne sustenta et governa,
et produce diversi fructi con coloriti flori et herba.

Laudato si', mi' Signore, per quelli ke perdonano per lo tuo amore
et sostengo infirmitate et tribulatione.

Beati quelli ke 'l sosterrano in pace,
ka da te, Altissimo, sirano incoronati.

Laudato si', mi' Signore, per sora nostra morte corporale,
da la quale nullu homo vivente pò skappare:
guai a-cquelli ke morrano ne le peccata mortali;
beati quelli ke trovara ne le tue sanctissime voluntati,
ka la morte secunda no 'l farrà male.

Laudate e benedicete mi' Signore et rengratiate
e serviateli cum grande humilitate.

## St. Francis of Assisi

*Hymn of the Creatures (or The Canticle of Brother Sun)*

Highest, omnipotent, good Lord,
Yours are the praises, the glory, the honor and every blessing.

To you alone, Highest, do they belong,
for no man is worthy to say your name.

Praised be you, my Lord, with all your creatures,
especially our harvester Brother sun,
who is the day and lights our way.
For he is beautiful and radiant with great brightness:
from you, Highest, he takes meaning.

Praised be you, my Lord, for Sister Moon and the stars:
with them you've made us clarity, value and beauty.

Praised be you, my Lord, for Brother Wind
and the air, clouds, calm and all our weather,
by which you give your creatures sustenance.

Praised be you, my Lord, for Sister Water,
who is very useful, humble, worthy and pure.

Praised be you, my Lord, for Brother Fire,
with whom you illumine the night:
for he is beautiful, cheerful, robust and strong.

Praised be you, my Lord, for our sister Mother Earth,
who sustains and governs us,
and produces many fruits with colored flowers and herbs.

Praised be you, my Lord, for those you pardon with your love,
nurturing the sick and suffering.

Praised be those who will live in peace,
who you, Highest, will crown.

Praised be you, my Lord, for our sister Bodily Death,
from whom no one can escape:
woe to those who will die in mortal sin;
blessed are those you find with your holiest will,
for damnation will not harm them.

Praise and bless my Lord – thank
and serve him with great humility.

# Giacomo da Lentino
## (active 1233–1246)

A notary at the Imperial Court of Emperor Federico II (1194–1250), Giacomo went far beyond his imperial charge of attesting official documents, acts and laws with his innovations in Italian poetry.

First, he adapted the love poetry of the troubadours of Provence to the Sicilian dialect. As refreshing as we might judge this adaptation today, serious food for thought comes from Francesco de Sanctis, 19th century Italian literary critic, who thought that, '...Sicilian culture had an original sin. Coming from outside, the lifestyle of courtly love, mixed with Eastern coloring, had no matching equivalent in our national life...it remained extraneous to our real soul and our real life...this poetry was not a powerful effusion of the soul, but a distraction, a comfort, an amusement, a style, a gallantry.' (see his *Storia della letteratura italiana*, Milano: Biblioteca universal Rizzoli, 1983, 69–71).

Second, since there are no earlier examples of the sonnet, Giacomo is generally credited with its invention. Of the sonnet, Jakob Burckhardt, 19th century Swiss historian of the Italian Renaissance, observed, 'The sonnet seems to us to have been an unspeakable blessing for Italian poetry. The clearness and beauty of its structure, the invitation to elevate the thought in the second and more rapidly moving second half, and the ease by which it could be learned by heart, made it loved and valued by even the greatest masters...The sonnet became a condenser of thoughts and emotions such as was possessed by the poetry of no other modern people.' Burckhardt continues that by studying the sonnet, 'the world of Italian sentiment comes before us in a series of clear, concise pictures which are most effective in their brevity.'

The poem *Meravigliosamente*, a *canzonetta* with verses consisting of the seven beat *settenario*, presents a refined consideration of the ecstasy of love. *Or come pote sì gran donna entrare* is a sonnet with *quartine a rime alterne* and *terzine di due rime alterne* that relates the beauty and power of woman.

## Giacomo da Lentino

1
Meravigliosamente
un amor mi distringe
e mi tene ad ogn'ora.
 Com'om che pone mente
in altro exemplo pinge
la simile pintura,
 cosi, bella, facc'eo,
che 'nfra lo core meo
porto la tua figura.

 In cor par ch'eo vi porti,
pinta como parete,
e non pare di fore.
 O Deo, co' mi par forte.
 Non so se lo sapete,
con' v'amo di bon core:
 ch'eo son si vergognoso
ca pur vi guardo ascoso
e non vi mostro amore.

 Avendo gran disio,
dipinsi una pintura,
bella, voi simigliante,
 e quando voi non vio,
guardo 'n quella figura
e par ch'eo v'aggia avante:
 come quello che crede
salvarsi per sua fede,
ancor non veggia inante.

 Al cor m'arde una doglia,
com'om che ten lo foco
a lo suo seno ascoso,
 e quando piu lo
allora arde piu loco
e non po stare incluso:
 similemente eo ardo
quando pass'e non guardo
a voi, vis'amoroso.

## Giacomo da Lentino

1
Marvelously
a love binds
and holds me every moment.
 Like a man, who keeps in
mind another image as he paints
a similar portrait,
so, My Beauty, do I,
for within my heart
I carry your likeness.

 It appears that I carry you in my heart,
painted as you appear,
and not any different.
 O God, how she seems so strong.
I don't know if you know it,
how I love you with a true heart:
 since I'm so ashamed,
I only glance at you secretly
and never show you my love.

 Having great desire,
I painted a picture,
My Beauty, resembling you—
 for when I don't see you,
I look at that image,
and it seems I have you before me:
 like one who believes
in saving himself for his faith,
I don't see you before me.

 A sorrow burns in my heart,
like a man who keeps a fire
hidden in his breast,
 because the more he covers it,
the more it burns
and is unable to stay hidden:
 similarly I burn
when I pass and don't look
at you, my Loving Face.

S'eo guardo, quando passo,
inver' voi, non mi giro,
bella, per risguardare.
 Andando, ad ogni passo
getto uno gran sospiro
che facemi ancosciare;
 e certo bene ancoscio,
c'a pena mi conoscio,
tanto bella mi pare.

Assai v'aggio laudato,
madonna, in tutte parti
di bellezze ch'avete.
 Non so se v'è contato
ch'eo lo faccia per arti,
che voi pur v'ascondete.
 Sacciatelo per singa,
zo ch'eo no dico a linga,
quando voi mi vedrite.

 Canzonetta novella,
va' canta nova cosa;
lèvati da maitino
 davanti a la più bella,
fiore d'ogni amorosa,
bionda più c'auro fino:
 "Lo vostro amor, ch'è caro,
donatelo al Notaro
ch'è nato da Lentino."

If I look, when near,
toward you, I don't turn,
My Beauty, to look again.
 Walking, every step
I let out a great sigh
that makes me suffer;
 and certainly I suffer well—
I know pain:
it seems so beautiful to me.

 I've completely praised you,
Lady, in all the
beauties that you have.
 I don't know if it matters
that I did it by means of art—
for you're still hiding from me.
 You know by appearances,
when you see me,
what I don't say with words.

 New little song,
go sing something new.
Set out in the morning
 for the most beautiful one,
flower of everything loving,
fairer than pure gold:
 "Your love, which is precious,
give it to the Notary
who was born in Lentino."

## Giacomo da Lentino

2
Or come pote si gran donna entrare
per gli oc[c]hi mei, che si pic[c]ioli sone?
e nel mio core come pote stare,
che 'nentr'esso la porto laonque i' vone?

[Lo] loco laonde entra gia non pare,
ond'io gran meraviglia me ne done;
ma voglio lei a lumera asomigliare,
e gli oc[c]hi mei al vetro ove si pone.

Lo foco inchiuso, poi passa di fore
lo suo lostrore, sanza far rot[t]ura:
cosi per gli oc[c]hi mi pass'a lo core,

no la persona, ma la sua figura.
Rinovellare mi voglio d'amore,
poi porto insegna di tal criatura.

## Giacomo da Lentino

2
Now how could so great a Lady enter
my eyes which are so tiny?
and how could she stay in my heart,
that I carry her in it wherever I go?

The spot she enters is not seen,
whence I give myself great surprise—
but I want to compare her to a lamp,
and my eyes to its glass.

The fire closed within then passes its
luster outside without shattering:
thus through my eyes it passes to my heart—

not her person, but her image.
I want to renew myself with love,
then I'll carry the image of such a creature.

# Lauda dei Servi della Vergine

Perhaps invented by Guittone D'Arezzo (see the next section), the *lauda* (a religious form of the *ballata*) became a popular devotional form in the Duecento, more often than not sung. In addition to devotional *laude*, some became the vehicle for dramatic presentations and were one of the sources for the development of Italian theater. In Umbria such *laude drammatiche* were called *devozioni*, while in Tuscany, with the addition of other material derived from the liturgy, they were known as *sacre rappresentazioni*. *Il sodalizio dei Servi della Vergine* (the Society of the Servants of the Virgin), begun sometime before 1211 in Bologna, had as one of its goals the recitation in the vernacular the Office of the Madonna during every of the nine canonical hours. In the Ducento, groups using the title of *Servi* sprang up as lay societies of volunteer citizens interested in promoting a variety of causes. Composed in the dialect associated with the Po Region in northern Italy, the *lauda* consists of a *lassa* of Alexandrines grouped according to rhyme. If Lentino's *Meravigliosamente* tells of the rapture of terrestrial love, the *Lauda* expresses the love directed toward the Virgin that is at once officially and publicly correct, yet possessing a delicacy that cannot but appeal to an individual's private self.

*Lauda dei Servi della Vergine*

Rayna possentissima,   sovr'el cel sì asaltaa.
Sovra la vita ancelica   vu sij sanctificaa.
Scala de sapiencia, mare de reverencia,  vu sì purificata,
spoxa de Iesu Cristo,  in celo humiliada.
Denanci al re de gloria  vu siti incoronata.
De le vertu altissime  tuta ne sì ornata.
[Ma]donna perfectissima, de Ioachin fusti nata.
Per salvar[e] lo segolo  fusti al mondo creata,
stella dolce clarissima,  gema glorificata.
Sovra le grande flore  vuy sì magnificata.
Corona sij d'imperio  a fin or fabricata,
palma preciosissima, stella del mondo ornata,
entro el cardin olentissimo roxa ingarofolata,
humiliata purissima,  viola [in]violata.
Colona sij del segolo,  in alto sij fermata.
Alma de penitencia, mare de reverencia, vu sì purificata,
forteca de Ierusalem  d'intorno circundata.
Lo fruto che portasti, madona, in Betelem, a nu la vita ha data.
Vuy siti sapiencia, presa de reverencia, columba sagellata.
Verga d'ubidiencia, polcella d'astinencia, vu sì amaistrata.
Vuy sì fontana de gracia,  madona aprexiata,
inguento olentissimo, oliva replantata,
balsemo olentissimo, manna dal cel mandata.
Sovra la mel dolcissima, vu sì humiliata.
Sovra tute le vercene  vuy sì luxe abraxata.
Vuy siti sacrificio  olente, cira colada,
de sal de sapiencia da Deo resuscitata.
Tanto sì stata, madre  dei miseri, aspetata.
Bia sera quell'anema  che de vuy sera aidata.
Vostra possanca altissima oltra fine e grandissima, in cel fortificata.

Lucerna splendidissima, soave e dolcissima, da Cristo aluminata,
vostra vita cerdssima  sempre avera durata.
Donsella cortexissima, d'adornese adornada,
sovra la flor de gloria  vui sì la piu aflorata,
mira e sacrificio  da Cristo asaminata,
piovando da le nuvole dal cel fresca roxata,
cum lo vostro fiolo  dai tri magi adorata.
Preta fermissima ch'al sorno e fondata,
sovra le dodexe prete vuy sì la piu afflorata.
Chi a vuy torna cum lagreme,  l'anima desperata
da vuy parte cum gaudio,  cum soia consolata
Dal destro la' sanctissimo fora ne vene undata
del vostro fiol carissimo, che sparse a tal derata

*'The Hymn of the Servants of the Virgin*

Most powerful Queen,         you've ascended to Heaven.
Above the Angelic realm     you've been sanctified.
Stairway of wisdom,     sea of reverence,    you are purified,
wife of Jesus Christ,     humble in Heaven.
In the presence of the King of glory   you are enthroned.
With the highest virtues     you are completely adorned.
Most perfect woman,     born of Joachim.
In order to save the ages    you were created for the world,
gentle, most bright star,    glorified gem.
Beyond the greatest flowers   you are magnified.
You are the imperial Crown   made from fine gold,
most precious palm,    adorned star of the world,
within the most fragrant garden   scented rose,
most pure humility,    inviolate violet.
You are the Pillar of the Ages,   fixed on high.
Soul of Penitence,    sea of reverence,   you are purified.
Fortress of Jerusalem    walled all around.
The fruit you bore,    Lady, in Bethlehem,  has given life to us.
You are wisdom,    prize of reverence,  confirmed Dove.
Rod of obedience,    sprout of abstinence,  you are most wise.
You are the source of Grace,   most worthy Lady,
most fragrant salve,    replanted olive,
most sweet balsam,    manna sent from heaven.
Above the sweetest flower,   you are humbled.
Above all the virgins    you are luster ablaze.
You are sacrifice    fragrant, a raised candle,
the salt of wisdom    resuscitated by God.
So much have you been, mother  of the suffering, desired.
Blessed will be that soul   that you will help.
Your highest power   grand beyond measure  fortified in Heaven.

Most splendid lamp, pleasant and most sweet, illuminated by Christ,
your most certain life    will endure forever.
Most courtly Lady,    adorned adornment,
above the flower of glory   you are the most blossomed,
goal and sacrifice    examined by Christ,
raining from the clouds   from the rosy fresh sky,
with your Son    adored by the three Magi.
Staunchest priestess   who is established at daybreak,
above the twelve priests   you are the most ornamented.
He who turns to you with tears,  a desperate soul,
leaves you with gladness,   consoled with joy.
From the holiest right side   fury came out
of your dearest son,    who spilled such quantities

lo sangue dilectissimo  che fo aqua roxata,
che confermo 'I batexemo unde l'alm' e salvata.
In vu cace la sentencia,  madona de gran sciencia, versen rayna iustificata.

Vuy sì piena de gracia,   da l'angel salutata.
Recordive de l'anima   che sta mortificata.
L'alma di vostri Servi   ve sia recomandada,
chi ha compli questa ystoria  per vuy, vercen sacrata:
aidati lor e l'anima,   sempre vercen biata.

of his beloved blood that made rose water
that confirms baptism whence the soul is saved.
In you lies judgment, Lady of great knowledge, proven virgin Queen.

You are so full of Grace, greeted by the angel.
You remember the soul who is shamed.
The souls of your Servi are committed to you,
Souls who have completed this story for you, Sacred Virgin:
Help those souls, always, Blessed Virgin.

# Guittone d'Arezzo
## (c. 1230–1294)

Considered the possible inventor of the *lauda*, Guittone d'Arezzo had a full and interesting life divided into two distinct callings. In the first half of his life, he led a worldly existence. His father was the treasurer of the city of Arezzo. Of this Guittone writes to a friend, recalling his youth, "And you saw me as a little boy help him often in the town hall." He married a beautiful woman named Archina, a union that produced three children. During the first half of his life, Guittone helped to develop the first school of love poets in Tuscany, based in the main on what the Sicilians had done in emulating the troubadours of Provence. *Poi pur di servo* is a sonnet in this vein. The second half of his life began when he underwent a religious conversion sometime around 1265 and became a member of the *Milites Beatae Viriginis Mariae*, popularly called the *Frati Godenti*. The ultimate source of his change of heart may have been spurred by the bloodshed and slaughter he saw at the Battle of Montaperti in 1260, when the Florentines were defeated by their rival, the city of Siena. No longer Guittone, but Frate Guittone, he transformed his verse into something religious and moralistic. In fact, Guittone and Frate Guittone write as if they were two completely different people, and perhaps, in the religious sense of being reborn, they were. *Ben saccio de vertà* characterizes the piety of his second style. Of his transformed style, De Sanctis writes that "that harsh and rough form has truly original and characteristic features, a moral elevation, a certain energy of expression...His verses aren't immediate representations of life, but subtle and ingenious discourses." Although considered, because of his moral tone, a Tuscan predecessor of Dante, Dante wrote in his *De volgari eloquentia*, "May they cease, the followers of ignorance who praise Guittone d'Arezzo." Whether one agrees or disagrees with Dante's judgment, the harshness of the master certainly indicates the strong literary following Guittone had in his own time.

## Guittone D'Arezzo

1
Poi pur di servo star ferm'ho 'l volere,
vorrea per lei me fosse comandato;
ma servigio non chesto è più 'n piacere
a chi 'l riceve, e 'l servo è più laudato;

e sta a servente mal farsi cherere,
e lo signor de chesta è affannato;
e al signore tocca in dispiacere
similemente merto adimandato.

Ch'adimandare affanna e falla il servo,
e lo signore anoia e par forzato,
sì che non guaire ha de mertar onore.

A non cheder ni far cheder m'aservo;
seraggio tal, non credo esser blasmato,
e la mia donna en se spero migliore.

2
Ben saccio de verta che 'l meo trovare
val poco, e ha ragion de men valere,
poi ch'eo non posso in quel loco intrare
ch'adorna l'om de gioia e de savere.

E non departo d'a la porta stare
pregando che, per Deo, mi deggia aprere:
allora alcuna voce audir me pare
dicendome ch'eo sia di bon sofrere.

Ed eo sofert'ho tanto lungiamente
che devisa' de me tutto piacere
e tutto cio ched era in me valente:

per ch'eo rechiamo e chero lo savere
di ciascun om ch'e prode e canoscente
a l'aiuto del meo grande spiacere.

## Guittone D'Arezzo

1
Since I always want to be a servant,
I would like her to command me;
but service not requested is more a pleasure
to who receives it, for the servant is praised more;

and woe to the servant who asks again,
for the master of the request is annoyed,
the master is displeased,
similarly deserving to be asked.

Because the servant tires of asking and fails,
and the master troubles and seems forced,
not whining merits honor.

Neither asking nor making me ask satisfies me;
I would suppress such—I don't believe I can be blamed—
for I expect better in my Lady.

2
Well do I truly know that my seeking
matters little, and with reason matters less,
since I am not able to enter that place
that adorns man with joy and knowledge.

And I don't stop praying before
the door that, for god's sake, I must open:
then I appear to hear some voice
telling me that I am suffering for goodness.

And I have suffered so long
that I have separated myself from all pleasure
and all that was worthy in me:

because I desire and draw upon the knowledge
of each brave and sage man
who can help with my great displeasure.

# Jacopone da Todi
## (1230–1306)

Born in Todi in Umbria, Jacopo Benedetti studied law at the University of Bologna, becoming a notary and district attorney in his native town. He married Vanna di Bernardino di Guidone, of the family of the Counts of Coldimezzo. Soon after, tragedy struck, with Vanna dying in the collapse of a dancing floor at a festival. Jacopone changed his life entirely, joining the Order of the Flagellants, immersing himself in a denial of the flesh and eventually becoming an ardent supporter of the Franciscan Spirituals. Part of the Spiritual embassy sent to Pope Celestino V in 1294, he wrote a satire against him. He also played a central role in the intrachurch struggle against Pope Boniface VIII, signing the manifesto that declared the Pontiff's election invalid. He was subsequently excommunicated and spent the next six years in an underground prison in Palestrina. Benedetto XI freed him and he spent the rest of his life in the Franciscan monastery with the Clarists of San Lorenzo in Collazzone near Todi. His poetry, of which there are more than 100 *laude*, is based on his mystical visions or what he came to call his '*nova pazzia*' (new madness). This particular selection, *De elatione fratrum*, is indicative of the sarcasm an ascetic could muster against the worldly comfort and seemingly frivolous intellectual pursuits that were part of Church life. The response to the opening hemistich, '*non ci è relïone*,' is today, in the form of '*Non c'è più religione*,' an oft heard observation in Italy on the tail of a specific action that is part of what we in America have come to call "declining manners and morals."

## Jacopone da Todi

*De elatione fratrum*

Tale qual è, tal è:                              non ci è relione.

Mal vedemmo Parisci,                        —che hane destrutto Asisi:
co la lor lettoria                            —messo l'ho en mala via.

Chi sente lettoria,              —vada en forestaria;
gli altri en refettorio,        —a le foglie coll'olio.

Esvogliara el lettore:          —servito emperatore;
enfermera el cocinere,          —e nol vorra l'om vedere.

Adunansi ai capitoli           —a far li molti articoli:
el primo dicitore              —e 'l primo rompetore.

Vedete el grande amore         —che l'uno all'altro ha en core:
lo vardalo co' muletto,        —per dargli el calcio en petto.

Si no gli dai la voce,         —porrati nella croce,
porrati puoi le 'nsidie,       —che moia a Renderenie.

Tutto 'l di sto a cianciare,              —co le donne beffare;
si fratello gli avarda,                    —e mandato a la malta.

Si e figlio de calzolaio                  —o de vil macellaio,
menera tal grossore                        —co' figlio de 'mperatore.

# Jacopone da Todi

*On the Elation of the Brothers*

Such that is, such is:          there is no more religion.

We saw evil Paris,             —that destroyed Assisi:
with their professor's degree    —I've placed it on the evil path.

Whoever listens to professors,    —wanders in the wilderness;
the others in the refectory,      —to the leaves with oil.

The lecturer will grow weary     —the commander served;
the cooking weakened,          —and one will not want to see anything.

They assembled at the capitals    —to make many articles:
the first speaker              —is the first breaker.

You see the great love         —that one and another has in his heart:
watch him with a mule        —giving it a kick in its side.

If you give him a 'no' vote     —he'll put you on the Cross,
he'll give you such deceptions,  —that you'll die at Renderenie.

All the day he trifles           —with mocking women;
if a brother sees him,          —he's sent to prison.

It he's the sock maker's son     —or of the lowly butcher,
he will raise such stench        —with the commander's son.

# Brunetto Latini
## (c.1225–1294)

Brunetto Latini was born in Florence, was a member of the Guelf party and, due to the touchy political situation for a Guelf in Florence after the party's indirect defeat at the Battle of Monaperti on September 4, 1260, was sent to Paris as an ambassador. In other words, he was exiled. After the Florentine victory at the Battle of Benevento in 1266, he returned to Florence to hold several important positions: Protonotary for Charles of Anjou, Chancellor of the Commune, Consul of the Art of Justices and Notaries, one of the Priors of the city, and a member of the Council of the One Hundred. Along with his full participation in the politics of Florence, he was one of the mainstays of lay education in Florence. In educating the young men of Florence, Latini emphasized the importance classical rhetoric and literature as an intellectual and spiritual underpinning of a citizen's obligation to participate in the governance of the Commune. Classical rhetoric supplied the general formal rules for grammatical usage, developing arguments, writing letters, and speaking publicly. Classical literature, beyond its natural ability to serve as concrete examples of good rhetorical usage, supplied the content from which to learn about human history and morals. This form and content were to stress the liberty of Florence, the liberty of her citizens, and the necessity of individual moral goodness as a fundamental requisite for the preservation of a republican form of government. Citizens were to convey this, following Latini's example of communicating 'in volgare.' (For more on this, see, Quentin Skinner, *The Foundations of Modern Political Thought*, (Cambridge: Cambridge University Press, 1978, 36-48.) Charles Till Davis explains that "Brunetto set forth the old Roman ideal of fame as the reward for virtue, which is true nobility; the rhetorician or orator should persuade his fellow citizens to live according to justice and reason." This theme is one of a handful that is central to understanding Dante's entire oeuvre and its impression on Dante is a testimony to the fact that good teaching does make a difference. (Charles Till Davis, 'Education in Dante's Florence,' *Speculum*, Vol. XL, No. 3, 415–35.) The selection here, which stresses the importance of writing in a concise, economical style in the vernacular, is from *Il Tesoretto*, Latini's shortened Italian version of *Livre dou Trésor*, an encyclopedia he wrote in French while in exile in Paris.

## Brunetto Latini

Verse 395-426 da *Il Tesoretto*

E percio che 'l me' dire
io lo voglio ischiarire,
si ch'io non dica motto
che tu non sappie 'n tutto
la verace ragione
e la condizione,
faro mio detto piano,
che pur un solo grano
non sia che tu non sacci:
ma vo' che tanto facci,
che lo mio dire aprendi,
si che tutto lo 'ntendi;
e s'io parlassi iscuro,
ben ti faccio sicuro
di dicerlo in aperto,
si che ne sie ben certo.
Ma percio che la rima
si stringe a una lima
di concordar parole
come la rima vuole,
che molte fiate
le parole rimate
ascondon la sentenza
e mutan la 'ntendenza,
quando vorro trattare
di cose che rimare
tenesse oscuritate,
con bella brevetate
ti parlero per prosa,
e disporro la cosa
parlandoti in volgare,
che tu intende ed apare.

## Brunetto Latini

Lines 395–426 from *Il Tesoretto*

And because it is my poem,
I want to clarify,
so that I won't say a word
for which you won't know
the entire reason
and condition—
I will make my words plain,
that even a single grain
won't be that which you don't know:
but I want to do this much,
so you learn from my speech,
so you understand all of it—
and if I were to speak unclearly,
I would make you well certain
of saying it openly,
so you would be well sure of it.
But because rhyme
is polished with a file
of harmonious words
as poetry demands,
so that many times
rhymed words
hide their meaning
and change their intention,
when I want to treat
things— that rhyming
would obscure—
with beautiful brevity,
I will speak in prose
and put the thing in order,
speaking to you in the vernacular,
so you understand and learn.

# Guido Guinizzelli
# (c.1230–1276)

In *Canto XXVI* (97–99), of the *Purgatorio*, Dante names Guido Guinizzelli his poetic '*padre mio*' and credits him with founding a new school of love poetry that comes to be called, using the words of Dante, the *Dolce stil nuovo* (Sweet or Subtle New Style). Dante considers that Guido gave "miglior, che mai rime d'amor usâr dolci e leggiadre" ("better use than ever of love poetry, subtle and elegant"). Guido was born in Bologna, where he studied law and then served as professor of law at its university, one of Europe's great centers of learning. He married Beatrice della Fratta, later taking his family in exile to Monselice in 1274 with other Ghibelline outcasts. Guido, part of the new scientific and philosophical culture at Bologna, successfully distilled what the new school of poetry would consider to be the essence of Provencal/Sicilian love poetry: the idea that love and a gentle, noble heart are one. This concept, which did exist in some Provencal poetry, represents a sharp break from feudal notion that nobility is the result of birth, of inheritance. Guido, instead, equates it with individual attainment regardless of one's social background. Guido then uses the analytical and speculative modes of the new learning at the university to generate a new subject matter for love poetry: a philosophical, physical and psychological exploration of the nature of love, virtue and nobility. As marvellous as this poetry reads, as philosophically expansive as its analogies are, De Sanctis is quick to point out that its weakness can be its very strength, for "this subtlety and fantasy on love and being in love is not the langauge of one head over heels in love (De Sanctis, 89)." For example, in the sonnet *Lo vostro bel saluto e 'l dolce sguardo* Guido he equates the glance of the beloved as entering one's eyes like lighting. He further relates that the eyes are a weakness like the window of a tower, and that the beating and cutting to pieces of what is inside ultimately leaves the lover like a brass statue. Does such a string of intellectually apt metaphors really express the emotion of love?

## Guido Guinizelli

Al cor gentil rempaira sempre amore
come l'ausello in selva a la verdura;
né fe' amor anti che gentil core,
nè gentil core anti ch'amor, natura:
ch'adesso con' fu 'l sole,
sì tosto lo splendore fu lucente,
né fu davanti 'l sole;
e prende amore in gentilezza loco
così proprïamente
come calore in clarità di foco.

Foco d'amore in gentil cor s'aprende
come vertute in petra prezïosa,
che da la stella valor no i discende
anti che 'l sol la faccia gentil cosa;
poi che n'ha tratto fòre
per sua forza lo sol ciò che li è vile,
stella li dà valore:
così lo cor ch'è fatto da natura
asletto, pur, gentile,
donna a guisa di stella lo 'nnamora.

Amor per tal ragion sta 'n cor gentile
per qual lo foco in cima del doplero:
splendeli al su' diletto, clar, sottile;
no li stari' altra guisa, tant'è fero.
Così prava natura
recontra amor come fa l'aigua il foco
caldo, per la freddura.
Amore in gentil cor prende rivera
per suo consimel loco
com'adamàs del ferro in la minera.

Fere lo sole lo fango tutto 'l giorno:
vile reman, né 'l sol perde calore;
dis'omo alter: "Gentil per sclatta torno";
lui semblo al fango, al sol gentil valore:
ché non dé dar om fé
che gentilezza sia fòr di corraggio
in degnità d'ere'
sed a vertute non ha gentil core,
com'aigua porta raggio
e 'l ciel riten le stelle e lo splendore.

## Guido Guinizelli

To a gently noble heart love always returns
like a bird in the wild to the greenery;
nature neither made love before a gentle heart,
nor a gentle heart before love:
for now the sun was with it,
so quick the brightness was shining,
nor was it before the sun;
and love stays in a gentle place
so naturally
like heat in the clarity of fire.

The fire of love kindles in a gently noble heart
like virtue in a precious stone,
for from the stars power descends to us,
rather than the sun making it a gently noble thing;
since the sun has drawn outside
with its force that which is vile to it,
the star gives it power:
so the heart which is made elect by
nature, even, gently noble,
the Lady, in the manner of a star, loves it.

Love for such a reason stays in a gently noble heart
like fire at the top of a torch:
it shines at its pleasure, clear, subtly;
it can do no other, so fierce it is.
So a deprived nature
opposes love like water does
the fire, with the cold.
Love lives in a gently noble heart
for its natural home,
like a diamond in the mineral of iron.

The sun beats the mud all day:
it stays vile and the sun loses no heat;
the conceited man man says: "I'm noble by birth";
I compare him to mud, noble worth to the sun:
for no one must hold
that gentle nobility is outside the heart
with the dignity of an heir,
if he doesn't have a gentle heart of virtue,
as water reflects the rays
and heaven holds the stars and splendor.

Splende 'n la 'ntelligenzïa del cielo
Deo crïator più che ['n] nostr'occhi 'l sole:
ella intende suo fattor oltra 'l cielo,
e 'l ciel vogliando, a Lui obedir tole;
e con' segue, al primero,
del giusto Deo beato compimento,
così dar dovria, al vero,
la bella donna, poi che ['n] gli occhi splende
del suo gentil, talento
che mai di lei obedir non si disprende.

Donna, Deo mi dirrà: "Che presomisti?"
sïando l'alma mia a lui davanti.
"Lo ciel passasti e 'nfin a Me venisti
e desti in vano amor Me per semblanti:
ch'a Me conven le laude
e a la reina del regname degno,
per cui cessa onne fraude."
Dir Li porò: "Tenne d'angel sembianza
che fosse del Tuo regno;
non me fu fallo, s'in lei posi amanza."

God Creator shines more on the intelligence
than the sun on our eyes:
and it understands its creator beyond heaven,
and heaven commanding, it obeys Him;
and with what follows, in the beginning,
the blessed perfection of a just God,
so should the beautiful lady, indeed,
give—when she shines in the eyes
of her noble—a desire
that never tears away from obeying her.

Lady, God will ask: "What did you presume?"
my soul being before him:
"You passed through heaven, finally came
and, in vain, love woke me through a comparison:
for the praises come to me
and the queen of the worthy realm."
I will say to Him: "She took the semblance of an angel
who was from your realm—
it was not my fault to arrive at loving her."

# Rustico di Filippo
## (c. 1230–95)

Rustico di Filippi, a Florentine *popolano* and friend of Brunetto Latini, left us around 60 sonnets which fall into two categories: satiric and amorous. Of the satiric vein, *Dovunque vai, con teco porti il cesso* gives a spirited example of breadth of expression the Italian sonnet was capable of. Its street level, bawdy humor is something that is still an essential part of the Florentine urban experience, whether it comes to describing another commune's soccer team, playing a joke on another citizen or simply making fun of someone for the sake of making fun. Rustico's amorous sonnets, of which we have included two examples, are indicative of the widespread practice of writing love sonnets when it was fashionable and almost commonplace. If we take an historical view of such a practice, we might agree with Burckhadt, whose appraisal of the sonnet itself was high. We might extend such praise to even Rustico's love poems. After all, in one sense they indicate a level of refinement and learning for their author, show that Florentine culture was open to both new and literary things, and indicate, in a broad social sense, an awareness of the tenuous nature of so many human relationships. However, as De Sanctis has amply criticized on aesthetic grounds, such verse is artificial – it contains no real insight into the notion of love, brings nothing new to the genre of love poetry, seems devoid of any but the simplest inspiration and is removed from any individuated expression of actual life.

## Rustico di Filippo

*(act. 1260–90)*

1
Dovunque vai, con teco porti il cesso,
oi buggeressa vecchia puzzolente,
ché qualunque persona ti sta presso
si tura il naso e fugge immantenente.

Li denti 'n le gengie tue ménar gresso,
ché li tàseva l'alito putente;
le selle paion legna d'alcipresso
inver' lo tuo fragor, tan'è repente.

Ché par che s'apran mille monimenta
quand'apri il ceffo: perché non ti spolpe
o ti rinchiude sì ch'om non ti senta?

Però che tutto 'l mondo ti paventa;
in corpo credo figlinti le volpe,
tal lezzo n'esce fuor, sozza giomenta!


2
Io non auso rizzar, chiarita spera,
inver' voi gli occhi, tan'ho gelosia;
e feremi nel viso vostra spera
e gli occhi abbasso e non so là ove sia.

Oi amorosa ed avvenante cèra,
non mi tardate la speranza mia:
ch'ad onta de la gente malparliera,
mi riterrete in vostra segnoria.

Deo, como son lontan dal me' pensiero
li falsi e li noiosi maldicenti,
ché là non volgo l'arco ov'eo ne fero!

Ma tuttavia mi fan soffrir tormenti:
ché spesso l'amoroso viso clero
s'asconde per li falsi parlamenti.

## Rustico di Filippo

*(act. 1260–90)*

1
Wherever you go, you smell like shit—
you lying, smelly hag—
because anyone standing next to you
plugs their nose and runs away!

The teeth in your gums are tartared and stained,
and they leave you with stinking breath;
the chamber pots seem made of the fragrant wood of cypress,
because of your stench that overwhelms.

Since it seems you open a thousand rotting graves
when you open your mouth: why don't you stop
and shut it so no one smells it?

Because all the world fears you,
I deeply believe the foxes brought you forth,
such a stench escapes you, filthy necessary!


2
I am not used to raising my eyes, luminous
ray, toward you, such is my anxiety;
your light hurts my eyes,
so I lower them and don't know where I am.

Alas, loving and graceful countenance,
don't delay my hope:
that, in spite of gossiping folk,
you pull me back into your power.

God, how the false and hateful blasphemers
are far from my thoughts,
for I don't direct the bow where I could injure with it!

But above all they make me suffer torments:
for often the clear loving face
hides itself because of false talk.

3

Quant'io verso l'Amor più m'umilìo,
a me più mostra fèra segnoria;
e più monta e più cresce il meo disio,
e più mirpiù tien doglioso notte e dia.

Adunque, lasso! como faraggio io,
se non mi soccorrete, donna mia?
Se mi tardate, bella, a lo cor mio
durar non pò più vita, anzi va via.

Ciascun mi guarda in viso e fa dimando,
veggendomi cangiato lo visaggio:
ed io celo la doglia mia in parlando.

E non ardisco dir lo meo coraggio,
per ch'io l'ho da la mia donna in comando;
oimè lasso, ch'attendendo morraggio!

3

The more I humble myself to love,
the more he shows me fierce power—
and the more my desire increases,
and the more night and day make me suffer.

Oh, how I suffer! What will I do,
if you don't aid me, my lady?
If you deny me, beautiful, in my heart,
life won't be able to last, but will leave.

Everyone looks me in the face and wonders,
seeing my changed expression:
for I hide my suffering with words.

And I don't dare speak my heart,
because my lady ordered me not to.
Helpless me! That in serving I will die.

# La Compiuta Donzella
## (second half of 13th century)

Little is known of this anonymous woman poet from Florence in the second half of the Duecento, other than she was recognized by her contemporaries as an educated lady, as her pseudonym, The Accomplished Maid, suggests. Guittone d'Arezzo addressed a letter to her – and after two (of her three extent) sonnets below, we have one of the two poems an anonymous poet exchanged with her. The subject matter of her poems – if autobiographical, and we have no evidence to suggest that they aren't – highlights the rarity of a right we too often take for granted today: self-determination. Forced by her father to marry against her will, our poetess sublimates her desire for any life of her own into a longing for a better life after death, a union with Christ, the healer of all wounds.

## La Compiuta Donzella

1
A la stagion che il mondo foglia e fiora
accresce gioia a tutti i fini amanti:
vanno insieme a li giardini, allora
che gli augelletti fanno dolzi canti:

la franca gente tutta s'innamora
e di servir ciascun traggesi innanti
ed ogni damigella in gioia dimora;
a me n'abondan marrimenti e pianti;

ca lo mio padre m'ha messo 'n errore
e tenemi sovente in forte doglia:
donar mi vòle, a mia forza, signore.

Ed io di ciò non ho disio né voglia
e 'n gran tormento vivo a tutte l'ore;
però non mi rallegra fior né foglia.


2
Lasciar vorria lo mondo, e Dio servire,
e dipartirmi d'ogni vanitate,
però che veggio credscere e salire
mattezza e villania e falsitate;

ed ancor senno e cortesia morire,
e lo fin pregio e tutta la bontate;
ond'io marito non vorria né sire,
né stare al mondo per mia volontate.

Membrandomi ch'ogn'uom di mal s'adorna,
di chiaschedun son forte disdegnosa,
e verso Dio la mia persona torna.

Lo padre mio mi fa stare pensosa,
ché di servire a Cristo mi distorna:
non saccio a cui mi vuol dar per isposa.

## La Compiuta Donzella

1
During the season when the world blooms and flowers,
joy grows in all refined lovers:
they go together to the gardens, when
little birds sing sweet songs.

Noble people fall completely in love
and each man moves forward to serve
and every maiden lives in joy—
but as for me, grief and tears abound.

because my father has made a terrible mistake
and often finds me in awful pain:
he wants to give me—against my will—a husband.

And I neither wish nor desire this,
living each moment in great torment—
so that neither flower nor leaf delights me.


2
I would like to leave the world and serve God,
and strip myself of every vanity,
because I see madness, outrage and deceit
grow and prosper—

and I see wisdom and courtesy,
refinement and goodness die—
for I want neither a husband nor master,
nor to willingly remain in the world.

Reminding myself that every man adorns himself with evil
and that each one is completely disdainful,
my person turns to God.

My father keeps me anxious,
because he discourages me from serving Christ:
I don't know to whom he wants to give me as a wife.

*Anonimo in tenzone con Compiuta donzella*

1
Gentil donzella somma ed insegnata,
poi c'ag[g]io inteso di voi tan'or[r]anza,
che non credo che Morgana la fata
né la Donna de[l] Lago né Gostanza

né fosse alcuna come voi presc[i]ata;
e di trovare avete nominanza
(ond'eo mi faccio un po' di mirata
c'avete di saver tant'abondanza):

però, se no sdegnaste lo meo dire,
vor[r]ia venire a voi, poi non sia sag[g]io,
a ciò che 'n tutto mi poria chiarire

di ciò ch'eo dotto ne lo mio corag[g]io;
e so che molto mi poria 'nantire
aver contia del vostro segnorag[g]io.

*An anonymous poet in exchange with Compiuta Donzella*

1
Gentle maiden, complete and cultured,
after I learned of your horror,
I don't believe that the Fate Morgana,
nor the Lady of the Lake, nor Gostanza,

nor anyone is as insightful as you;
then to discover you have a reputation
(for I've checked around
and your intelligence is renowned):

however, if you don't discount my advice,
I want to come to you since you don't know
what I want to clarify,

of what I, learned in my bravery—
because I know that I would submit
in order to know your sovereignty.

# Anonima Poetessa
## (later 13th century)

Nothing is known of this anonymous poetess, other than she, like many others involved in love, was jilted for another. Of particular note in this sonnet is very successful extended conceit of love analogized as hunting for birds with a trained sparrow-hawk.

## Anonima Poetessa

Tapina me che amavo uno sparviero,
amavol tanto, ch'io me ne moría,
a lo richiamo ben m'era maniero
ed unque troppo pascer no 'l dovía.

Or è montato e salito sì altero,
assai piú altero che non far solía;
ed è assiso dentro a un verziero,
e un'altra donna l'averà in balí.

Isparvier mio, ch'io t'avea nodrito,
sonaglio d'oro ti facea portare,
perché nell'uccellar fossi piú ardito;

or sei salito siccome lo mare,
ed hai volto li geti e sei fuggito
quando eri fermo nel tuo uccellare.

## Anonymous Poetess

Wretched me who loved a sparrow-hawk,
I loved him so such that I'll die from it:
at the sound of the bird call he was obedient,
and in no way did I feed him too much.

Now he's ascended to new heights,
much higher than he ever used to—
next he's seated in a garden
and another woman has him in her power.

My hawk, that I nourished,
I made him carry a golden bell,
for I was the boldest at hunting—

now you're as free as the sea,
having broken your bands, escaping
when you were caught in your own hunt.

# Iacopo da Lèona

Little is known of Jacopo da Lèona. The son of Tancredi da Lèona, he was both a judge and notary in Volterra until 1274. He also served as the notary for Bishop Ranieri degli Ubertini. His eight surviving sonnets run that gamut, from courtly love poetry to both the comic and obscene. *Amor m'auzide* is a sonnet that contains a dialogue between a smitten young man and his friend offering him advice.

## Iacopo da Lèona

—Amor m'auzide.—Per che?—Per ch'io amo,
—Cui?—La bella.—E non è ella saggia?
—Sì è.—Bene fai dunque.—Altro non bramo.
—Se non che?—Se non lei.—Fa sì che l'aggia.
—Como?—Servi.—Eo servo e merzé chiamo.
—Non ti val?—Non.—Dunqu'è ella salvaggia?
—Non è.—Che è?—Non la fere ancor l'amo.
—Dove?—Al core.—S'è d'amor loco, assaggia.
—Varrami?—Sì bene.—Omè, troppo tarda!
—Non tarda.—Non?—chéd ell'è già ripresa.
—Di cui?—Di te.—Altro 'l mio cor non guarda.
—Ricco se'.—Come?—Per far lung'attesa.
—Che n'ho?—La bella.—Prima vuol ch'io arda.
—Non vuol.—Come 'l sai?—Non fa più difesa.—

## Iacopo da Lèona

—Love kills me.—Why?—Because I love.
—Who?—The beauty.—Then, she isn't wise?
—Yes, she is.—Love her, then.—I dare nothing else.
—If not what?—If not her.—Make so you have her.
—How?—Serve.—I serve and call mercy.
—Does it work?—No.—So, she's hard-hearted?
—She isn't.—Who is?—I don't offend, but love.
—Where?—In the heart.—If it's of the place of love, taste.
—You would launch me?—Of course.—Alas, it seems too late!
—It isn't.—No?—She's ready to carry on.
—With who?—With you.—My heart sees no other.
—You're rich.—How so?—By making a long siege.
—What will I have for it?—The beauty.—First she wants me to burn.
—She doesn't.—How do you know?—She no longer defends.

# Chiaro Davanzati
## (act. 2nd half of 13th century)

Much like Rustico's love sonnets, Chairo Davanzati's poems demonstrate an incipient Renaissance culture in Florence that was open to new ideas. Moreover, there is a mellifluous flow to his verse that is in keeping with the idea that love is wonderful, his lady is beautiful and pure, etc. From our vantage point, both his and Rustico's verse give, by way of contrast, an idea of the innovative capacities of two of their successors: Guido Cavalcanti and Dante.

## Chiaro Davanzati

La splendïente luce, quando apare,
in ogne scura parte da chiarore;
cotant'ha di vertute il suo guardare,
che sovra tutti gli altri e 'l suo splendore:

così madonna mia face alegrare,
mirando lei, chi avesse alcun dolore;
adesso lo fa in gioia ritornare,
tanto sormonta e passa il suo valore.

E l'altre donne fan di lei bandiera,
imperadrice d'ogni costumanza,
perch' è di tutte quante la lumera;

e li pintor la miran per usanza
per trare asempro di sì bella cera,
per farne a l'altre genti dimostranza.

## Chiaro Davanzati

The shining light, when it appears,
enlightens every dark corner;
so full of virtue is her glance,
that her splendor transcends all the others:

so my Lady makes happy
any suffering soul who looks at her—
suddenly she makes their joy return,
so transcending is her worth.

And other women spread her fame,
Empress of every fashion,
because she is everyone's light;

And painters always look at her
in order to copy her beautiful face,
as an example to other nobility.

# Guido Cavalcanti
## (c. 1250–1300)

In his *Vita nuova*, Dante refers to Guido Cavalcanti as his best friend and credits him with the idea that poetry should be written in the vernacular. Francesco De Sanctis judged him "the first Italian poet worthy of this name, because he was the first who had a sense and feel of the real. The empty generalities of the troubadours, having become a scientific and rhetorical subject, are in him alive, because, when he wrote for pleasure or simply to vent, he rendered the impressions and sentiments of the soul. Poetry that before him thought and described, now narrated and represented, not in the simple and rough manner of the older poets, but with that grace and those refinements to which the language had come, managed with perfect mastery by Guido" (De Sanctis, 110). Cavalcanti was a complex man, by nature haughty and at times withdrawn, he was also an animated conversationist, a hot-headed protagonist for his own views and a student of rhetoric and philosophy. An advocate of the ideas of the Arab philosopher Averroës, Cavalcanti believed that a human being was divided into three elements: the vegetative, in which humans shared a similarity with plants, maintained the most fundamental functions; the sensitive, which humans shared with animals, allowed people to feel with their senses and experience such basic appetites as hunger for food, the desire for sex, the wish for bodily comfort, etc.; and, the intellectual, which gave humanity reason and enabled to think, communicate with words and, essentially, distinguish itself from plants and animals. Averroës held that the intellect was part of a universal consciousness that it returned to after an individual died. This meant that self-identity was not realized through the intellect, but achieved through the sensitive faculty. Moreover, higher consciousness, the bonum perfectum, was attained by balancing the intellectual and sensitive faculties. However, for Guido this was impossible because the power of love was so strong that when felt in the sensitive faculty, it completely overwhelmed the rational one. Love resulted, then, in the death of reason, the death of the mind. This pessimism is evident in both poems here. In *Noi siàn le triste pene isbigotite*, Cavalcanti's relates the suffering embodied in his own writing of love poetry through the personification of the implements used in writing: the quill and the knife used to sharpen it, along with the scissors used to cut the parchment. In *Donna me prega*, one of the masterpieces of Italian poetry, Cavalcanti relates his theory of love, the forces that work on the human consciousness, how parts of human consciousness react to love, the physiological response to love and the bittersweet nature of the total experience. Above all, Cavalcanti was able to successfully merge profoundly considered experiences of love with the deep and tangled emotions that sprang from it.

## Guido Cavalcanti

1
Noi siàn le triste pene isbigotite,
le cesoiuzze e 'l coltellin dolente,
ch'avemo scritte dolorosamente
quelle parole che vo' avete udite.

Or vi diciàn perché noi sià partite
e sià venute a voi qui di presente:
la man che ci movea dice che sente
cose dubbiose nel core apparite;

le quali hanno destrutto sì costui
ed hannol posto sì presso a la morte,
ch'altro non v'è rimaso che sospiri.

Or vi preghiàn quanto possiàn più forte
che non sdeg[i]ate di tenerci noi,
tanto ch'un poco di pietà vi miri.

SPIGOTIRE — TO STUN, TO DISMAY

NOI SIÀM WE ARE

CESOIUZZE — SHEARS

## Guido Cavalcanti

1
We sad, despondent quills,
sorrowing scissors and knife
have written in anguish
these words you've heard.

Now we speak to you leaving
and coming to your presence:
the hand moving us feels
doubtful things appear in the heart—

*COMPARE*
*w/*
*ORIGINAL(?)*  ←

so destroying him,
so taking him near death,
so but to sigh...

We ask how much stronger we must be
that you don't disdain us—
until you look with a little pity.

2

Donna me prega—per ch'eo voglio dire
d'un accidente-che sovente—è fero
ed è sì altero—ch'è chiamato amore:
sì chi lo nega—possa 'l ver sentire!
5   Ed a presente—conoscente—chero,
perch'io no spero—ch'om di basso core
a tal ragione porti canoscenza:
chè, senza—natural dimostramento
non ho talento—di voler provare
10   là dove posa, e chi lo far creare,
e qual sia sua vertute e sua potenza,
l'essenza—poi e ciascun suo movimento,
e 'l piacimento—che 'l fa dire amare,
e s'omo per veder lo pò mostrare.

15   In quella parte—dove sta memora
prende suo stato—sì formato—come
diaffan da lume—d'una scuritate
la qual da Marte—vène, e fa demora;
elli è creato—ed ha sensato—nome,
20   d'alma costume—e di cor volontate.
Vèn da veduta forma che s'intende,
che prende—nel possibile intelletto,
come in subietto—loco e dimoranza.
In quella parte mai non ha pesanza
25   perchè da qualitate non descende:
respende—in sé perpetüal effetto;
non ha diletto—ma consideranza;
sì che non pote largir simiglianza.

Non è vertute—ma da quella vène
30 ch'è perfezione—(ché si pone—tale),
non razionale—ma che sente, dico;
for di salute—giudicar mantene,
chè, la 'ntenzione—per ragione—vale:
discerne male—in cui è vizio amico.
35   Di sua potenza segue spesso morte,
se forte—la vertù fosse impedita,
la quale aita—la contraria via:
non perché, oppost' a naturale sia;
ma quanto che da buon perfetto tort'è
40 per sorte—non pò dire om ch'aggia vita,
ché, stabilita—non ha segnoria.
A simil pò valer quand'om l'oblia.

68

2

Woman asks me—for which I want to speak
of something extraneous—often—fierce
so proud—called love:
whoever denies it—can hear the truth!
5   about this—knowing—expert
as I don't expect—men with vile hearts
   to know:
because without—natural demonstration,
I haven't the desire—the will to prove
10   where it rests, and who makes it act,
   what are its virtues, its power,
its essence—each movement,
its predilection—making one call it love-ing,
demonstrably seen.

15   In that part—where memory
is—so formed—like
translucence from light—from a shadow
   of Mars—it came and lives,
created—judicious—named,
20   of a typical soul—and a willing heart.
   It came from the visible form of one in love,
it takes—in the potential intellect
as in the subject—position and residence,
never physical there,
25   since it descends not from matter:
shining—in its own perpetual effect,
not delighting—but reflecting
beyond all comparison.

   It's not virtue—but came from what
30   is perfectable—(one posits—such)
not rational—but feeling, I say
   beyond salvation—within judgment,
because its intention—by natural law—prevails:
recognizing evil—vice's friend.
35   Death often follows its power
if strong—virtue is impeded
that aids—the opposite way:
not because it violates nature,
   but based on how far sin is—by chance—from
40   'good perfection'—I can't explain to one alive
because stability—reigns not:
the same happens to one abstaining.

L'essere è quando—lo voler è tanto
ch'oltra misura—di natura—torna,
45   poi non s'adorna—di riposo mai.
   Move, cangiando—color, riso in pianto,
e la figura—con paura—storna;
poco soggiorna—ancor di lui vedrai
   che 'n gente di valor lo più—si trova.
50   La nova—qualità move sospiri,
e vol ch'om miri—'n non formato loco,
destandos' ira la qual manda foco
   (imaginar nol pote om che nol prova),
né mova—già però ch'a lui si tiri,
55 e non si giri—per trovarvi gioco:
né, cert'ha mente gran saver né, poco.

   De simil tragge—complessione sguardo
che fa parere—lo piacere—certo:
non pò coverto—star, quand'è sì giunto.
60   Non già selvagge—le bieltà son dardo,
ché tal volere—per temere—è sperto:
consiegue merto—spirito ch'è punto.

   E non si pò conoscer per lo viso:
compriso—bianco in tale obietto cade;
65   e, chi ben aude—forma non si vede:
dunqu' elli meno, che da lei procede.
   For di colore, d'essere diviso,
assiso—'n mezzo scuro, luce rade.
For d'ogne fraude—dico, degno in fede,
70   che solo di costui nasce mercede.

   Tu puoi sicuramente gir, canzone,
là 've ti piace, ch'io t'ho sì adornata
ch'assai laudata—sarà tua ragione
da le persone—c'hanno intendimento:
75   di star con l'altre tu non hai talento.

It exists when—desire is
   beyond measure—of nature—it comes,
45 then does not honor—never resting—
      it moves, changing—color, laughs to tears—
   and the victim—with fear—turns away
   of short duration—you'll see it
      more in people of worth.
50   Fresh—it causes sighs,
   wanting attention—in an ambiguous place,
   awakening an ire that causes fire,
      (unimaginable to the inexperienced)
   neither moving—for one is already drawn
55   and can't escape—to find delight,
   nor knowing anything certain.

      Similarly it extracts—a glance
   that appears—pleasurable—certain,
   unable to hide—or remain, once arrived.
60   Not initially savage—beauties are arrows,
   so excess desire—by fear—reigns
   attaining redemption—the spirit that is wounded,
      one's face reveals nothing:
   repressed—pallor overwhelming the victim
65   and, who hears well—sees nothing:
   therefore, Love leads, who from her proceeds.
      Colorless, a being divided,
   sealed—in the middle of darkness, light erasing light,
   beyond deceit—I say in good faith:
70   mercy comes only from Love.

      Go with certainty, my song,
   where you please, since I've so adorned you
   that so praised—will be your nature—
   by people—who are in love:
   you won't desire to stay with outsiders.

# Dante Alighieri
## (1265–1321)

Although not generally known, Dante was one of Karl Marx's favorite poets. This might seem surprising to us since Marx hated the very things that were the underpinnings of Dante's age: feudalism; an incipient capitalistic system; aristocratic political systems that were far from democratic; and, a view of the natural universe based on the seeming superstitious notions of Christian spiritualism, astrology and alchemy. Yet, Marx understood that artistic taste, or perhaps even more broadly, one's view of life, could not be explained by simple ideological schemes, even if he was (along with Friedrich Engels) the inventor of one such scheme. In keeping with this seeming ideological inconsistency – or cultural cosmopolitanism – Marx's favorite art was that of Classical Athens, a society based, in part, on imperial conquest and slavery. All this should, then, serve to warn that in aesthetic matters things are more complex than our ideological paradigms are capable of explaining. Rather than writing off this and that as so much political uncorrectness, we might be better off abiding by Marx's maxim: *Nihil humani a me alienum puto* (Nothing human is alien to me).

To the young student whose idea of extended study goes no further than the brief moment so enshrined by our sound-byte culture, Dante is indeed a monkey wrench thrown into the works. He took on his own age with poetry – lots of it. He disagreed with the majority of those in power. Further, he championed the idea that individuals do have choices and do make differences. To our relativistic ears, he may seem harsh because he does, in his *Divina commedia*, come to final judgments on a variety of individuals and issues. However, from his point of view in an age where business, politics and religion melded into a brazen game of acquisition and self-interest, a lone voice calling for some sense of sanity was not unreasonable. His position is something each and every of us should consider with more than casual attention.

Dante, a shortened version of Durante, was born in Florence in May of 1265. Both of his parents died in his youth and he was raised by well caring relatives. Around 1285, he was married to Gemma di Manetto Donati, the daughter of the powerful Donati clan, after having been formally betrothed to her in 1277. Being well connected, Dante had tremendous opportunities to learn in city like Florence, one of the metropolitan centers of Europe. Experientially, he was exposed to business, politics and culture. In his grammar school, he would have read in grammar school from Cato, Aesop and the Bible. He also received basic instruction in grammar and arithmetic, the contemporary essentials for commerce. In adolescence, he would have studied Boethius, Cicero, and Aristotle. We also know that the young Dante was familiar with many Provencal, Sicilian and classical poets. Of the latter, Dante speaks of Homer, Horace, Lucan, Ovid and Virgil in the *Vita Nuova*. Above all, Dante was strongly influenced by Brunetto Latini, who emphasized the importance classical rhetoric and literature as an intellectual and spiritual underpinning of a citizen's obligation to participate in the governance of the Commune.

Governing the commune was no easy task. At mid-13th century, Florence, an independent city-state or commune, was divided into two warring political factions, the Guelf party, mostly allied with the expansionist minded papacy, and the Ghibellines, often allied with the imperial designs of the Holy Roman Emperor. Their political struggle, intensified by the interests of foreigners, was driven locally by an intense economic struggle between the established landed aristocrats and the up-and-coming, cash-based middle class merchants. The stakes were simple, but tangible: control of Florence's booming economy. In 1260, the Ghibellines, with Sicilian help, defeated the Guelfs at the battle of Montaperti. In 1266, the Guelfs, with French help, triumphed over the Ghibellines at Benevento. The Ghibellines were banished from Florence forever. However, the dispute did not end there, for the Guelfs eventually split into two factions: the White Guelfs allied with the Ghibellines and the Black Guelfs, who favored the Papacy.

Dante came to the middle of this struggle. In 1300, he was elected to be one of the six *Priori*, the most powerful part of the Florentine government. Soon after his election, the hostility between the Whites and the Blacks erupted into open violence. Dante and his fellow Priors banished the leaders of both factions. Among Whites was Dante's best friend, Guido Cavalcanti. The Blacks plotted with Boniface VIII and Charles of Valois to return themselves to power. First, they had Dante called to Rome to discuss the situation with the Pope. Then, Charles of Valois entered Florence with his army, the Blacks returned, and the White's houses and businesses were looted for nearly a week. While Dante's house was sacked, his wife Gemma hid with relatives. Next, Dante was falsely convicted of selling government positions and soliciting bribery. For not answering these charges in person – he was still enjoying the company of the Pope – Dante was first exiled for two years and then condemned to be burnt to death. Dante heard of all this in Siena while returning from Rome. He was effectively *declassé*, separated from his family, deprived of his income, and possessing no citizenship with which to participate in politics. Indeed, from his point of view, virtue was left to wander without a home.

Given the treachery that he suffered in his political life, it is not surprising that two of Dante's main ideas are virtue and nobility, both of which he derived from Aristotle, Augustine Christianity and the philosophy of St. Thomas Aquinas. Central to Dante's system is the Aristotelian notion that human beings are different from any other beings in nature. "The specific capacity, then, which differentiates man is not merely being....nor animated being, for this is in plants; nor apprehension, for this is shared by the brutes; but apprehension by means of the possible intellect...." (*De monarchia*, I, iii, 45–55). According to Christian dogma, God wanted all humans to use their minds to come to know him through the study of the universe that he created for them. Such a life requires, then, both thought and action, respectively, the *vita contemplativa* and the *vita activa*. The end of the vita contemplativa was philosophy, or more precisely, the love of wisdom. The end of the vita activa, was to use this wisdom to achieve harmony with other human beings. Dante writes that "....it is the fact that in sedentary quietness the individual man is perfected in knowledge and in wisdom [the contemplative life], it is evident that in the quiet or tranquility of peace the human race is most freely and favourably disposed [the active life]....Whence it is manifest that universal peace is the best of all those things which are ordained for our blessedness" (*De monarchia*, I, iv).

The virtue of peace or harmony is achieved like any other virtue. Avoid excess and aim for the mean between two extremes. Avoid defects by striving for excellence. Avoid personal gain. Instead, strive for nobility, the state in which each thing has "the perfection of the nature peculiar to it." For human kind this is the habit of exercising right choice (*De monarchia*, IV, xvi) Finally, Dante writes: "And it is plain that man's nobility is nothing else than the seed of happiness dispatched by God to the soul that is in good setting, that is the soul whose body is perfectly adjusted in every part" (*De monarchia*, IV, xx). In conclusion, both the *vita contemplativa* and *activa* should end in the well-balanced harmony of seeking truth, avoiding personal gain and seeking peace with others.

At the end of the 13th century in Florence, Dante, Guido Cavalcanti, and to a lesser extent, Cino da Pistoia, Lapo Gianni, and Gianni Alfani developed a new poetic style called the *Dolce stil nuovo* (literally, the Sweet or Subtle New Style). While, the *stilnovisti* borrowed from both the Provencal troubadours and the Sicilian poets, they developed their own special qualities that set their poetry apart.

Vittorio Cian points out that the "truly beautiful and alive" elements in this poetry were "the sincerity, the spontaneity of inspiration, the truth and freshness of observation, the bent for representing the internal and external world, the psychological profundity, the affirmation of human individuality, the sense of the divine and infinite in a sweet mysticism materialized in human love along with that veil of melancholy and grieving sadness that inevitably accompanies it..." (Cian, 16).

Just as Dante and his peers believed that the tangible world was not the ultimate reality but simply an imperfect mirror of heaven, so they held that there were many possible meanings beyond the literal word and text. Consequently, Dante and his peers tended to look beyond the literal to multiple levels of allegorical meaning in poetry. For instance, while Dante literally tells of his love for Beatrice, woman he first saw in a dream, he himself explains allegorically that Beatrice embodies virtuous love and virtue itself. Further, there are other meanings beyond this, particularly Dante's emphasis on personal, communal, moral, and religious reconciliation that would serve as an antidote to the deterioration of political relationships in Florence. Mario Marti explains that "the new poetics did not blossom weakly in closed circles, but descended to the streets, totally laid bare, ready to sustain encounters and clashes that would leave their mark." Dante's poetry "takes us back to the bitter measures, the sense and color of a militant culture against the background of the life and history of the Commune [of Florence]" (Marti, 161–2).

Since translations of Dante's *Divina commedia* abound in our libraries, the selection of Dante's poetry in this volume is exclusively from his lyric poems.

*Alighieri*

1
*Dante ai fedeli d'amore*

> A ciascun'alma presa e gentil core
> nel cui cospetto ven lo dir presente,
> in ciò che mi riscrivan suo parvente,
> salute in lor segnor, cioè Amore.
>
> 5  Già eran quasi che atterzate l'ore
> del tempo che onne stella n'è lucente,
> quando m'apparve Amor subitamente,
> cui essenza membrar mi dà orrore.
>
> Allegro mi sembrava Amor tenendo
> 10  meo core in mano, e ne le braccia avea
> madonna involta in un drappo dormendo.
>
> Poi la svegliava, e d'esto core ardendo
> lei paventosa umilmente pascea:
> appresso gir lo ne vedea piangendo.

2
*Guido Cavalcanti a Dante in risposta al Sonetto 1*

> Vedeste, al mio parere, onne valore
> e tutto gioco e quanto bene om sente
> se foste in prova del segnor valente
> che segnoreggia il mondo de l'onore,
>
> 5  poi vive in parte dove noia more
> e ten ragion nel casser de la mente:
> sì va soave per sonni a la gente,
> che i cor ne porta sanza far dolore.
>
> Di voi lo cor ne portò, veggendo
> 10  che vostra donna la morte chedea;
> nodrilla de lo cor, di ciò tememdo.
>
> Quando v'apparve che ne gia dogliendo,
> fu dolce sonno ch'allor si compiea,
> ché 'l su' contraro lo venia vincendo.

*Alighieri*

1

*Dante to Love's Faithful*

> To each captive and nobly gentle heart
> in whose sight comes this present poem,
> returning to me his response,
> of greeting to their Lord, that is, Love.
>
> Already it was four am,
> at that time when every star shines,
> when love suddenly appeared to me,
> whose essential form gives me horror to remember.
>
> Happily Love seemed to hold
> 10 my heart in his hand—and in his arm
> had my Lady wrapped in a mantle sleeping.
>
> Then he woke her and this burning heart
> to fearful her humbly fed—
> then I saw him turn away...crying...


2

*Guido Cavalcanti to Dante in response to Sonnet 1*

> If it were mine, you'd see every value
> and joy and good feeling
> if you knew of the worthy lord
> who rules the world of honor,
>
> 5  living where trouble dies,
> reasoning in the mind's citadel:
> visiting people's dreams,
> painlessly transporting their hearts.
>
> He took your heart away, seeing
> 10 your Lady ask for your death,
> nourishing her with your trembling heart...
>
> ...when you see it leave sorrowing,
> the sweet trance ends—
> defeated by its enemy.

3

*Cino da Pistoia (o Terino da Castelfiorentino) a Dante in risposta al Sonetto 1*

Natualmente chere ogni amadore
di suo cor la sua donna far saccente,
e questo per la vision presente
intese di mostrare a te l'Amore

5   in ciò che de lo tuo ardente core
pascea la tua donna umilmente,
che lungamente stata era dormente,
involta in drappo, d'ogne pena fore.

Allegro si mostrò Amor, venendo
10  a te per darti ciò ch 'l cor chieda,
insieme due coraggi comprendendo;

e l'amorosa pena conoscendo
che ne la donna conceputo avea,
per pietà di lei pianse partendo.

4

*Dante da Maiano a Dante Alighieri in risposta al Sonetto 1*

Di ciò che stato sei dimandatore,
guardando, ti rispondo brevemente,
amico meo di poco canoscente,
mostrandoti del ver lo suo sentore.

5   Al tuo mistier così son parlatore:
se san ti truovi e fermo de la mente,
che lavi la tua coglia largamente,
a ciò che stinga e passi lo vapore

lo qual ti fa favoleggiar loquendo;
10  e se gravato sei d'infertà rea,
sol c'hai farneticato, sappie, intendo.

Così riscritto el meo parer ti rendo;
né cangio mai d'esta sentenza mea,
fin che tua acqua al medico no stendo.

3

*Cino da Pistoia (or Terino da Castelfiorentino) to Dante in response to Sonnet 1*

Every lover naturally seeks
to make his Lady know his heart
and this with the present vision
is intended to show Love to you,

5    whereby your Lady humbly
eats your burning heart,
distantly sleeping,
wrapped in a mantle—beyond every pain.

Quickly Love appeared, seeing
10 what your heart asked for,
putting two hearts together—

then—knowing the amorous grief
he saw in your Lady,
he cried in pity for her...parting...

4

*Dante da Maiano to Dante Alighieri in response to Sonnet 1*

To what you've asked,
reflecting, I respond briefly,
my friend of little knowledge,
giving you true advice.

5    I speak of your need—
if you are healthy and of sound mind—
Wash your balls in cold water,
so the vapor—which makes you fantasize—

passes and extinguishes itself;
10 and if you're infirm,
I imagine you're only delirious—may you know—

As such I send my poetic view on this matter;
I won't change my judgment,
until a doctor looks at your urine.

*[handwritten marginalia: WTF — cold WATER? ACQUA FREDDA IN A BOOK w/ BIZARRE TRANSLATIUM — THIS IS ONE STANDS OUT]*

5

Cavalcando l'altr'ier per un cammino,
pensoso de l'andar che mi sgradia,
trovai Amore in mezzo de la via
in abito leggier di peregrino.

5  Ne la sembianza me parea meschino,
come avesse perduto segnoria:
e sospirando pensoso venia,
per non veder la gente, a capo chino.

Quando mi vide, mi chiamò per nome,
10 e disse: "Io vengo di lontana parte,
ov'era lo tuo cor per mio volere;

e recalo a servir novo piacere."
Allora presi di lui sì gran parte,
ch'elli disparve, e non m'accorsi come.

5

Horseback riding the day before yesterday,
pensive about this trip that disgusts me,
I found Love in the middle of the road
in the elegant clothes of a pilgrim.

5 His face appeared wretched
as if he lost his reign:
and sighing he came pensively,
avoiding the multitude, his head down.

When he saw me, he called my name
10 and said—"I come from far away,
where your heart serves my will;

and I lead it to serve new pleasures."
Iust as I was completely taken in by him,
he disappeared...and I didn't know how.

6

Donne ch'avete intelleto d'amore,
i' vo' con voi de la mia donna dire,
non perch'io creda sua laude finire,
ma ragionar per isfogar la mente.
5 Io dico che pensando il suo valore,
Amor sì dolce mi fa sentire,
che s'io allora non perdessi ardire,
farei parlando innamorar la gente.
E io non vo' parlar sì altamente,
10 ch'io divenisse per temenza vile;
ma tratterò del suo stato gentile
a rispetto di lei leggeramente,
donne e donzelle amorose, con vui,
ché non è cosa da parlarne altrui.

15 Angelo clama in divino intelletto
e dice: "Sire, nel mondo si vede
maraviglia ne l'atto che procede
d'un anima ch 'nfin qua su risplende".
Lo cielo, che non have altro difetto
20 che d'aver lei, al suo segnor chiede,
e ciascun santo ne grida merzede.
Sola Pietà nostra parte difende,
ché parla Dio, che di madonna intende:
"Diletti miei, or sofferite in pace
25 che vostra spene sia quanto me piace
là 'v' è alcun che perder lei s'attende,
e che dirà ne lo inferno: O mal nati,
io vidi la speranza de' beati".

Madonna è disiata in sommo cielo:
30 or voi di sua virtù farvi savere.
Dico, qual vuol gentil donna parere
vada con lei, che quando va per via,
gitta nei cor villani Amore un gelo,
per che onne lor pensero agghiaccia, e pere;
35 e qual soffrisse di starla a vedere
diverria nobil cosa, o si morria.
E quando trova alcun che degno sia
di veder lei, quei prova sua vertute,
ché li avvien, ciò che li dona, in salute,
40 e sì l'umilia, ch'ogni offesa oblia.
Ancor l'ha Dio per maggior grazia dato
che non pò mal finir chi l'ha parlato.

6

Women who have intellects of Love,
I go with you to speak of my Lady,
not believing I can complete her praises,
but in order to vent my mind.
5   I say thinking of her power and worth,
Love so sweet makes me feel
I would never lose that boldness,
speaking I would make people love her.
And I don't want to speak so nobly
10  that I become cowardly from fear;
but I will treat her noble state
gently for her sake,
gentle loving women, with you,
for there is nothing to say to others.

15  An angel invokes divine intellect
saying: "Lord, in the world we see
marvelous actions proceeding
from her soul shining above."
Heaven, having no other defect
20  than having her, asks the Lord
as each Saint cries out for Mercy.
Only Pity defends our cause,
until God who loves my Lady speaks:
"My delights you would suffer in peace,
25  if your hope were as great as I would like
there where those lost souls await her,
and who will say in Hell: O evil born
I have seen the hope of the blessed."

My Lady is desired at Heaven's summit:
30  now I want to make you know her Virtue
I say, she who wants to be a gentle lady
go with her when she goes out,
Love casts a chill in rude hearts,
so that all their thoughts freeze...and fade;
35  and who suffers to see her
would become noble...or die.
Then when she finds one worthy of
seeing her, he recovers his virtue,
from what she gives as salvation,
40  and she so humbles him, he forgets every fault.
Again, God has given her such Grace
whoever speaks of her can come to no bad end.

Dice di lei Amor: "Cosa mortale      A
come esser pò sì adorna e sì pura?"      B
45 Poi la reguarda, e fra se stesso giura      B
che Dio ne 'ntenda di far cosa nova.      C
Color di perle ha quasi, in forma quale      A
convene a donna aver, non for misura:      B
ella è quanto de ben pò far natura;      B
50 per essemplo di lei bieltà si prova.      C
De li occhi suoi, come ch'ella li mova,      C
escono spiriti d'amore inflammati,      D
che feron li occhi a qual che allor la guati,      D
e passan sì che 'l cor ciascun retrova,      C
55 voi le vedete Amor pinto nel viso,      E
là 've non pote alcun mirarla fiso.      E

Canzone, io so che tu girai parlando
a donna assai, quand'io t'avrò avanzata.
Or t'ammonisco, perch'io t'ho allevata
60 per figliuola d'Amor giovane e piana,
che là 've giugni tu dichi pregando:
"Insegnatemi gir, ch'io son mandata
a quella di cui laude so' adornata".
E se non vuoli andar sì come van,
65 non restare ove sia gente villana:
ingegnati, se puoi, d'essere palese
solo con donne o con omo cortese,
che ti merranno là per via tostana.
Tu troverai Amor con esso lei;
70 raccomandami a lui come tu dei.

Love says of her: "How could a
mortal thing be so complete and so pure?"
45 Then he considers her and swears to himself
that God intends to make a new thing.
She has the color of pearl in the form
necessary for a woman not beyond comprehension:
she is as much good nature can make;
50 selecting her as an example of beauty.
From her moving eyes—as only she can—
come inflamed spirits of Love,
injuring onlooking eyes,
passing to each seeking heart:
55 you see Love painted in her face
where no one dare look.

Canzone, I know that you will go about speaking
enough to ladies after I have polished you.
Now I warn you, for I have raised you
60 for the young and clear daughter of Love,
there where you arrive you say imploringly:
"Teach me to stretch out for I am sent
to her with whose praises I am adorned."
And if you don't want to go in vain.
65 don't stop with vile people:
strive, if you can, to be at home
only with courtly ladies and gentlemen
who will lead you on the quickest path.
You will find Love with her;
70 speak favorably of me to him as you must.

*A LITTLE*
*OVERCOOKED*

## 7
## Risposta d'anonimo alla Canzone 6 in nome delle donne e della canzone

Ben aggia l'amoroso e dolce core
che vol noi donne di tanto servire,
che sua dolze ragion ne face audire,
la qual è piena di piacer piagente;
5 che ben è stato bon conoscidore,
poi quella dov'è fermo lo disire
nostro per donna volerla seguire,
perché di noi ciascuna fa saccente,
ha conosciuta sì perfettamente
10 e 'nclinatosi a lei col core umile;
sì che di noi catuna il dritto istile
terrà, pregando ognora dolzemente
lei cui s'è dato, quando fia con noi,
ch'abbia merzé di lui co gli atti suoi.

15 Ahi Deo, com'have avanzato 'l su' detto
partendolo da noi in alta sede!
e com'have 'n sua laude dolce fede,
che ben ha cominzato e meglio prende!
Torto seria tal omo esser distretto
20 o malmenato di quella al cui pede
istà inclino, e sì perfetto crede,
dicendo sì pietoso, e non contende,
ma dolci motti parla, sì ch'accende
li cori d'amor tutti e dolci face;
25 sì che di noi nessuna donna tace,
ma prega Amor che quella a cui s'arrende
sia a lui umilitata in tutti lati
dov'udirà li suoi sospir gittati.

Per la vertù che parla, dritto ostelo
30 conoscer può ciascun ch'è di piacere,
ché 'n tutto vol quella laude compiere
c'ha cominzata per sua cortesia;
ch'unqua vista né voce sott'un velo
sì vertudiosa come 'l suo cherere
35 non fu ned è, per che de' om tenere
per nobil cosa ciò che dir disia
ché conosciuta egli ha la dritta via,
sì che le sue parole son compiute.
Noi donne sem di ciò in accordo essute,
40 che di piacer la nostra donna tria;

# 7
## Anonymous Response to Canzone 6 in the Name of Ladies and the Canzone

Blessed be the sweet and loving heart
that so wants to serve us Ladies,
for his reasonings announce
something full of pleasing pleasures;
5　he is as truly learned
as our desire to follow our
Lady is strong,
for she makes each of us wise,
he knows her so perfectly
10　bowing toward her with a humble heart;
just as the proper path will
draw each of us who sweetly pray
to her presence, to whom we surrender,
for she shows mercy to his poems.

15　Alas God—how he has improved his song
leaving us for a higher authority!
And how his praises have a sweet faith
that began well and became even better!
A grave injustice were such a man tormented
20　or misled by her at whose feet
he kneels and so perfectly believes,
speaking so kindly and not arguing
but reciting sweet poems igniting
all amorous hearts and making them sweet;
25　so that none of us ladies keep silent,
but pray to Love that she to whom he surrenders
be humble to him in every place
where she will hear his sorrows.

Of the virtue that he speaks, each is able to directly
30　know the seat of pleasure ,
for he wants to finish the praise
that he began with her courtesy;
for neither a face nor voice softly veiled
so virtuous like her intercession
35　never was nor is—so that deeming noble
what a man wants to say
because he has known the proper path,
that his words are complete.
We Ladies agree with this,
40　for our Lady pleases to choose him;

e sì l'avem per tale innamorato,
ch'Amor preghiam per lui in ciascun lato.
Audite ancor quant'è di pregio e vale:
che'n far parlare Amor sì s'assicura
45 che conti la bieltà ben a drittura
da lei dove 'l su' cor vol che si fova.
Ben se ne porta com'om naturale,
nel sommo ben disia ed ha sua cura,
né in altra vista crede né in pintura,
50 né non attende né vento né plova;
per che faria gran ben sua donna, po' v'ha
tanta di fé, guardare a li suoi stati;
poi ched egli è infra gl'innamorati
quel che 'n perfetto amar passa, e più gio' v'ha;
55 noi donne il metteremmo in paradiso,
udendol dir di lei c'ha lui conquiso.

—Io anderò, né non già miga in bando;
in tale guisa sono accompagnata,
che sì mi sento bene assicurata,
60 ch'i' spero andare e redir tutta sana.
Son certa ben di non irmi isviando,
ma in molti luoghi sarò arrestata:
pregherolli di quel che m'hai pregata,
fin ched i' giugnerò a la fontana
65 d'insegnamento, tua donna sovrana.
Non so s'io mi starò semmana o mese,
o se le vie mi saranno contese:
girò al tu' piacer presso e lontana;
ma d'esservi già giunta io amerei,
70 perché ad Amor ti raccomanderei.-

and have we fallen in love with him,
so in every way we pray to Love for him.
Hear again how worthy he is:
in making Love speak he proves
45 that he values her beauty
by wanting his heart to burn.
He truly behaves as a natural man,
he desires the highest good and her healing power,
and does not believe in other images,
50 nor does he mind the wind or rain;
because his Lady will create harmony,
he believes in his poetic motives;
with all this he is among the in-love
who pass on to perfect love, he is the more joyous;
55 we Ladies will admit him to Paradise,
hearing him speak of her who has conquered him.


—I will go, but never in exile—
I will be accompanied
so I feel safe,
60 expecting to go and return whole.
I am certain to not go badly,
but in many places I will be stopped:
I will pray for those who have prayed for me,
until I arrive at the fountain
65 of learning, your sovereign Lady.
I don't know if I'll be gone a week or a month
or if my path shall be contested:
I will go for your pleasure near and far;
but I would love to already be there
70 because I would commend you to Love...

8

Tanto gentil e tanto onesta pare
la donna mia quand'ella altrui saluta,
ch'ogne lingua deven tremando muta,
e li occhi no l'ardiscon di guardare.

5 Ella si va, sentendosi laudare,
benignamente d'umiltà vestuta;
e par che sia una cosa venuta
da cielo in terra a miracol mostrare.

Mostrasi sì piacente a chi la mira,
10 che dà per li occhi una dolcezza al core,
che 'ntender no la può chi no la prova:

e par che de la sua labbia si mova
un spirito soave pien d'amore,
che va dicendo a l'anima: Sospira.

8

...so gentle and honest appears
my lady when she greets others,
that every tongue quivers mute
and their eyes don't dare look...

5   Hearing praises, she goes
kindly dressed in humility—
she seems a thing come
to earth from Heaven to reveal miracles.

Appearing so pleasant to whoever looks,
10 she sends a sweetness through their eyes to the heart,
you can't understand without experiencing it:

and appearing to move from her lips,
a sweet spirit full of Love
says to my soul: ...sigh...

9

    Quantunque volte, lasso!, mi rimembra
    ch'io non debbo già mai
    veder la donna ond'io vo sì dolente,
    tanto dolore intorno 'l cor m'assembra
5  la dolorosa mente,
    ch'io dico: "Anima mia, ché non ten vai?
    ché li tormenti che tu porterai
    nel secolo, che t'è già tanto noioso,
    mi fan pensoso di paura forte".
10  Ond'io chiamo la Morte,
    come soave e dolce mio riposo;
    e dico "Vieni a me" con tanto amore,
    che sono astioso di chiunque more.

    E' si raccoglie ne li miei sospiri
15  un sono di pietate,
    che va chimando Morte tuttavia:
    a lei si volser tutti i miei disiri,
    quando la donna mia
    fu giunta da la sua crudelitate;
20  perchè 'l piacere de la sua bieltate,
    partendo sé da la nostra veduta,
    divenne spirital bellezza grande,
    che per lo cielo spande
    luce d'amor, che li angeli saluta,
25  e lo intelletto loro alto, sottile
    face maravigliar, sì v'è gentile.

9

Whenever I remember
I was never again
to see my Lady, I wander suffering
my heart unites so much pain
5  in my suffering mind
that I ask—my soul, why don't you leave?
for the torments you will endure
in the future, already a burden,
make me imagine greater fears—
10  so I call for Death
a smooth and sweet relief
and I say with much love "come to me"
for I'm envious of those who die.

Then in my sighs a unity
15  of mercy gathers
that directly calls Death:
to it all my desires turn
when my Lady
was taken by its cruelty;
20  for the pleasure of her beauty,
leaving our sight,
became a great spiritual beauty
that spans the heavens
with the light of love that angels greet
25  and their subtle, lofty intellects
marvel at her so gentle nobility.

10
*Guido Cavalcanti a Dante*

I' vengo il giorno a te infinite volte
e trovote pensar troppo vilmente:
molto mi dol de la gentil tua mente
e d'assai tue vertù che ti son tolte.

5     Solevanti spiacer persone molte,
tuttor fuggivi l'annoiosa gente;
di me parlavi sì coralmente,
che tutte le tue rime avie ricolte.

Or non ardisco per la vil tua vita
far mostramento che tuo dir mi piaccia,
né in guisa vegno at te che tu mi veggi.

Se 'l presente sonetto spesso leggi,
lo spirito noioso che t'incaccia
si partirà da l'anima invilita.

10
*Guido Cavalcanti to Dante*

Each day I come to you an infinity of times
finding you with base thoughts:
I mourn the loss of your noble mind
and your many virtues.

5  The many often displeased you,
you've always fled the tedious;
you've spoken warmly of me,
so I've gathered all your poems.

Now I publicly dare neither
10 to praise your song nor even
approach you because of your vile life.

If you often read my sonnet,
the troublesome spirit haunting you
will leave your disheartened soul.

11

*Primo cominciamento*

Era venuta ne la mente mia
la gentil donna che per suo valore
fu posta da l'altissimo signore
nel ciel de l'umilitate, ov'è Maria.

*Secondo cominciamento*

Era in venuta ne la mente mia
quella donna gentil cui piange Amore,
entro 'n quel punto che lo suo valore
vi trasse a riguardar quel ch'eo facia.

5  Amor, che ne la mente la sentia,
s'era svegliato nel destrutto core,
e diceva a' sospiri: "Andate fore';
per che ciascun dolente si partia.

Piangendo uscivan for de lo mio petto
10  con una voce che sovente mena
le lagrime dogliose a li occhi tristi.

Ma quei che n'uscian for con maggior pena,
venian dicendo: "Oi nobile intelletto,
oggi fa l'anno che nel ciel salisti."

11
*First beginning*

> Had come into my mind
> the gentle Lady who for her value
> was taken by the most high Lord
> in the Heaven of humility, where Mary is.

*Second beginning*

> Had come into my mind
> that gentle lady Love cries for,
> in that moment that her power
> draws you to look at what I've done.

> 5    Love, who feels her in his mind,
> was awakened by the heart's destruction,
> saying to the Sighs: "Go out."
> ...so each one left suffering.

> Crying they left my chest
> 10   with a voice that led
> the sorrowing tears from sad eyes.

> But those who left with greater pain
> came to say "You noble intellect,
> today is a year since she ascended to Heaven."

12

Un dì si venne a me Malinconia
e disse: "Io voglio un poco stare teco";
a parve a me ch'ella menasse seco
Dolore e Ira per sua compagnia.

5   E io le dissi: "Partiti, va via";
ed ella mi ripose come un greco:
e ragionando a grande agio meco,
guradai e vidi Amore, che venia

vestito di novo d'un drappo nero,
10   e nel suo capo portava un cappello;
e certo lacrimava pur di vero.

Ed eo li dissi: "Che hai, cattivello?".
Ed el rispose: "Eo ho guai e pensero,
ché nostra donna mor, dolce fratello".

12

One day Melancholy came to me
and said: "I want to be with you a moment,"
and she appeared to lead
Pain and Discord with her.

5   Then I said to her: "Leave! Go away!"
and she responded like a Greek:
arguing with me a lot,
I looked and saw Love, who came

newly dressed in a black outfit,
10  on his head he wore a hat,
and was truly crying.

Then I said to him: "What's wrong, poor wretch?"
And he replied: "I'm afraid that our Lady is dead,
sweet brother."

13

Così nel mio parlar voglio esser aspro
com'è ne li atti questa bella petra,
la qual ognora impetra
maggior durezza e più natura cruda,
5   e veste sua persona d'un diaspro
tal, che per lui, o perch'ella s'arretra,
non esce di fareta
saetta che già mai la colga ignuda:
ed ella ancide, e non val ch'om si chiuda
10  né si dilunghi da' colpi mortali,
che, com'aveser ali,
giungono altrui e spezzan ciascun'arme;
sì ch'io non so da lei né posso atarme.

Non trovo scudo ch'ella non mi spezzi
15  né loco che dal suo viso m'asconda;
ché, come fior di fronda,
così de la mia mente tien la cima:
cotanto del mio mal par che si prezzi,
quanto legno di mar che non lieva onda;
20  e 'l peso che m'affonda
è tal che non potrebbe adequar rima.
Ahi angosciosa e dispietata lima
che sordamente la mia vita scemi,
perché non ti ritemi
25  sì di rodermi il core a scorza a scorza,
com'io di dire altrui chi ti dà forza?

Ché più mi triema il cor qualora io penso
di lei in parte ov'altri li occhi induca,
per tema non traluca
30  lo mio penser di fuor sì che si scopra,
ch'io non fo de la morte, che ogni senso
co li denti d'Amor già mi manduca;
ciò è che 'l pensier bruca
la lor vertù sì che n'allenta l'opra.
35  E' m'ha percosso in terra, e stammi sopra
con quella spada ond'elli ancise Dido,
Amore, a cui io grido
merzé chiamando, e umilmente il priego;
ed el d'ogni merzé par messo al niego.

13

I want to be as rare and biting in my poetry
as this beautiful stone is in her actions,
every moment she petrifies
into a harder and cruder substance,
5   covering her person in jasper
so, because of him or because she retreats,
an arrow from a quiver
never finds her unprotected:
and she kills no matter if a man shuts himself off
10  or distances himself from mortal blows,
that—as if they had wings—always
overtake, breaking all defenses to pieces;
I don't know how to protect myself from her.

I can't find a shield that she doesn't destroy
15  nor a place to hide myself from her face;
for like a flower on a branch,
she's at the top of my mind:
she appears to appreciate my poor verse,
as a boat at sea gentle waves;
20  and the weight that sinks me
is such my rhyme could never counteract.
Ah-h-h!! anguishing and merciless mud
that secretly rots my life,
why don't you restrain yourself
25  from corroding my heart layer by layer,
as I from telling others who gives you your strength?

For my heart trembles the more I think
of her where other's eyes occasion,
my thought doesn't shine through
30  for fear that it will be discovered,
so I do nothing but die when Love
chews up my every sense...
...that is what eats the virtue
of my thoughts—so weakening their ability to work.
35  He's knocked me to the ground standing above me
with the sword he killed Dido with.
Love to whom I scream
for mercy—humbly begging for it—
and he seems decided against any pity.

40 Egli alza ad ora la mano, e sfida
    la debole mia vita, esto perverso,
    che disteso a riverso
    mi tiene in terra d'ogni guizzo stanco:
    allor mi surgon ne la mente strida;
45 e 'l sangue, ch'è per le vene disperso,
    fuggendo corre verso
    lo cor, che 'l chiama; ond'io rimango bianco.
    Elli mi fiede sotto il braccio manco
    sì forte, che 'l dolor nel cor rimbalza:
50 allor dico: "S'elli alza
    un'altra volta, Morte m'avrà chiuso
    prima che 'l colpo sia disceso giuso".

    Così vedess'io lui fender per mezzo
    lo core a la crudele che'l mio squatra!
55 poi non mi sareb'atra
    la morte, ov'io per sua bellezza corro:
    ché tanto dà nel sol quanto nel rezzo
    questa scherana micidale e latra.
    Ohmè, perché non latra
60 per me, com'io per lei, nel caldo borro?
    ché tosto griderei: "Io vi soccorro";
    e fare 'l volentier, sì come quelli
    che ne' biondi capelli
    ch'Amor per consumarmi increspa e dora
65 metterei mano, e piacere' le allora.

    S'io avessi le belle trecce prese,
    che fatte son per me scudisco e ferza,
    pigliandole anzi terza,
    con esse passerei vespero e squille:
70 e non sarei pietoso né cortese,
    anzi farei com'orso quando scherza;
    e se Amor me ne sferza,
    io mi vendicherei di più di mille.
    Ancor ne li occhi, ond'escon le faville
75 che m'infiammano il cor, ch'io porto anciso,
    guarderei presso e fiso,
    per vendicar lo fuggir che mi face;
    e poi le renderei con amor pace.
    Canzon, vattene dritto a quella donna

80 che m'ha ferito il core e che m'invola
    quello ond'io ho più gola,
    e dàlle per lo cor d'una saetta;
    ché bell'onor s'acquista in far vendetta.

40 Over and over he raises his hand threatening
my enfeebled life—this perverse one
who pins my back to the ground
too tired to struggle:
then cries rise in mind
45 and the blood dispersed in my veins
—fleeing—runs to the
heart that calls it—so I become pale...
Love wounds me so sharply under my left
arm that pain rebounds in my heart:
50 then I say: "If he threatens
again, Death will have closed me off
before the blow descends."

Oh-h-h, could I see him split in half
the heart of the cruel woman who quartered mine!!
55 then death would not seem black
to me when I run to her beauty:
because this homicidal and thieving she-assassin
strikes as much in the sun as in the shade.
...ah-h-h-h!! why doesn't she steal for
60 me in the hot ravine as I do for her?
for quickly I'd cry: "I'll help you."
Gladly then I would please her by
putting my hand in the blond hair
that Love curls and gilds
65 in order to consume me.

If I would have taken those beautiful locks
that are my whip and lash,
grabbing them before tierce,
I'd pass through Vespers's bells:
70 and would be neither merciful nor courtly
but rather like a bear when he plays
and if Love whips me
I would revenge myself a thousand time
still I would stare in her eyes that
75 issue sparks that inflame my heart that
I carry murdered
to avenge her making me flee
and then with love I would give her peace.
Canzone, go straight to that woman

80 who wounded my heart, stealing
what I most hunger for—
shoot her heart with an arrow,
for one gains fine honor in taking revenge.

# Giovanni Boccaccio
## (1313–1375)

Because of his father's work for the formidable Florentine Bardi family and their banking interests, Giovanni Boccaccio enjoyed a very cosmopolitan upbringing. He was born in Paris to a French mother and a Tuscan father. Although Giovanni showed an early interest in literature, his father wanted to urge him toward a career in business. For this reason, young Giovanni was sent to Naples where he studied canon law and developed a working knowledge of banking and commerce representing Bardi banking interests at the court of the Neapolitan King, Robert of Anjou. Needless to say, young Giovanni took advantage of these contacts and the enriching activities available in circles of higher culture and learning. Further, his business activities afforded him a broad view of everyday life, something that would add both color and detail to all of his writings, especially his boisterous *Decamerone*. During his stay in Naples, Boccaccio wrote such poems as *Caccia di Diana*, *Filostrato* and *Teseida*, as well as the prose romance *Filocolo*. After returning to Florence around 1340 (probably due to the Bardi bankruptcy), he spent the next decade of his life writing such poems as *Ninfale d'Ameto*, *L'amorosa visione* and the *Elegia di Madonna Fiammetta*. He would write his prose masterpiece, the *Decamerone*, between 1349–51, after the Black Death ravaged Europe.

In 1350, Boccaccio befriended Petrarch in Florence, a relationship that would lay the foundations for much subsequent Italian Renaissance humanism. Boccaccio wrote several humanistic works in Latin, among them the encyclopedic account of pagan mythology, *Geneologia deorum gentilum*; his *Bucolicum carmen*, a series of allegorical eclogues on contemporary issues and events; and, *De claris mulieribus*, an account of famous women in history that paralleled Petrarch's *De viris illustribus*, an account of famous men in history. He also encouraged the recovery of classical Latin texts by such authors as Varro, Martial, Apuleius, Seneca, Ovid and Tacitus. Contrary to Petrarch, Boccaccio admired the poetry of Dante. He wrote a *Vita* or *Trattatello in laude di Dante*, actually performed public readings in 1373 in Florence at San Stefano di Badia and began a commentary on the *Divina commedia*. Boccaccio underwent a change of heart after the Black Death, gradually turning away from his worldly attitude toward a more somber Christian one. He actually considered burning his literary works and selling his library, but Petrarch convinced him not to.

The selection of his poetry in this volume is from his *Rime*, a series of occasional sonnets drawing from the Sicilians, the *Dolce stil nuovo* and, of course, his friend Petrarch. These poems reflect a meditation on time and place that reveals a deep empathy with Italy's Ancient Roman past.

## Giovanni Boccaccio

1

Mai non potei, per mirar molto fiso
i rossi labri et gli occhi vaghi et belli,
il viso tutto et gli aurei capelli
di questa, che m'è in terra un paradiso,

nell' intellecto comprender preciso
qual più mirabil si fosse di quelli:
come ch'io stimoo di preporre ad elli
l'angelico leggiadro et dolce riso.

Nel qual, quando scintillan quelle stelle
che la luce del sol fanno minore,
par s'apra il cielo et rida il mondo tutto.

Ond'io, che tutto 'l cor ò dritto a quelle,
esser mi tengo molto di megliore,
sentend' in terra sì celeste fructo.

2

Che fabrichi? che tenti? che limando
vai le catene, in che tu stesso entrasti—
mi dice Amore – et te stesso legasti
senza mio prego et senza mio comando?

Che latebra, che fuga vai cercanclo
vi drieto a me, al qual tu obligasti
la fede tua, allor che tu mirasti
l'angelica belleza desiando?

O stolte menti, o animali sciocchi!
Poi che t'avrai co' tua inganni sciolto
et volando sarai fuggito via,

una parola, un riso, un muover d'occhi,
un dimonstrarsi lieto, il vago volto
fara tornarti piu strecto che pria.

3

Cesare, poi ch'ebbe, per tradimento
de l'egitan duttor, l'orrate chiome,
rallegrossi nel core, en vista come
si fa quel che di nuovo è discontento.

## Giovanni Boccaccio

1
Never could I—in order to focus on
the red lips, graceful, beautiful eyes,
the face and golden hair
of this one, who is a paradise on earth—

precisely understand in my intellect
which is the most admirable of these:
even though I prefer to them
her angelic grace and sweet smile.

In those, when those stars sparkle
that sunlight dims,
appears to open the sky and the whole world laughs.

Whence I, who has directed all his heart to them,
think myself to be much better,
sensing such heavenly fruit on earth.


2
What do you make? what do you attempt? that you go
perfecting the chains in which you yourself have entered—
Love says to me—and you have bound yourself
without my wish and without my command?

What dark corner, what escape are you seeking
directly to me, to which you've pledged
your faith, now that you've seen
the angelic beauty desiring?

O stupid minds, o blind animals!
Since you've freed yourself with your deceptions
and flying you've fled—

a word, a smile, a glance,
a happy demonstration, the graceful turn
will make you more closed than before.


3
Cesare—since he had, through the treatment
of the Egyptian doctor, golden tresses—
delighted in his heart, but in his face
acted as one newly discontented.

E'llora ch'Anibal ebbe 'l presento
del capo del fratel, ch'aveva nome
Asdrubal, ricoprì suo' grave some
ridendo alla suo' gente, ch'era in pianto.

Per somigliante ciascun uom tal volta
per atto allegro o per turbato viso
mostra 'l contrario di ciò che 'l cor sente.

Però, 'i' canto, non dimostro riso:
fo per mostrare a cchi mi mira e ascolta
Ch'ai dolor gravi i' sia forte e possente.


4
Se mi bastasse allo scriver, l'ingegno,
la mirabil bellezza e 'l gran valore
di quella donna, a cui diede il mio core
Amor, della mia fede eterno pegno;

et anchora l'angoscia c'io sostegno
o per lo suo o per lo mio errore
Veggendo me della sua gratia fore
esser sospinto da crudele sdegnoo:

io mostrerrei assai chiaro et aperto
che 'l pianger mio et mio essere smorto
maraviglia non sia, ma ch'io sia vivo.

Ma poi non posso, ciaschedun sia certo
che gli è assai maggiore il duol ch'io porto,
che 'l mio viso monstra ch'io non scrivo.


5
Intra 'l Barbaro monte e 'l mar tyrrheno
sied' il lago d'Averno, intorniato
da calde fonti, et dal sinistro lato
gli sta Pozzuolo et a dextro Miseno;

il qual sent'ora ogni suo grmbo pieno
di belle donne, avendo racquistato
le frondi la verdura e 'l tempo ornato
di feste di diletto et di sereno.

And when Hannibal was presented
the head of his brother, who was named
Asdrubal, he covered his heavy burden
laughing at his people, for he was in tears.

For like each man sometimes,
by a happy act or troubled face,
shows the contrary of what his heart feels.

However, if I sing, I don't show happiness:
I act—in order to show whoever looks and listens
that you have great suffering—strong and powerful.


4
If it were enough for me to write, my genius,
of the admirable beauty and great power
of that woman, to whom I gave the love of
my heart, of my eternal faith pledged;

and of the anguish I still sustain,
either for her or my fault,
seeing me outside her grace,
shunned by cruel disdain—

I would show clearly and openly enough
that my crying and my deathly pallor
are not surprising, but that I am alive.

But, then I can't, every individual is certain
the suffering I bear is important enough to him,
that my face does not show and that I do not write.


5
Between the Swiss Alps and the Tyrrhenian Sea
sits the Lake of Averno, surrounded
by hot springs, and on the left side
is Pozzuolo, on the right Miseno;

which now feels its very bosom full
of beautiful women, having recovered
the bough, the greenery and the weather adorned
with festivals of pleasure and joy.

Questi con la bellezza sua mi spoglia
ogn' anno, nella più lieta stagione,
di quella donna ch'è sol mio desire.

A sé la chiam, et io contr' a mia voglia,
rimango senza il cuore, in gran quistione
qual men dorriemi, il viver o 'l morire.


6
L'aspre montagne et le valli profonde,
i folti boschi et l'acqua e 'l ghiaccio e'l vento,
l'alpi selvaggie et piene di spavento,
et de' fiumi et del mar le torbid' onde,

et qualunqu'altra cosa più confonde
il pover peregrin, che, mal contento,
da' sula s'allunga, non ch'alcun tormento
mi desser, tornand'io, ma fur gioconde:

tanta dolce speranza mi recava,
spronato dal desio di rivederti,
qual ver me ti lascai, donna, pietosa.

Or, oltr' a quel che io, lasso, stimava,
truovo mi sdegni, et non so per quai merti:
per che piange nel cor l'alma dogliosa.

Et maledico i monti l'alpi e 'l mare,
che mai mi ci lasciaron ritornare.


7
Ipocrate, Avicenna o Galieno,
diamante, zaphir, perla o rubino,
brettonica, marrobbio o rosmarino,
psalmo evangelio et oration vien menlo;

piova né vento, nuvol né sereno,
mago né negromante né indovino,
tartaro né giudeo né saracino
Né povertà né doglia, ond'io son pieno,

These rob me with her beauty
every year, in the happiest season,
of that woman who is my sole desire.

To them she calls, and I, against my will,
remain without heart, in great doubt
which will bear me life or death.


6
The harsh mountains and deep valleys,
the  thick forests and the water, ice and wind,
the savage Alps, full of terror,
and the turbulent waves of the rivers and seas,

and whatever other thing more confuse
the poor pilgrim—who, malcontent,
removes himself from her—not that these tormented
me, returning, but were joyful:

such sweet hope carried me,
spurred by the desire of meeting you again,
who towards me—I left you, Lady—compassionate.

Now, beyond that which I, alas, esteemed,
I find you disdain me, and I don't know for what reason:
because my suffering soul cries in my heart.

And I curse the mountains, the Alps and the sea,
that will never let me return there.


7
Hippocrates, Avicenna or Galen,
diamond, sapphire, pearls or rubies,
horehound or rosemary,
psalm, gospel amd oration count less;

neither rain nor wind, clouds nor calm sky,
magician nor wizard nor sorcerer,
neither Tartar nor Jew nor Saracen,
neither poverty nor suffering, of which I'm full,

poteron mai del mio pecto cacciare
questo rabbioso spirito d amore,
ch' a poco a poco alla morte mi tira.

Ond' io non so che mi debba sperare;
et ei d' ogn' altro affar mi caccia fuore,
et, come vuol, m' affligge et mi martira.

8
Saturno al coltivar la terra puose
gia lungo studio, et Pallade lo ingegno
ad le mecaniche arti, et Hercul degno
si fe' di eterna fama l'orgogliose

fiere domando; et 'opre virtuose
de' buon Romani el nome loro e 'l regno
ampliaro ultra ad ogni mortal segno,
et Alexandro le imprese animose.

Così philosophia fece Platone,
Aristotele et altri assai famosi
et Homero et Vergilio i versi loro.

Hoggi seria reputato un montone
chi torcesse el camin da li studiosi
di perder tempo ad acquistar thesoro.

9
Dormendo, un giorno, in somno mi parea'
quasi pennuto volar verso il cielo
drieto all' orme di quella, il cui bel velo
cenere è facto, et ella è facta dea.

Quivi sì vaga et lieta la vedea,
ch' arder mi parve di più caldo gielo
ch'io non solea, et dileguarsi il gelo
ch' in pianto doloroso mi tenea.

Et, guardando, l'angelica figura
la man distese, come se volesse
prender la mia; et io mi risvegliai.

will be able to chase from my heart
this rabid spirit of love
that is slowly pulling me toward death.

Whence I don't know what I must expect;
and it chases from me every other quality,
and, as it wants, afflicts and martyrs me.


8
To cultivate the land, Saturn undertook
long study and Pallas devised
the mechanical arts and worthy Hercules
made prideful, spirited demands

of eternal fame—and the virtuous works,
the name and reign of the good Romans
extended beyond every mortal trace
and Alexander's undertakings.

Thus Plato, Aristotle and other famous
ones made philosophy,
and Homer and Virgil their verses.

Today, deemed serious, a stupid man
would twist his path from his studies
to lose time in acquiring riches.


9
Sleeping one day in a dream,
almost feathered to fly toward the sky
on the trail of her whose beautiful veil
is made of ashes and she is made a goddess.

Here she seemed so graceful and happy
that the ardor seemed more hot ice
that I wasn't used to—and the ice disappeared
which kept me suffering in tears.

And looking, the angelic figure
extended her hand as if she wanted
to take mine—then I woke up.

O quanta fu la mia disaventura!
Chi sa, se ella allor preso m' avesse,
et s' io quaggiu piu ritornava mai?


10
Dura cosa è et horribile assai
la morte ad aspettare, et paurosa,
ma cosi certa et infallibil cosa
né fu né è né, credo, sarà mai;

e 'l corso della vita è breve, ch'ài,
et volger non si può né dargli posa;
né qui si vede cosa sì gioiosa,
che 'l suo fine non sia lagrime et guai.

Dunque perché con operar valore
Non c'ingegniamo di stender la fama
et con quella far lunghi e brevi giorni?

Questa ne dà, questa ne serva honore,
questa ne lieva degli anni la squama,
questa ne fa di lunga vita adorni.

O how great was my misfortune!
Who knows, if she would have taken me,
and I down here would ever return?


10
A cruel, horrible and fearful enough
thing it is to wait for death,
but such a certain and infallible thing
never was, nor is, nor will be—I believe;

and the course of life is brief,
and one can neither turn it around nor stop it;
nor does one see a thing so joyous
that its end isn't tears and woe.

Then why with power to do
don't we strive to extend fame
and with it make long and short days?

This happens to it, this keeps its honor,
this scrapes the scales from the years,
this makes it adorned with long life.

# Francesco Petrarca
## (1304–74)

The first Italian humanist and, for many, the first modern lyric poet, Francesco Petrarca (called Petrarch, in English) was born in Arezzo, July 20, 1304 to Ser Pietro di Ser Parenzo, a notary, and Eletta Canigiani. Francesco, whose father was exiled from Florence in 1302, never lived there, but was brought up to speak its language and always thought of himself as Florentine. In 1312, his father became a notary at the papal court in Avignon and, in 1316, Francesco began law studies at Montpellier, which he further continued in Bologna from 1320 to 1326. He returned to Avignon after his father's death in 1326. Receiving the tonsure in 1330, he appeared to do so only to hold Church benefices, never actively advancing to the priesthood. In 1331, well off from his benefices, he moved to Vaucluse, an enchanting valley near Avignon. He would later wander as the welcome guest of the ruling powers in Parma, Milan, Padua and Venice. His ability for writing poetry in Latin was given the highest acclaim when he was crowned poet laureate in Rome in 1340, the first such coronation since Antiquity.

Petrarch's literary achievements fall into three categories: Latin poetry and prose, among which are prose and poetic letters which Petrarch kept copies of and assembled into collections; his Latin *Secretum Meum* (My Secret), a private meditation not intended for publication in which he has an imaginary dialogue with St. Augustine about his desire for earthly fame and earthly love in the face of his deep-seated belief that true Christian salvation demanded a rejection of earthly things; and, his Italian poems, consisting of *I Trionfi* (The Triumphs), a long narrative poem about the triumphs of love, chastity, death, fame, time and eternity, and his collection of 366 poems in Italian called by either its more common name *Canzoniere* (The Songbook), or the definitive title Petrarach gave it, *Rerum vulgarium fragmenta* (Vernacular Pieces).

Petrarch's fame is due to his *Canzoniere* and it is from it that the selections in this volume are taken. The *Canzoniere* consisted of sonnets, ballads, canzones and madrigals. Petrarch worked on it for most of his adult life, writing and re-writing various poems, completing one and then beginning and completing another manuscript until he finally left for posterity his definitive text, the MS. Vatican Latinus 3195 in the Vatican Library. The subject of the *Canzoniere* is the profound, extended and subtle exploration of Petrarch's feelings of unrequited love for Laura, his ideal lady. Although we know that Petrarch had socially known several women who had the name Laura, which lady is the Laura of the *Canzoniere* remains a mystery, for Petrarch kept her real identity a secret. Moreover, the Laura of his poetry may be no woman, but simply a metaphor for the motivation of his unquenched and unceasing desires.

De Sanctis writes that "Dante expanded his Beatrice to the universe, to which he gave a conscience and a voice. Petrarch shrank the entire universe into Laura and made his world of her and himself. This was his life and this was his glory. It seems a step backward, but it's really a step forward. This world is smaller, a fragment of the vast Dantean synthesis, but it is a fragment made into a finished and rich totality – a world full, concrete, developed, analyzed, explored in its most intimate recesses...here is neither symbol nor concept, but feeling. And the lover, who is always on stage, gives you the history of his soul...but it is not a history marked with fixed points – rather it is a vague continuum between the most contrary impressions, determined by the moment and state of his soul at any given time."

# A Brief Note on Petrarchism

Dozens of poets in Italy wrote collections of sonnets both before Petrarch and after. Many of these collections do not consist of extended sonnet sequences meant to be taken as one complete literary work. Instead, they simply consist of a collection of sonnets (and other lyric forms) written over a given span during a particular poet's life. Dante's *Vita nuova* is a notable exception, consisting of an extended poetic sequence (in addition to sonnets, it contains ballads and canzoni) interspersed with prose narrative. Petrarch, then, was the first poet to compose an extended poetic sequence about one subject – his love for Laura. Because of the accolades given Petrarch's achievement and the popularity of the *Canzoniere* itself, imitators of Petrarch sprung up almost immediately. This phenomenon of imitating Petrarch's *Canzoniere* in an extended sonnet (or poetic) sequence is referred to as Petrarchism. In the two centuries following his death, Petrarch's poems were read and studied in their own right, but also used a model for poets in Italy, France, Spain, Portugal, Germany, Dalmatia, Hungary and England. In Italy, Petrarch was a much more admired poet during the Renaissance than Dante, who was considered too rough, unpolished and direct in comparison to Petrarch, the smooth, refined and allusive (i.e., sophisticated) poet.

If Petrarch was popular during the late 14th and throughout the 15th century in Italy, Petrarchism as a literary genre exploded in the 16th, first in Italy and then throughout Europe. The man responsible for this was another poet in this volume, Pietro Bembo, who was so taken with Petrarch that, according to Lodovico Dolce, one of Bembo's contemporaries, it was "as if he is Petrarch or Petrarch is him." It is safe to assume that one of the key reasons for Petrarch's popularity lay in the fact that his exploration of human feelings about love fit universally with the then growing Renaissance sensibility about living a life that was, in comparison to the traditional medieval one, more secular and which encouraged an individual to recognize and cultivate his (and to a lesser extent) her personality. It would be hard to argue with the fact that love plays a central role in almost everyone's personality.

According to Arturo Graf, a 19th century critic, Petrarchism, which he describes as "a chronic ailment of Italian literature," existed for very important social reasons, even though those reasons are not especially admirable. Graf begins with the observation that Bembo was "a man of mediocre creativity, but deeply and broadly erudite, educated in all the refinement and cosmopolitanism of that culture." Graf explains that the Cinquecento preferred Petrarch over Dante for the very reason that Giovanni della Casa gives in *Il Galateo*, his treatise on manners from 1555: one cannot learn to be 'grazioso' from Dante. And what was seen as Petrarch's 'grace' (or what we today would call 'polish') was the central quality needed to succeed in Italy's aristocratic courts. In addition, Petrarch's subtlety and nuances about love, for better or worse, fit perfectly with the frivolous and superficial games of love that were the norm in any Cinquecento court. Further, any knowledge of Petrarch could be parlayed into an image of seeming literate and well educated. Finally, there was a purism in Petrarch's Florentine that allowed the aristocrats and those with aristocratic pretensions to separate themselves from their lessers who could express themselves only – horrors! – in their own local dialects.

Making a simple observation about Petrarchism's failure to produce any great poetry in Italy, Benedetto Croce observed, "Among the so-called lyricists of the Cinquecento, there weren't any great poets." Croce also points out that the real heirs to Petrarch's tradition were such later Italian poets as Vittorio Alfieri, Ugo Foscolo, Giacomo Leopardi and Giosue Carducci, each of whom studied and understood Petrarch, but took a step beyond what he had done. Taking the next step is not always easy and is often discouraged for we find comfort in looking back, enveloped in the security of tradition, well-worn rules and authority. We have trouble with going into the unknown, ready to adapt, as the sustaining of life always requires. But Karl Popper, a 20th century philosopher, reminds us, "...if we want to remain human, then there is only one way...we must go into the unknown, the uncertain, and the insecure, using what reason we have to plan as well as we can for both security and freedom." Petrarchism does not permit us that.

## Francesco Petrarca

1

Era il giorno ch'al sol si scoloraro
per la pietà del suo fattore i rai;
quando i' fui preso, e non me ne guardai,
che i be' vostr'occhi, Donna, mi legaro.

Tempo non mi parea da far riparo
contr'a' colpi d'Amor; però m'andai
secur, senza sospetto; onde i miei guai
nel commune dolor s'incominciaro.

Trovommi Amor del tutto disarmato,
et aperta la via per gli occhi al core,
che di lagrime son fatti uscio et varco.

Però, al mio parer, non li fu onore
ferir me de saetta in quello stato,
a voi armata non mostrar pur l'arco.

2

Solo et pensoso i più deserti campi
vo mesurando a passi tardi e lenti,
e gli occhi porto per fuggire intenti
ove vestigio uman la rena stampi.

Altro schermo non trovo che mi scampi
dal manifesto accorger de le genti,
perché negli atti d'allegrezza spenti
di fuor si legge com'io dentro avvampi;

sì ch'io mi credo omai che monti et piagge
e fiumi e selve sappian di che tempre
sia la mia vita, ch'è celata altrui.

Ma pur sì aspre vie né sì selvagge
cercar non so, ch'Amor non venga sempre
ragionando con meco, et io con lui.

## Francesco Petrarca

1

It was the day when the sun's rays paled
from the pity of its maker
that I was taken and did not defend myself—
for your beautiful eyes, Lady, bound me.

It did not seem to me a time to defend myself
against the blows of Love; so I went
in certainty, without suspicion, whence
my troubles in common suffering began.

Love found me completely disarmed
and opened the path to my heart through my eyes,
which are made from the opening and passage of tears.

However, it seems to me it did him no good
to wound me with an arrow in that state,
to not even show his bow to you, so secure.


2

Alone and pensive the most deserted fields
I go measuring with slow, hesitant steps,
and I keep my eyes alert to avoid
any human trace in the sand.

No other shield do I find to protect me
from people openly knowing,
because in extinguished acts of happiness
one can read from without how I burn within—

so I believe by now that mountains and shores
and rivers and woods know what temper
my life has, which is hidden from others.

But still I don't know how to find paths
so harsh or savage that Love does not always come
talking with me, and I with him.

3

Volgendo gli occhi al mio novo colore,
che fa di morte rimembrar la gente,
pietà vi mosse, onde benignamente
salutando teneste in vita il core.

La fraile vita, ch'ancor meco alberga,
fu de' begli occhi vostri aperto dono
e de la voce angelica soave;
da lor conosco l'esser ov'io sono;
che, come suol pigro animal per verga,
così destaro in me l'anima grave.
Del mio cor, Donna, l'una e l'altra chiave
avete in mano, e di ciò son contento,
presto di navigare a ciascun vento:
ch' ogni cosa da voi m'è dolce onore.

4

Io son già stanco di pensar sì come
i miei pensier in voi stanchi non sono,
e come vita ancor non abbandono
per fuggir de' sospir sì gravi some;

e come a dir del viso e de le chiome
e de' begli occhi ond'io sempre ragiono
non è mancata omai la lingua e 'l suono,
dì e notte chiamando il vostro nome;

e che' piè miei non son fiaccati et lassi
a seguir l'orme vostre in ogni parte,
perdendo inutilmente tanti passi;

et onde vien l'enchiostro, onde le carte
ch'i' vo empiendo di voi; se 'n ciò fallassi,
colpa d'Amor, non già defetto d'arte.

3

Turning your eyes to my new color
that makes people think of death,
pity moved you—in kindly
greeting me, you kept my heart alive.

The fragile life that still lives with me
was an open gift of your beautiful eyes
and smooth angelic voice;
I see that the being I am is from them—
that, as a lazy animal is used to the rod,
so I rouse my serious side.
You have, Lady, one and the other keys
to my heart in your hand—and that makes me happy,
ready to navigate each wind:
for eveything from you is sweet honor to me.


4

Already wearied of thinking how
my thoughts of you are tireless
and how I don't abandon life
to flee such a heavy burden of pain,

and how I always speak of you face
and hair and beautiful eyes,
not yet dead my voice and sound
calling your name day and night,

and that my feet aren't broken and tired
of following your every step,
uselessly wasting so many steps,

and whence the ink comes whence the pages
I fill with you (if I fail in that,
blame Love, not my lack of art).

5

Dicesette anni à già rivolto il cielo
poi che 'mprima arsi, e già mai non mi spensi,
ma quando avèn ch'al mio stato ripensi
sento nel mezzo de le fiamme un gelo.

Vero è 'l proverbio, ch'altri cangia il pelo
anzi che 'l vezzo, e per lentar i sensi
gli umani affetti non son meno intensi;
ciò ne fa l'ombra ria del grave velo.

Oi me lasso! e quando fia quel giorno
che mirando il fuggir de gli anni miei
esca del foco e di sì lunghe pene?

Vedrò mai il dì che pur quant'io vorrei
quell'aria dolce del bel viso adorno
piaccia a quest'occhi, e quanto si convene?

6

Come talora al caldo tempo sòle
semplicetta farfalla al lume avezza
volar negli occhi altrui per sua vaghezza,
onde avven ch'ella more, altri si dole;

così sempre io corro al fatal mio sole
de gli occhi onde mi ven tanta dolcezza,
che 'l fren de la ragion Amor non prezza,
e chi discerne è vinto da chi vole.

E veggio ben quant'elli a schivo m'ànno
e so ch'i' ne morrò veracemente,
ché mia vertù non po contra l'affanno;

ma sì m'abbaglia Amor soavemente
ch'i' piango l'altrui noia e no 'l mio danno,
e cieca al suo morir l'alma consente.

5

Seventeen years the Heavens turned
since I first burned and am still unextinguished,
when it happens that I think of my state,
I feel cold in the middle of the flames.

True is the proverb one's hair will change
before one's habits, and because of the slowing of
senses human emotions aren't less intense—
the wicked shadow of considered pretext does that to us.

Suffering me! When comes the day
seeing the years passed,
I leave the fire and such long suffering?

Will I ever see the wanted day
when that sweet look of her beautiful face
will please these eyes as much is needed?

6

As now and then happens in the hot weather,
the simple butterfly drawn to the light,
because of its desire, flies in someone else's eyes,
where it dies and that someone is hurt:

so always I run to my fatal sun
of the eyes where such sweetness comes to me—
for Love doesn't care about the restraint of reason—
so one who thinks is defeated by one who wants.

Then I really see how much they've shunned me
and I know that I'll truly die from it—
for my virtue doesn't have power over the pain;

but so sweetly does Love dazzle me
that I mourn another's pain and not my own—
and my blind soul consents to its own death.

7

O passi sparsi, o pensier vaghi et pronti,
o tenace memoria, o fero ardore,
o possente desire, o debil core,
oi occhi miei, occhi non già, ma fonti;

o fronde, onor de le famose fronti,
o sola insegna al gemino valore;
o faticosa vita, o dolce errore,
che mi fate ir cercando piagge et monti;

o bel viso, ove Amor inseme pose
gli sproni e 'l fren ond'el mi punge e volve
come a lui piace, e calcitrar non vale;

o anime gentili et amorose,
s'alcuna à 'l mondo, e voi, nude ombre e polve,
deh, ristate a veder quale è 'l mio male.


8

I' vo pensando, e nel penser m'assale
una pietà sì forte di me stesso,
che mi conduce spesso
ad altro lagrimar ch'i' non soleva:
ché vedendo ogni giorno il fin più presso,
mille fiate ò chieste a Dio quell'ale
co le quai del mortale
carcer nostr'intelletto al ciel si leva:
ma infin a qui niente mi releva
prego o sospiro o lagrimar ch'io faccia;
e così per ragion conven che sia,
ché chi possendo star cadde tra via
degno è che mal suo grado a terra giaccia.
Quelle pietose braccia
in ch'io mi fido, veggio aperte ancora;
ma temenza m'accora
per gli altrui esempli, e del mio stato tremo;
ch'altri mi spronea e son forse a l'estremo.

7

O squandered steps, o eager, quick thoughts,
o tenacious memory, o fierce ardor,
o powerful desire, o weak heart,
o my eyes (not eyes but fountains)—

o leaves, honor of famous brows,
o single crest of twin powers,
o difficult life, o sweet error
that makes me wander shores and mountains—

o beautiful face where Love has united
the spurs and reins whence he pricks and turns me
at pleasure, useless to resist—

o souls gentle and loving,
if there are any in the world, and you, bare shades and dust—
alas, stay to see what is my suffering.

8

I go thinking and such a strong
self-pity assails my thoughts
that it often leads me
to another weeping I'm not used to:
because seeing the end nearer every day,
I've asked God with a thousands breaths for
those wings which lift our minds
to Heaven from its mortal prison:
but up to here no prayer or sigh
or tear I make relieves me—
and so it reasons to be,
for one strong enough to stand falls on the way,
deserving to lie unwillingly on the ground.
I see those merciful arms
in which I trust still open,
but fear chases me
through examples of others—and I tremble for my state
that others spur me and I am—perhaps—near death.

L'un penser parla co la mente, et dice:
"Che pur agogni? onde soccorso attendi?
misera, non intendi
con quanto tuo disonore il tempo passa?
Prendi partito accortamente, prendi,
e del cor tuo divelli ogni radice
del piacer, che felice
nol po mai fare, e respirar nol lassa.
Se già è gran tempo fastidita e lassa
se' di quel falso dolce fuggitivo
che 'l mondo traditor può dare altrui,
a che ripon' più la speranza in lui?
che d'ogni pace e di fermezza è privo.
Mentre che 'l corpo è vivo
ài tu 'l freno in bailia de' penser tuoi.
Deh stringilo or che pòi,
ché dubbioso è 'l tardar, come tu sai,
e 'l cominciar non fia per tempo omai.

Già sai tu ben quanta dolcezza porse
agli occhi tuoi la vista di colei,
la qual anco vorrei
ch'a nascer fosse, per più nostra pace.
Ben ti ricordi, e ricordar ten dei,
de l'imagine sua, quand'ella corse
al cor, là dove forse
non potea fiamma intrar per altrui face.
Ella l'accese, e se l'ardor fallace
durò molt'anni in aspettando un giorno
che per nostra salute unqua non vene,
or ti solleva a più beata spene
mirando 'l ciel che ti si volve intorno
immortal et adorno:
ché dove del mal suo qua giù sì lieta
vostra vaghezza acqueta
un mover d'occhi, un ragionar, un canto,
quanto fia quel piacer, se questo è tanto?"

One thought speaks to my mind and says:
"What do you desire? from where do expect help?
Miserable one, don't you understand
how time your your dishonor spends?
Decide wisely, decide,
and tear out every root
of the pleasure that can never
make you happy and never let you breathe.
If you are already disgusted and tired
of that false fleeting sweetness
that the traitorous world can give others,
why do you put any more hope in it?
For it lacks any peace or security.
As long as your body is alive,
you have the power to stop your own thoughts.
Alas, grab it now, not then—
for delaying is dubious—as you know—
and beginning now is not in time.

"You already know how much sweetness
the sight of her has given your eyes,
she who I wish were yet to be born,
for more our peace.
You remember well and must remember
her image, when it raced
to your heart, where perhaps
the flame from another torch couldn't enter.
She set it on fire and if that false desire
lasted many years in expecting a day
of salvation that never comes,
now soothe yourself with a more blessed hope
looking at the immortal and adorned sky
that that revolves around you—
for down here where a glance, a pursuasion, a song
calms your desire—
so happy in its pain—
what will be that pleasure, if this is so much?"

Da l'altra parte un pensier dolce et agro,
con faticosa e dilettevol salma
sedendosi entro l'alma,
preme 'l cor di desio, di speme il pasce;
che sol per fama glorisoa ed alma
non sente quand'io agghiaccio o quand'io flagro,
s'i' son pallido o magro;
e s'io l'occido, più forte rinasce.
Questo d'allor ch'i' m'addormiva in fasce
venuto è di dì in dì crescendo meco,
e temo ch'un sepolcro ambeduo chiuda:
poi che fia l'alma de le membra ignuda
non po questo desio più venir seco.
Ma se 'l latino e 'l greco
parlan di me dopo la morte, è un vento:
ond'io, perché pavento
adunar sempre quel ch'un'ora sgombre,
vorre' 'l ver abbracciar, lassando l'ombre.

Ma quell'altro voler di ch'i' son pieno
quanti press'a lui nascon par ch'adugge,
e parte il tempo fugge
che scrivendo d'altrui di me non calme;
e 'l lume de' begli occhi che mi strugge
soavemente al suo caldo sereno
mi ritien con un freno
contra cui nullo ingegno o forza valme.
Che giova dunque perché tutta spalme
la mia barchetta, poi che 'nfra li scogli
è ritentua ancor da ta' duo nodi?
Tu che dagli altri che 'n diversi modi
legano 'l mondo in tutto mi disciogli,
signor mio, ché non togli
omai dal volto mio questa vergogna?
Che 'n guisa d'uom che sogna
aver la morte inanzi gli occhi parme,
e vorrei far difesa e non ò l'arme.

On the other hand, a sweet and bitter thought—
with a difficult and pleasing burden
sitting in my soul—
presses my heart with desire, feeds it with hope,
but for glorious and nourishing fame,
it doesn't feel when I freeze or burn,
if I'm pale and wasted—
and if I kill it, it's reborn stronger.
Day by day growing in me, this,
since I slept in swaddling,
and I fear one tomb will close us both—
seeing that my soul, bare of its body,
this thought will not be able to come with it.
But if the Latins and the Greeks
speak of me after my death, it's merely wind—
whence I, because I'm always afraid
to bring together what one hour clears away,
I would like to embrace the truth, leaving the shadows.

But the other desire of which I'm full
seems to overshadow others born next to it,
and time flies
while writing of another, not calming myself;
and the light of those beautiful eyes, gently
destroying me with its clear heat,
holds me with a bit
against which no wit or force prevails.
Why, then, do I tar all my
little boat, since it's held
on the reef by your two knots?
You who completely untie me from the
other knots that bind the world in many different ways,
my Lord—why don't you take
this shame from my face?
For like a man who dreams
I seem to have death before my eyes,
and I would like to defend myself and have no weapons.

Quel ch'i' fo, veggio, e non m'inganna il vero
mal conosciuto, anzi mi sforza Amore,
che la strada d'onore
mai nol lassa seguir chi troppo il crede;
e sento ad ora ad or venirmi al core
un leggiadro disdegno, aspro e severo
ch'ogni occulto pensero
tira in mezzo la fronte, ov'altri 'l vede;
ché mortal cosa amar con tanta fede
quanto a Dio sol per debito convensi,
più si disdice a chi più pregio brama.
E questo ad alta voce anco richiama
la ragione sviata dietro ai sensi;
ma perchi'ell'oda ee pensi
tornare, il mal costume oltre la spigne
et agli occhi depigne
quella che sol per farmi morir nacque,
perch'a me troppo et a se stessa piacque.

Né so che spazio mi si desse il cielo
quando novellamente io venni in terra
a soffrir l'aspra guerra
che 'ncontra me medesmo seppi ordire:
né posso il giorno che la vita serra,
antiveder per lo corporeo velo;
ma variarsi il pelo
veggio e dentro cangiarsi ogni desire.
Or ch'i' mi credo al tempo del partire
esser vicino o non molto da lunge,
come chi 'l perder face accorto e saggio,
vo ripensando ov'io lassai 'l viaggio
da la man destra, ch' a buon porto aggiunge:
e da l'un lato punge
vergogna e duol che 'ndietro mi rivolve;
dall'altro non m'assolve
un piacer per usanza in me sì forte
ch'a patteggiar n'ardisce co la morte.

I see what I'm doing and the ill-known truth
doesn't deceive me—rather forced by Love
who doesn't let anyone who too believes
him follow that the path of honor—
and from time to time I feel coming in my heart
an elegant disdain, harsh and severe,
that drags every secret thought
before my face, where others see them—
for loving a mortal thing with as much faith
one owes to God,
the more you deny one who desires more value.
And this loudly calls back
my reason, diverted behind my senses:
but because it hears and thinks
to return, my bad habit pushes it further
and paints for my eyes
she born only to make me die,
for she pleased me and herself too much.

Nor do I know how much time heaven gave me
when I first came down to earth
to suffer the bitter war
I learned to weave against myself—
nor am I able to foresee, through my bodily
veil, the day life ends—
but I see my hair
and every inner desire changing.
Now I believe I'm near, or not very far
from the time of parting—
like one who loss made wary and wise,
I consider where I left the voyage
on the right, which leads to a good port:
for shame and suffering—revolving around
me—pierce one side,
and from the other a pleasure, so strong a habit,
doesn't free me,
but dares to bargain with Death.

Canzon, qui sono ed ò 'l cor via più freddo
de la paura che gelata neve,
sentendomi perir senz'alcun dubbio,
ché pur deliberando ò vòlto al subbio
gran parte omai de la mia tela breve;
né mai peso fu greve
quanto quel ch'i' sostengo in tale stato
ché co la Morte a lato
cerco del viver mio novo consiglio;
e veggio 'l meglio et al peggior m'appiglio.

9

Oimè il bel viso, oimè il soave sguardo,
oimè il leggiadro portamento altero!
Oimè il parlar ch' ogni aspro ingegno et fero
facevi imile ed ogni uom vil, gagliardo!

Et oimè il dolce riso onde uscio 'l dardo
di che morte, altro bene omai non spero!
Alma real dignissima d'impero
se non fossi fra noi scesa sì tardo:

Per voi conven ch'io arda e 'n voi respire,
ch'i' pur fui vostro; e se di voi son privo
via men d'ogni sventura altra mi dole.

Di speranza m'empieste e di desire
quand'io parti' dal sommo piacer vivo:
ma 'l vento ne portava le parole.

Poem, here I am and with a heart much colder
with fear than frozen snow,
feeling myself perish without any doubt,
because still deliberating I have now woven
the better part of my brief fabric—
nor was a weight ever so heavy
as what I carry now in this mode of life:
with Death at my side
I seek new counsel on my life,
for I see the better but attach myself to the worst.


9


Alas that beautiful face, alas that soft glance,
alas that elegant, proud manner!
Alas that speech that made every cutting and
rough-edged man humble and every cowardly one brave.

And alas the sweet smile from which came the dart
that I expect no other good than death!
Royal soul, worthy of empire
if you hadn't descended to us so late!

For you I must burn, I must breathe,
I've been only yours—and if I'm deprived of you,
it pains me much more than any other misfortune.

You filled me with hope and desire
when I left the highest pleasure still alive:
but the wind carried away the words.

10

Che fai? che pensi? che pur dietro guardi
nel tempo che tornar non pote omai,
anima sconsolata? che pur vai
giugnendo legno al foco ove tu ardi?

Le soavi parole e i dolci sguardi,
ch'ad un ad un descritti et depinti ài,
son levati de terra, et è, ben sai,
qui ricercarli intempestivo e tardi.

Deh, non, rinovellar quel che n'ancide,
non siguir piu penser vago fallace,
ma saldo et cero ch'a buon fin ne guide;

cerchiamo 'Ciel, se qui nulla ne piace,
ché mal per noi quella beltà si vide
se viva e morta ne devea tor pace


11

Mentre che 'l cor dagli amorosi vermi
fu consumato e 'n fiamma amorosa arse,
di vaga fera le vestigia sparse
cercai per poggi solitari et ermi,

ed ebbi ardir, cantando, di dolermi
d'Amor, di lei che sì dura m'apparse;
ma l'ingegno e le rime erano scarse
in quella etate ai pensier novi e 'nfermi.

Quel foco è morto e 'l copre un picciol marmo
che se col tempo fossi ito avanzando
come gia in altri infino a la vecchiezza,

di rime armato ond'oggi mi disarmo,
con stil canuto, avrei fatto, parlando,
romper le pietre et pianger di dolcezza.

10

What are you doing? thinking? that you
look back to a time that can never return,
disconsolate soul? why do you add
wood to the fire you burn in?

The smooth words and sweet glances
that you've painted one by one
are raised from the earth, and it is, you know,
untimely to seek them here.

Alas, don't renew what kills us,
don't follow a vague, false thought—
but a solid certain one that leads us to a good end.

Let us try Heaven if nothing pleases us here,
for, ill to us, we saw that beauty,
whether living or dead, must take our peace.


11

While my heart was eaten by the worms of Love
and burned in an amorous flame,
I searched lonely hills
or scattered traces of a wandering beast—

and I dared, singing, to complain
of Love of she who appeared so cruel to me,
but subtlety and poetry were rare
in that season of new and weak thoughts.

That fire is dead, covered by a little marble
that, if it had advanced to old
age as it did with others,

armed with poems of which I'm disarmed today,
with a mature style, I would have made speaking
break the stones and weep with sweetness.

12

Quel rosignuol che si soave piagne
forse suoi figli o sua cara consorte
di dolcezza empie il cielo e le campagne
con tante note sì pietose e scorte,

e tutta notte par che m'accompagne
e mi rammente la mia dura sorte,
ch'altri che me non ò di chi mi lagne,
ché 'n dee non credev'io regnasse Morte.

O che lieve e inganar chi s'assecura!
Que' duo bei lumi assai più che 'l sol chiari
chi pensò mai veder far terra oscura?

Or cognosco io che mia fera ventura
vuol che vivendo e lagrimando impari
come nulla qua giù diletta e dura!

12

That nightingale that so sweetly weeps,
perhaps for his children or dear consort,
fills the sky and fields with sweetness
with so many notes sorrowing and prudent,

and all the night he appears to me
and reminds me of my cruel fate—
for, other than me, I have no one to grieve me,
no one who didn't believe Death reigned over goodness.

O how easy it is to deceive one who is sure!
Those two lights brighter than the sun,
whoever thought to see them made humble soil?

Now I know my savage fate
wants, living and weeping, to learn
how nothing down here pleases and lasts.

13

Standomi un giorno solo a la fenestra
onde cose vedea tante et sì nove
ch' era sol di mirar quasi già stanco,
una fera m'apparve da man destra
con fronte umana da far arder Giove,
cacciata da duo veltri, un nero un bianco,
che l'un et l'altro fianco
de la fera gentil mordean sì forte
che 'n poco tempo la menaro al passo,
ove chiusa in un sasso
vinse molta bellezza acerba morte:
et mi fe' sospirar sua dura sorte.

Indi per alto mar vidi una nave
con le sarte di seta et d'or la vela,
tutta d'avorio e d'ebeno contesta;
e 'l mar tranquillo e l'aura era soave
e 'l ciel qual è se nulla nube il vela,
ella carca di ricca merce onesta;
poi repente tempesta
oriental turbò sì l'aere e l'onde
che la nave percosse ad uno scoglio.
O che grave cordoglio!
Breve ora oppresse et poco spazio asconde
l'alte ricchezze a null'altre seconde.

In un boschetto novo i rami santi
fiorian d'un lauro giovenetto e schietto
ch'un delli arbor parea di paradiso,
e di sua ombra uscian sì dolci canti
di vari augelli e tant'altro diletto
che dal mondo m'avean tutto diviso;
e mirandol io fiso
cangiossi 'l cielo intorno e tinto in vista
folgorando 'l percosse e da radice
quella pianta felice
subito svelse: onde mia vita è trista
ché simile ombra mai non si racquista.

13

Standing alone one day at the window
where I saw so many new things,
I was exhausted from just looking—
a wild creature appeared to me on the right
with a human face enough to make Jove burn,
hunted by two greyhounds, one black, one white,
with one and the other biting
so fiercely at the flanks of the gentle one
that shortly they led it to the pass—
where trapped by a rock,
bitter death defeated beauty
and made me bemoan its harsh fate.

Then one the high seas I saw a ship
all made from ivory and ebony,
with lines of silk and sails of gold—
and the sea was calm, the breeze soft
with no cloud veiling the sky—
she was loaded with rich, honest goods—
then a violent eastern storm
so disturbed the air and the waves
that the ship struck a reef.
O what serious grief!
A moment's time overpowers and a tiny space hides
those lofty riches second to no others.

In a fresh grove holy boughs of a
young, straight laurel flowered
that it seemed one of the trees of paradise—
and from its shade came such sweet songs
and other delight of different birds
that they completely severed me from the world—
then looking, I focused on it—
the entire sky changed and tinted to the eye,
flashing, it struck—and by the roots
that happy plant
was suddenly torn—whence my life is sad,
for such shade is never regained.

Chiara fontana in quel medesmo bosco
sorgea d'un sasso, ed acque fresche et dolci
spargea soavemente mormorando;
al bel seggio riposto ombroso et fosco
né pastori appressavan né bifolci,
ma ninfe et muse, a quel tenor cantando;
ivi m'assisi, e quando
più dolcezza prendea di tal concento
e di tal vista, aprir vidi uno speco
e portarsene seco
la fonte e 'l loco: ond' ancor doglia sento
e sol de la memoria mi sgomento.

Una strania fenice, ambedue l'ale
di porpora vestita e 'l capo d'oro,
vedendo per la selva altera e sola,
veder forma celeste ed immortale
prima pensai, fin ch'a lo svelto alloro
giunse ed al fonte che la terra invola.
Ogni cosa al fin vola:
ché mirando le frondi a terra sparse
e 'l troncon rotto e quel vivo umor secco,
volse in sé stessa il becco,
quasi sdegnando, e 'n un punto disparse:
onde 'l cor di pietate e d'amor m'arse.

Alfin vid'io per entro i fiori e l'erba
pensosa ir sì leggiadra e bella Donna
che mai nol penso ch'i' non arda e treme,
umile in sé, ma 'ncontra Amor superba;
ed avea in dosso sì candida gonna,
sì testa ch'or e neve parea inseme,
ma le parti supreme
eran avvolte d'una nebbia oscura;
punta poi nel tallon d'un picciol angue,
come fior colto langue
lieta si dipartìo, non che secura:
ahi nulla altro che pianto al mondo dura!

Canzon, tu puoi ben dire:
Queste sei visioni al signor mio
àn fatto un dolce di morir desio.

In that same forest a clear fountain
rose from a stone and sweet, fresh water
spread gently murmuring—
neither shepherds nor cowherds drew near
that beautiful, shady, dark seat,
but nymphs and muses sang to that mood—
there I sat and when
I took more sweetness from such harmony
and such a view, I saw a cave open
and carry away
the fountain and the place—whence I still grieve
and am terrified by the memory.

A strange phoenix, both wings
clothed with purple and its head with gold,
seen in the forest proud and alone,
at first I thought to see heavenly
and immortal form, until it arrived at the
uprooted laurel and the fountain that the earth stole.
Everything flies to its end:
because seeing the leaves spread on the earth
and the trunk broken and the living spring dry,
it turned its beak on itself,
almost in disdain....and in an instant disappeared—
whence my heart burned with pity and love.

Finally, I saw among the flowers and grass
walking thoughtfully such a joyous and beautiful lady
that I never think of her without burning and trembling—
humble in herself but proud against Love—
and she wore such a pure gown,
so woven, that gold and snow appeared together,
but the highest parts
were wrapped in a dark mist—
pierced then in the heel by a little serpent
as a picked flower languishes,
she leaves happy, not merely confident:
alas, nothing other than tears endure the world!

Canzone, you may well say:
"These six visions have given my
lord a sweet desire to die."

# Coluccio Salutati
## (1331–1406)

Lino Coluccio di Piero Salutati was born in Stignano in Valdinievole. After a few months, he was sent to his father, Piero, who was in exile in Bologna. As a youth, he studied law, and, with an indication of an interest in classical literature, fashioned the nickname 'pierius,' which signifies both "the son of Piero" and "a devotee of the Pierides," another name for the Muses of Greek mythology. Salutati remained in Bologna until 1351, having become a notary sometime in the late 1340s. He became the Chancellor of Todi in 1367, of Lucca in 1371, and then spent a brief time in the *Curia romana* in Viterbo with Urban V. Beginning in 1377, he became Chancellor of the Florentine Signoria, a position he held for 30 years. He participated in the lively politics of the Commune with such virtue and fervor, that Sant'Antonino, Archbishop of Florence in the mid-Quattrocento, would historically refer to him as "virum iustum and rectum" (a just and righteous man). In his letters, collected into 14 volumes, Coluccio continued the philological and humanistic criticism begun by Petrarch. In fact, he began the practice that would be further developed by later humanists of comparing the variations of a given text as found in numerous manuscripts. His humanism, however, was not the arid study of texts in the isolation of a library, but consisted, more properly, of an evaluation of the great writings for what they might contribute in the conduct and judgments one makes in real life, politics and society. Among his works are *De tyranno* (On Tyranny), *De nobilitate legum e medicinae* (On the Nobility of Law and Medicine), *De laboris Herculis* (On the Labors of Hercules), and the selection presented here, his sonnet *Invectiva...in Antomium Luscum de [florentina] republica male sentientum*.

In 1399, Gian Galeazzo Visconti, ruler of Milan and her territories, bought Pisa and seized Siena. In 1400-01, he captured Perugia, Lucca and Bologna. In 1402 he was ready to invade and then annex Florence. Salutati led Florence in her bid to remain an independent republic. Coluccio wrote his most famous work as these events unfolded. In his sonnet, *Coluccio* equates the desires and motives of the Milanesi with numerous figures of dubious reputation from Antiquity and the Old Testament. The response of the Visconti was composed by Antonio Loschi (1365-1441), who in addition to working for Visconti interests at this time, served later as a secretary, apostolic writer and notary in the *Curia romana*. Loschi left collections of letters, many orations, a commentary on 11 orations by Cicero and the famous sonnet, which begins with the accusation that Florence was as vain as Cleopatra, the pagan Egyptian Queen. Note that Loschi, in responding to Salutati, follows the convention of the day by copying the rhyme of Salutati's sonnet, indeed asserting that Milan was not only as smart, but even more moral than Florence. Gian Galeazzo died September 3 of the plague as he was beginning his siege against the city. The rest, as one might say of subsequent Florentine accomplishments in art, literature, music and learning, was history.

## Coluccio Salutati

O scacciato dal ciel da Micael,
o ruina della sede d'aquilon,
o venenoso serpente Fiton,
o falso ucciditor del giusto Abel;

o mal commettitore Architophel,
o successor d'incanti d'Eriton;
maladicati l'alto Iddio, Sion,
che benedisse i figli d'Israel.

Contro ti sia la fede d'Abraam,
e l'oration che fe' Melchisadech,
e l'angiol che diè storpio a Balaam;

nascer possa per te nuovo Lamech.
che 'l sangue vendicò del fi' d'Adam,
tal sia tuo fin qual fu d'Abimlech.

Contro ti sia la gratia di Jacob,
poi che procacci crescer pene a Job.

*Antonio Loschi*

O Cleopatra, o madre d'Ismael,
o gran Semiramis di Babilon,
io son più pio che 'l figliuol d'Amon,
perché mi guarda l'angiol Rafael.

Ippolito, Narciso e Daniël
sempre ò nel cor, né già come Sansone
vinto sarò, né come Salomon,
né come il gran martiro d'Antrachel.

Il fuoco t'arda che arse Araam,
in odio venga a Dio come Ismalech,
o come al suo vicino Canaam;

o sventurata sí come Isposech,
o come Sedechia o Roboam,
nel tuo campo non nasca Semelech.

Se non ti basta, abbi di quel di Job,
io senta la gratia di Jacob.

## Coluccio Salutati

Oh, one chased from Heaven by Michael,
oh, ruin of the seat of Aquilon,
oh, venomous serpent Python,
oh, false murderer of the just Abel;

oh, evil transgressor Architophel,
oh, follower of the sorcery of Eriton;
damned of the high God, Zion,
who blessed the sons of Israel.

The faith of Abraham is against you,
and the preachings of Melchisedech,
and the angel who hindered Balaam;

the new Lamech was able to be born because of you,
whose blood avenged the sons of Adam,
such will be your end as was Abimlech's.

The grace of Jacob is against you,
since you strive to increase Job's suffering.


*Antonio Loschi*

Oh, Cleopatra, mother of Ishmael,
Oh, great Semiramis of Babylon,
I am more pure than the son of Amon,
because the angel Raphael watches me.

I always have Hippolytus, Narcissus
and Daniel in my heart, nor will I be
defeated like Samson, nor like Solomon,
nor like the great martyrdom of Antrachel.

The fire burns you that burned Araam,
you come to God in hate like Ismalech,
or like your cousin Canaam;

and so unhappy like Isposech,
or like Sedechia or Roboam,
Semelech would not be born on your side.

If it isn't enough, may you have that of Job,
then I might feel the grace of Jacob.

# Leonardo Bruni
# (1370–1444)

Leonardo Bruni was born in Arezzo in 1370. He was a secretary to the Papal chancery, with a few brief interruptions, between 1405 and 1415. He served as the Chancellor of the Florentine Republic from 1427 to his death on March 9th 1444. In addition to his political career, Bruni was a diligent humanist and man of letters, leaving an elegant translation of such writers from antiquity as Demosthenes, Xenophon, Plutarch, Plato and Aristotle. He also wrote lives of Dante and Petrarch, and wrote a defense of the vernacular. His major literary work, *Historiarum florentini populi libri XII*, a history of Florence from the beginnings of the Commune to 1404, was notable since it was the first history of Florence that relied on a critical examination of primary source material. Translated into Italian by Donato Acciaiuoli, it was widely read during the Renaissance. The selection presented here is a canzone in which Bruni praises Venus and explains the qualities beauty possesses. As a poem, its clear exposition and measured pace recall the style inherent in Cicero's orations. As a historical document, it sheds some light on certain aspects of early Quattrocento Florentine aesthetics. Bruni is buried in Santa Croce in a tomb by Bernardo Rossellino.

## Leonardo Bruni

*Canzone a laude di Venere*

O Venere formosa, o sacro lume,
o salutar fulgore, o alma stella,
bella sopra ogni bella,
che dal sublime cielo amor diffondi—
qual lingua, quale stilo o qual volume,
quale eloquenzia prisca over novella
può con mortal favella
gl'immortal don contar che ne fecondi?
Da te provengon tutti e ben giocondi;
tu 'l cielo illustri con tua santa lampa,
e giù nel mondo avampa
ogni animante, sì che tua potenza
perpetuar constrigne lor semenza.

Quando prim'entra il luminar del cielo
in quella region, la qual disegna
l'aurata sovransegna
del triangol celeste, allor s'esplica
la tua virtù, e saccia vento e gielo.
Voluttà, gioia e amicizia regna,
e la terra si degna
di fior vestirsi e diventar aprica;
il mar pon giù la guerra sua antica
e placido si fa e a te ride;
e gli angelletti stride,
percossi da tua forza, gittan fuore,
e tutto 'l mondo grida: amore, amore!

Non monti eccelsi, non rapaci fiumi,
non valli tenebrose o selva scura
ostan, chè senza cura
trapassan, quando sprona il tuo impero.
Tu dea permuti gli antichi costumi
e fai placido tal che prima fura;
e l'armi tue secura
rendono ogn'alma, e di coraggio altero.
Per ogni bosco e per ogni sentiero
pace, amicizia e concordia si vede;
e l'uno all'altro crede
placido senza fraude e in fe pura:
e per questo salute il mondo dura.

# Leonardo Bruni

*A Poem in Praise of Venus*

O buxom Venus, o sacred light,
o healthy radiance, o nourishing star—
beauty above every beauty,
who spreads love from the sublime heavens—
what language, what style, what book,
what ancient eloquence
can explain with mortal speech the news
of the immortal gifts
with which you are so fertile?
From you flourishes all nature;
you clarify the heavens with your sacred light,
and down in the world you enflame
every being, so that your power
compels their seed to flower.

When the star of heaven enters
that region, which draws
the golden sign
of the celestial triangle, your virtue
reigns and chases away wind and ice.
pleasure, joy and friendship reign,
and the earth is pleased
to dress herself in flowers and become sunny—
the sea puts its ancient battle down
and becomes calm, smiling at you—
and the little angels sing out,
hit with your power, they shout
and all the world cries: "Love, love!"

Not high mountains, not wild rivers,
not dark valleys or black woods
resist, for they are overcome
with no worry when you use your power.
You, goddess, barter the ancient customs
and calm the thieves—and your certain weapons
make every soul proud and courageous.
In every forest and every byway
one sees peace, friendship and harmony—
and one and all believe in
serenity without fraud and in pure faith:
so, the world prospers in this well-being.

D'esta virtù ch'io t'ho mostrato e veggio
nasce l'amore o insensata turba.
Certo chi in lui si turba
degno è che in estremo odio al mondo gema.
L'alma gentil che fu nell'alto seggio
vidde beltade vera senza turba;
poi giù, quando s'inurba,
se simil vede a quella alta e suprema,
attonita la guata, e pare iscema
d'ogni altro senso e propinquar disia.
E questa fantasia
distragge l'alma, o Dio! mirabil cosa,
che fuor di sè la mente in altri posa.

Chi amor crede biasimare, il loda,
quando insano e furente in suo dir chiama
colui che fervente ama;
perchè divin furore è ben perfetto.
La Sibilla non mai il vero isnoda,
se non quand'è furente, matta e grama;
e la divina trama
cerne il commosso, e non il sano petto;
e gli vaticinanti ch'àn predetto
furenti vider. Sicchè non è rio
il furor che da Dio
discende nella mente. E così amore
da Vener nasce, ed è divin furore.

Essa beata cogli occhi ridenti
su dal colmo del ciel guarda nostre opre,
e d'intorno la copre
l'Auriga colle sue dorate spalle.
Le picciole Virgilie lucenti
alli suo' piè festeggiano, e di sopre
del destro omero scopre
Perseo armato con sue stelle gialle;
con l'altra mano, in sul sinistro calle,
la fiera coma d'Orion minaccia;
e quei si rimbonaccia,
e pon giù l'ira e l'armi: e tale aspetto
spande nel mondo un fiume di diletto.

Questo inno a tuo onor, Ciprigna bella,
ha fatto un'alma che su nel ciel forse
dentro a tue rote corse,
dove impronata fu della grazia;
però di te lodar non fia mai sazia.

From this virtue that I've shown you and I see,
Love or irrational emotion is born.
Certainly he who is so touched
is pleased to moan in extreme hate to the world.
The gently noble soul who was in the lofty throne
saw, without agitation, true beauty—
then down here, when he enters a city,
if he sees something similar to that lofty and supreme,
he looks at it astonished, appears to lack
every other sense and desires to be next to her.
Then this fantasy
distracts the soul—Oh, God!—what a wonderful thing
that the mind rests outside itself in another.

He who believes in cursing love, praise him,
when, in his speech, he calls the one he
fervently loves insane and mad—
because the divine fury is truly perfect.
The Sybil isn't loose with the truth,
except when she's frenzied, delirious and tormented—
so the divine weaver
chooses the emotional, not the sane—
and the prophets have foretold
of seeing the crazed. So that the fury that
descends to the mind
from God is not evil. And so love
is born from Venus—and it's a divine madness.

Blessed with smiling eyes,
she watches our works from the heights of heaven—
and the Charioteer covers
her golden shoulders all around.
The little shining Virgos
celebrate fleet of foot—and above
Perseus armed with his yellow stars
uncovers her right shoulder,
with the other hand, on the left side,
he threatens the proud tresses of Orion—
then, all this calms down,
putting aside anger and arms: and such an aspect
spreads a river of pleasure across the world.

Beautiful Cypriot, this hymn in your honor
has made a soul who races to heaven, if
allowed, to be within your orbit,
where he is stamped with your grace—
however, we can never praise you enough.

# Filippo Brunelleschi
## (1377–1446)

In his *Istorie fiorentine* of 1427, Giovanni Cavalcanti writes that Gentile da Fabriano and Pesello were the two greatest artists of his time. Although we have scant documentation on and no remaining works by Pesello, Gentile da Fabriano worked solely in the International Gothic, a style whose roots go well back into the previous century. By contrast, Leon Battista Alberti does not mention either Gentile or Pesello in the epistle dedicated to Filippo Brunelleschi in the Italian translation of his treatise *De pictura* in 1436. Instead, Alberti mentions five artists – Brunelleschi, Donatello, Masaccio, Ghiberti and Luca della Robbia – who had, with their new art, surpassed even the greatest works of the ancients. Although we tend to see Leonardo, Raphael and Michelangelo as the pinnacle of Renaissance creativity, a strong argument could be made that Donatello, Masaccio and, above all, Brunelleschi were more than their equals.

Actually, it is not implausible to say that Brunelleschi was the most creative of all Renaissance artists. His bronze relief The Sacrifice of Isaac, which lost the 1401 competition for the second set of bronze doors for the Baptistery, ushered in an entirely new form of dramatic realism in the visual arts. In 1418, his original design and subsequently successful coordination of the construction of the cupola of the Duomo in Florence was both an engineering marvel, since it was built without any centering, and an aesthetic success, since its 'swelling tension' resonated off the hills surrounding Florence and encapsulated the then existing proportions of the city into a dynamic whole. Finally, Brunelleschi's invention of linear perspective, with proportionally receding transversal lines, created an entirely new way of measuring and creating a three-dimensional space on a two-dimensional surface.

It is not surprising, then, that Filippo would respond sharply to the sonnet by Giovanni da Prato (1367-1442/46) that mocks his attempt to build the Duomo's cupola. Domenico de Robertis, a 20th century critic, refers to Brunelleschi's sonnet as "perhaps the most beautiful sonnet of the entire Quattrocento... (De Robertis, 406)." With its faith in the capacity of the human mind to solve problems and discover new things, it encapsulates the Renaissance 'can-do' spirit in just fourteen lines.

## Giovanni da Prato

*a Filippo Brunelleschi*

O fonte fonda e nissa d'ignoranza,
pauper animale ed insensibile,
che vuoi lo 'ncerto altrui mostrar visibile,
ma tua archimia nichil habet possanza;

la insipida plebe sua speranza
omai perduta l'ha, ed è credibile:
ragion non dà che la cosa impossibile
possibil facci uom sine sustanza.

Ma se 'l tuo Badalon che in acqua vola
viene a perfezion, che non può essere,
non ched i' legga Dante nella scuola,

ma vo' con le mieman finir mio essere,
perch'io son certo di tuo mente fola,
ché poco sai ordire e vie men tessere.


*Filippo Brunelleschi in risposta*

Quando dall'alto ci è dato speranza,
o tu c'hai efigia s'animal resible,
perviensi all'uom, lasciando il corruttibile,
e ha da giudicar Somma Possanza.

Falso giudcicio perde la baldanza,
ché sperïenza gli si fa terribile:
l'uom saggio non ha nulla d'invisibile,
se non quel che non è, perc'ha mancanza.

E quella fantasia d'un senza scola,
ogni falso pensier non vede l'essere
che l'arts dà quando natura invola.

Adunque i versi tuoi convienti stessere,
c'hanno rughiato in falso la carola,
da poi che 'l mio "impossibil" viene all'essere.

## Giovanni da Prato

*to Filippo Brunelleschi*

O deep source and nexus of ignorance,
poor and insensible animal,
you want to make the uncertain visible to others,
but your alchemy has no power.

By now the insipid mob has
lost its hope and it's understandable:
reason dictates the man can't do
an impossible thing without substance.

But if your large fig that flies in water
comes to perfection, which it can't do—
not because I read Dante in school—

but because I want to finish my being with my own hands,
since I'm certain of your mental folly,
as you know little of weaving and your fabric fails.

*Filippo Brunelleschi in Response*

When impetus comes from on high,
oh you who has the aspect of a mocking animal,
it reaches man, leaving the corruptible,
desiring to be the Supreme Good.

False judgment loses self-confidence,
for experience treats it badly:
the wise man has nothing invisible,
but that which isn't, because it is deficient.

And those imaginings of one without learning—
each phony thought doesn't see the being
that art gives when nature disappears.

Therefore, your verses must unravel,
they have falsely interrupted the dance,
since my "impossible" comes to be.

# Leon Battista Alberti
# (1404–1472)

Man of letters, philosopher, sculptor, architect and theorist of art, Leon Battista Alberti embodied all that was Renaissance humanism. Born in Genoa on February 14, 1404, the son of an exiled Florentine nobleman, he demonstrated an early talent for excelling. While studying law at Bologna, he wrote a Latin comedy *Philodoxeos* (c.1424) that his contemporaries mistook for a lost Roman play. In 1434, he became papal secretary. In 1435, he wrote *De pictura*, a Latin treatise on painting in which he both recognized and explained the new art of a new generation of artists that included Brunelleschi, Donatello, Masaccio, Ghiberti and Luca della Robbia. In a culture whose mainstream art was International Gothic, this was no insignificant achievement. The next year Alberti translated the treatise into Italian for Brunelleschi who couldn't read Latin. In the 1437-8, Alberti wrote the first three books of *Della famiglia*, a philosophical treatise on the education and ethics of domestic life. In 1441, he wrote the fourth book on the subject of friendship. In 1450, he wrote *De re aedificatoria*, an architectural treatise modeled on Vitruvius that discusses ancient and modern building design as well as the theory of mathematical proportions inherent in both music and good architecture. Between 1447 and 1450 he designed a new exterior for the church of San Francesco in Rimini. Among his other archtectural achievements were such projects as the churches of San Sebastiano (1460) and Sant'Andrea (1472) in Mantua, the facade of Santa Maria Novella in Florence (1470) and the facade of the Palazzo Rucellai (1455-58) in Florence. In 1472, he completed *De scultura*, a treatise on sculpture.

Alberti also wrote on a wide variety of subjects that included domestic animals, religion, the priesthood, law, politics, government, mathematics, mechanics, literature and language. Regarding the latter, he was one of the champions of the vernacular in Florence. He and Piero de' Medici promoted the *Certame coronario*, a competition held on October 22, 1441 in Florence's Duomo in which several poets wrote vernacular poetry on the theme *La vera amicitia* (True Friendship). Examples of Alberti's poetry in this volume include some Petrarchan sonnets; *Corymbus*, the first pastoral poem written since Antiquity; *Versioni poetiche*, Italian translations of various ancient authors; and, *De Amicitia*, his poem on friendship for the *Certame coronario* that emulates Latin hexameters. The hexameter is a verse of six feet, with the first four usually dactyls or spondees, with the fifth a dactyl or spondee, and the sixth a spondee or trochee.

## Leon Battista Alberti

1
Chi vòl bella victoria e star sicuro,
e contra il morbo far un scudo forte,
siegua di Amor la glorïosa corte,
che confusion non teme o tempo oscuro.

Amor dinanci al cor è un marmo duro,
contra cü non val veneno o morte.
Amor da sé discazza ogni altra sorte;
in l'alma dov'el sta, fa l'aere puro.

Amor è un foco dentro al gentil pecto,
che brusa e che consuma ogni altro umore;
e Morte fugge il suo real aspecto.

Amore fa in uom mortal vivace il cuore;
né può morir, mentre ha per suo obiecto
Amor, che sempre il pasce in vivo ardore.

Però seguiti Amore,
o gentil' spiriti, e voi, madonne oneste,
che amor vi camparà da mortal peste.


2
Per li pungenti spin', per gli aspri istecchi,
per le turbe marin', per cruda guerra,
dove io mi varchi, un pensier mi sotterra,
e vuol che innanzi tempo imbianchi e 'nvecchi.

Tanto son facti e miei pensier' parecchi,
che sì e non nel capo mi s'aferra:
quand'un si chiude, e l'altro si riserra,
onde di duol mestier sarà ch'io assecchi.

Ma tu, Padre sincer, che l'opre e 'l core
cognosci di noi, gente maladetta,
ché non provedi a tanto nostro errore?

La tu' iustitia, ché tanto s'aspecta?
Ben dice Dante, ond'io prendo vigore:
La spada di lassù non taglia in fretta.

## Leon Battista Alberti

1
Whoever wants a beautiful victory and security,
and to make a strong shield against ill,
follow the glorious court of Love,
that fears neither confusion nor dark weather.

Love before a heart is hard stone
against which prevails neither venom nor death.
Love by itself dismisses every other motive—
in the soul where it stays, it makes the air pure.

Love is a fire inside a gentle heart
that burns and consumes every other humor—
Death flees in his tangible presence.

Love makes a mortal's heart quicken,
nor can it die while its object is
Love, who always feeds it with living passion.

For these reasons follow Love,
o gently noble spirits, and you virtuous ladies,
who Love will save from mortal plagues.


2
Through the prickly thorns, the sharp twigs,
the stormy seas, cruel war,
wherever I go, a thought takes me away,
and before I know it, makes me gray and old.

My deeds and thoughts are so many
that "yes" and "no" grapple in my head:
when one stops, the other rallies,
whence I must dry my sorrow.

But you, sincere Father, who know the
deeds and hearts of us, cursed people,
why don't you compensate for our sin?

Your justice, why do you linger so much?
Dante said well, whence I take strength:
The sword above doesn't swing in haste.

3
*Corymbus*

M.B.   Corimbo, giovinetto avernïese,
       bello, prudente, virtuoso, onesto,
       in cui eran d'Amore le faci incese,
       di selva in selva giva solo, mesto,
       spegnendo con le lagrime la vampa,
       qual a sé stesso lo rendeva infesto.
       Spesso "Infelice" dicea "chi inciampa
       in questi lacci tuoi, crudel Cupido!
       Felice chi da' tuoi strali campa!
       Che è a dir, ch'i' fuggo ov'io stessi mi guido
       e duolmi troppo quel che più mi piace,
       e troppo temo, ov'io troppo mi fido?
       Accendo co' sospiri in me le face,
       qual' pure i' copro, e pur vorrei scoprire"
       mio dolore entro prega, e di fuor tace.

Cor-   Piango cantando. Oimè, debb'io morire?
imbo   Misero me, misero me, i' moro,
       e io stessi m'accoro;
       i' fuggo ogni salute al mio languire.

       Misero chi si crede
       aminuir l'ardore,
       discoprendo la fede,
       ch'altrui li fa signore;
       oimè, coperto amore
       convien serva a sua posta e libertade,
       benché l'altrui pietade
       c'inviti a confidar nel ben servire.

       Aimè, ch'i' mi pensai
       rallentar mïa doglia,
       e parte mi fidai
       discoprir mïe voglia.
       Infelice chi spoglia
       l'arme che col soffrir molto l'aita!
       Meglio è finir sua vita,
       che dover senza merto altrui servire.

3
*Corymbus*

M.B.    Corymbus, young Vernian,
        handsome, wise, virtuous, honest,
        in who the torches of Love burn,
        of the wood, walking alone in the wood, sad,
        extinguishing with tears passion,
        which by itself made him hostile.
        often "Unhappy" he said "who stumbles
        in your place, cruel Cupid!
        Happy he who lives far from your arrows!
        Which is to say, do I flee from where I take myself
        and suffer too much what pleases me more
        and fear too much where I trust myself too much?
        Lighting the torches in me with sighs,
        which I, moreover, cover and nevertheless
        would like to uncover:
        my pain within wishes and outside is silent."

Cor.    I weep singing. Alas, must I die?
        miserable me, miserable me, I die
        and I alone know what I am going through;
        I avoid every remedy of my weakening.
        Miserable he who believes
        to lessen the passion,
        discovering the faith
        that other make master;
        alas, concealed love
        must preserve its place and license,
        although pity invites others
        to feel sure in serving well.

        Alas, that I thought I
        could lessen my suffering
        and, for my part, I could trust
        myself to discover my will.
        Unhappy he who lowers
        his weapons to help them with much suffering!
        Better to end his life
        than having to serve another without reward.

Ripenso, duolmi, spasimo,
e meco ne fo storia;
lodo, [i]spero, biasmo,
e riduco a memoria
che pure egli è vittoria
poter, perdendo, adoperar sue armi.
Io andai a legarmi,
e né posso tacer, né gliel so dire.

Invidiosa fortuna,
anzi i' fui stolto;
non sapev'io che niuna,
benché la serva molto,
soffrì mai sie sciolto
da' lacci, con che amor ne inreta e tiene?
Or painger ne convien,
stolti, che al fuoco entràn credendo uscire.

A noi, meschini amanti,
qual dura non si pieghi,
udendo nostri pianti,
nostri sospiri e prieghi?
Chi sarà che dinieghi
che un fedel servir merti merzede?
O Iddio, altri pur vede
che fede e onestà mi fa soffrire.

M.B.    Che fai, Corimbo? Stolto chi si crede
pietà trovar più in altri che 'n sé stessi!
Prendi da Amore quanto ti concede.
Stolto, Corimbo, stolto se credessi
con libertà poter viver suggetto:
potresti assai, se te stesso vincessi.
Ma' sempre suole Amor chiuso nel petto
più palesarsi quanto più l'ascondi:
non val contra l' iddii l'uman concetto.
Che fai, Corimbo? Te stessi confondi.
Ben scorge chi tu servi in un sospiro
qua' sieno de' pensier' tuoi i più profondi.
Se 'l ciel porge a voi sdegnoso e diro,
miseri amanti, vincete soffrendo.
Matura il tempo ogni vostro disiro.

I reflect, I grieve, I burn with passion
and make it my testament;
I praise, I hope, I lament
and I call to my mind
that he is victory—
able, losing, to take up his arms.
I went to make a relationship,
and I can neither be silent nor know how to tell him

Invidious Fortune,
before, I was stupid.
I knew no one,
although I served her much,
would I ever suffer were I freed
from the snares with which Love ensnared and trapped?
Now I must weep,
foolish, for I entered the fire believing to escape.

To us, wretched lovers,
doesn't that hardness yield,
hearing our tears,
our sighs and prayers?
Who will it be who denies
that a faithful servant deserves mercy?
O God, others see
that faith and honesty make me suffer.

M.B.    What are you doing, Corymbus? Stupid he who believes
to find pity more in others than in himself!
Take from Love as much as he concedes you.
Stupid, Corymbus, stupid if you'd believe
yourself able to live with liberty when enslaved:
you would be well able to, were you to conquer yourself.
Never ever get used to Love bound in your heart
more revealing the more you hide him:
the human mind has no power against the gods
What are you doing, Corymbus? You confuse yourself.
He guides well who you serve in a sigh,
which is the most profound of your thoughts.
If the heavens bestow you disdain and cruelty,
wretched lovers, defeat suffering.
Time matures every desire of yours.

4

S'i' sto doglioso, ignun si maravigli,
poiché sì vuol chi può quel che le piace,
né so quando aver debba omai più pace
l'alma, ismarrita infra tanti perigli.

Misero me, a che convien s'appigli
mia vana speme, debile e fallace?
Né rincrescer mi può chi ciò mi face:
Amor, che fai? perché non mi consigli?

Ben fôra tempo ad avanzar tuo corso,
ché la stanca virtù ognor vien meno,
né molto d'amendue già mi confido.

Ma s'ancora a pietà s'allarga il freno,
tengo ch'assai per tempo fia il soc[c]orso;
se non, tosto udirai l'ultimo istrido.

4

If I'm sorrowing, no one would be surprised,
since my power is tied to wanting what she wants,
nor do I know when my soul must have more
peace, lost among so many dangers.

Miserable me, to what must my vain hope
attach itself, weak and unfounded?
Nor can who makes me burden me:
Love, what are you doing? why don't you counsel me?

Very out of sync for you to hurry,
for tired virtue always faints,
nor have I much trust in either.

But if he allows mercy more freedom,
I believe the aid will be early enough—
 if not, soon you will hear the last scream.

*Versioni poetiche*

1

"Disse Oratio Flacco poeta:

Qualunque corse ad acquistarsi laude
giovane, cose molte e dure e gravi
sofferse, al freddo e al caldo; e ben se asten[n]e
fuggendo con virtù Venere e Bacco".

2

"Come dice Valerio Martiale di Mitridate,

Qual, uso spesso a guastar el veleno,
rendette in sé natura sua sì fatta,
che più niun tossico gli potea noiare".

3

"Adunque non iniuria dicea Ovidio poeta:

Con ambigüi passi la Fortuna
erra, né segue certa in alcun luogo,
ma or si porge lieta ed ora acerba.
Solo una legge serba: in essere lieve".

4

"Versi di Giuvenale, optimo poeta satiro:

Pena fu data a chi molto ci vive
che, iterata sempre clade in casa
con molti pianti e perpetuo merore
s'invecchi adolorato in veste nera".

5

"Sono versi di Lucretio, poeta vetustissimo:

Già poi che 'l tempo con sue forze in noi
straccò e nervi ed allassò le membra,
claudica el piede e l'ingegno e la lingua,
persin che manca ogni cosa in tempo".

*Poetic Translations*

1
The poet Horace Flaccus said:

"Whoever runs to acquire new
praise, suffers many hard and serious
things, from cold to hot; and well better he abstain
fleeing Venus and Bacchus with virtue."

2
As Valerius Martial of Mitridate says:

"One who is used to destroying venom
makes in himself a nature so made
that no more poison can trouble him."

3
Therefore, Ovid the poet used to say don't offend:

"With ambiguous steps Fortune
wanders, not following certainty in any place,
but presenting herself now happy, now cruel.
Only one law endures: transcend."

4
Verses of Juvenal, the best satiric poet:

"Pain is given to one who lives fully
until, repeated disasters at home,
with many tears, perpetual suffering,
aging, tormented, wearing black."

5
These are verses of Lucretius, most ancient poet:

"Truly, since time with its force
tires and fatigues our bodies and nerves,
stops our feet, our minds and our voices,
until each of them is missing after a while."

6

"Ma basti qui a noi tanto asseguire quanto Valerius Martial, festivissimo poeta;
ne ammonisce suo epigramma:

"S'ancora forse dài a farti amare,
poi ch'io te vedo attorniato d'amici,
cedemi, Ruffo, se t'avanza, un luogo;
e non mi recusare perch'io sia nuovo,
che si fur tutti quei tuoi antiqui amici.
Tu tanto guarda chi ti s'apparechia,
se potrà farsi a te buon vec[c]hio amico."

7

"Faremo secondo che ammoniva Fenix quel buon vecchio presso di Homer,
qual dicea ad Achille:

Doma questo tuo animo sbardellato,
quando gl'idii, quali certo ti superano
di virtù e dignità, sono flexibili."

8

"Sono versi qui di Baptista in suoi poemi toscani, in quali imitò Virgilio:

Grave più cose già sofrim[m]o altrove,
e darà el tempo a queste ancor suo fine."

9

"Appresso d'Homer Hector ferito a morte consolava sé stessi con sperare a sé gloria immortale et
eterna fama. E dicea:

Satisfeci al mio fato, esco di vita
forse in età non matura, ma esco
non sanza qualche piena e bene appresa
glorïa, quando feci più e più cose
degne di memoria e posterità.

6

But suffice here that we follow how much Valerius Martial, most celebrated poet, admonishes in his epigram:

"If still perhaps you're annoyed by love,
considering I see you surrounded by friends,
cede to me, Rufus, if it occurs to you, a place
and don't refuse me because I'm young,
because all those are old friends of yours.
You look so much at whoever readies for you,
as if he will make you a good friend."

7

We will act according to how Phoenix warned, that good old man close to Homer, who said to Achilles:

"Tamed this unchained soul of yours,
when the gods, who will certainly surpass you
with virtue and dignity, are flexible."

8

These are verses here of Baptista in his Tuscan poems, in which he imitated Virgil:

"We have already suffered more serious things elsewhere,
and time will give to these yet its end."

9

According to Homer, Hector, wounded to death, consoled himself with the expectation of immortal glory and eternal fame:

"I satisfied my destiny, I leave this life
perhaps not yet old, but I leave
not without some full and well earned
glory, when I did many things
worthy of memory and posterity."

*De Amicitia*

*Exametri*

Dite, o mortali, che sì fulgente corona
ponesti in mezzo, che pur mirando volete?
Forse l'Amicitia, qual col celeste Tonante
tra·lli Celicoli è con maiestate locata,
ma, pur sollicita, non raro scende l'Olimpo,
sol se subsidio darci, se comodo posse?
Non vien nota mai, non vien comperta, temendo
l'invida contra lei scelerata gente nimica.
In tempo e luogo veg[g]o che grato sarebbe
a chi qui mira manifesto poterla vedere.
S'oggi scendesse, qui dentro accolta vedrete
sì la sua effigie e' gesti, sì tutta la forma.
Dunque voi, che qui venerate su' alma corona,
leggerete i mie' monimenti, e presto saràvi
l'"inclita forma sua molto notissima, donde
cauti amerete poi. Così starete beati.

*On Friendship*

*Hexameters*

Do you say, o mortals, what you want, beholding so
shining a crown that you have taken up the challenge?
Perhaps Friendship—which is located with majesty
among Heaven's dwellers with Zeus, the celestial thunderer—
yet, does she merely entice, doesn't she rarely descend Olympus
to give aid only if it is convenient?
She is never observed, she never draws attention, fearing
the hatred of wicked, hostile people.
On earth, I see that she would be kind
to whoever strives at being able to see her clearly.
If she were to descend today, here assembled inside you
would see her appearance and manner—in fact all her being.
Therefore, you, who here venerate her immortal crown,
will read my monuments and, immediately, her celebrated form
will be very recognized, whence
you will surely love. Thus you will be blessed.

# Selections from the *Certame coronario*

On October 22, 1441, eight poets participated in the *Certame coronario* (Silver Laurels) in the Duomo of Florence. Each recited or had someone recite his original vernacular poem on the theme of *De vera amicitia* or 'True Friendship.' The jury consisted of ten papal secretaries. The audience consisted of the Archbishop of Florence, the Orator of the Republic of Venice and a large crowd of onlookers. The winner was to receive a crown of laurel made from silver. The contest was promoted by Leon Battista Albeti, Piero di Cosimo de' Medici and the administrators of the University of Florence. It was modeled after ancient poetry contests and more contemporary ones in France, Flanders and Spain. The goal of the *Certame* was to promote the idea that the vernacular was as capable of noble expression as Latin. Interestingly, the ten judges, all Latin humanists, decided that the recited poetry was weak and awarded no one the silver laurel. The Florentines, not to be dictated to by papal secretaries from Rome, accused the panel of jealousy, which, had the second *Certame* taken place (it did not), would have served as its theme.

Regardless of how the papal judges felt, the poetry of the *Certame* had some interesting developments. Among the innovations, both Alberti and Leonardo Dati created the first Italian examples of *metrica barbara* with their respective attempts to emulate classical meter. The term *metrica barbara* was coined by Giosuè Carducci, the late 19th and early 20th century poet and winner of the Noble Prize in Literature in 1906, to label Italian poetry that attempted to imitate the quantitative quality of both Greek and Latin poetry. (It was barbaric in the sense that it was written in a language other than Greek or Latin.) Quantitative verse is based on the alternation of long and short syllables, syllables classified on how long it takes to pronounce them. (One of the few poets to try this in English was the 16th century English poet Thomas Campion.) Normally, Italian poetry was qualitative, based on stressed and unstressed syllables. A further innovation by Dati was his use of the Sapphic strophe in the third part of his poem. The Sapphic strophe is a four line stanza invented by Sappho, 6th century BCE poet. Its first three lines are 11 syllables long. Each 11 syllable line can be divided into 5 poetic feet, each of which is two syllables long, usually trochaic, except for the third, which is a trisyllabic dactyl. The fourth line is 5 syllables long, usually a dactyl followed by a spondee.

The selections here are by Alberti, Benedetto Accolti, Ciriaco d'Ancona and Leonardo Dati. Each of them indicates an almost meditatively profound response to the *Certame's* theme of 'True Friendship.'

Leon Battista Alberti, covered in the previous section of this volume, wrote a poem in *metrica barbara*, an attempt in the vernacular to emulate Latin hexameters

Benedetto Accolti (1415-1466), humanist and attorney, taught public and canon law at Volterra, Bologna and then Florence. He succeeded Poggio Bracciolini as the Chancellor of Florence. He wrote a four book Latin poem on the First Crusade, *De bello a Christianis contra barbaros gesto*, and a defense of modern over ancient culture, *Dialogus de praestantia virorum sui aevi*. Domenico de Robertis refers to his *Certame* poem *Se mai gloria d'ingegno altri commosse* as the "most organic and unified" of the competition.

Ciriaco d'Ancona (1391-1452) was a traveler, antiquarian and autodidactic humanist. His family's business interests enabled him to begin travels by the age of nine that, into his adulthood, would reach as far as Constantinople and Egypt. In his now lost *Commentarii* he described gems, statuettes, medals, manuscripts and epigraphic material he discovered during his many travels. De Robertis decribes his *Qel Sir, che socto l'idëale stampa* as "the most exquisite sonnet."

Leonardo Dati (1408-1472), humanist, served as papal secretary for Callixtus II, Pius II, Paul II and Sixtus IV. He became the bishop of Massa in 1472. His Latin writings include letters, lyric poems, eclogues and a one-act tragedy *Hiempsal*. De Robertis characterizes his *Scena* for the *Certame* "the only interesting experiment" of the group.

## Leon Battista Alberti

*De Amicitia*

*Exametri*

Dite, o mortali, che sì fulgente corona
ponesti in mezzo, che pur mirando volete?
Forse l'Amicitia, qual col celeste Tonante
tra·lli Celicoli è con maiestate locata,
ma, pur sollicita, non raro scende l'Olimpo,
sol se subsidio darci, se comodo posse?
Non vien nota mai, non vien comperta, temendo
l'invida contra lei scelerata gente nimica.
In tempo e luogo veg[g]o che grato sarebbe
a chi qui mira manifesto poterla vedere.
S'oggi scendesse, qui dentro accolta vedrete
sì la sua effigie e' gesti, sì tutta la forma.
Dunque voi, che qui venerate su' alma corona,
leggerete i mie' monimenti, e presto saràvi
l'inclita forma sua molto notissima, donde
cauti amerete poi. Così starete beati.

# Leon Battista Alberti

*On Friendship*

*Hexameters*

Do you say, o mortals, what you want, beholding so
shining a crown that you have taken up the challenge?
Perhaps Friendship—which is located with majesty
among Heaven's dwellers with Zeus, the celestial thunderer—
yet, does she merely entice, doesn't she rarely descend Olympus
to give aid only if it is convenient?
She is never observed, she never draws attention, fearing
the hatred of wicked, hostile people.
On earth, I see that she would be kind
to whoever strives at being able to see her clearly.
If she were to descend today, here assembled inside you
would see her appearance and manner—in fact all her being.
Therefore, you, who here venerate her immortal crown,
will read my monuments and, immediately, her celebrated form
will be very recognized, whence
you will surely love. Thus you will be blessed.

## Ciriaco d'Ancona

Quel Sir, che socto l'idëale stampa
dié forma a l'alme substanze superne,
a Delio, a la sorella, all'altre eterne
nymphe, che 'l celo adorna e 'l mondo avampa,
con quei liquenti corpi, con che accampa
Amphitrite la terra, ove concerne
omni animal che vive, sente e cerne
socto li raggi de Sua chiara lampa,
per l'universo ornar d'omni delicia
produsse in forma, in acto e in potenza
tante e diverse al mondo crëature
substanze e accidenze miste e pure
dandoli in don più degno a la Sua essenza
util, iucunda, honesta, alma Amicizia.

## Ciriaco d'Ancona

That Lord, who during the ideal shaping
gave form to the divine, immortal substances—
to the Delian, his sister and other eternal
nymphs, who adorn the heavens and illuminate the earth
with those watery bodies, with which Amphitrite
encamps the earth, which concerns
every animal that lives, feels and discerns
under the rays of his clear light—
throughout the universe the adornment of every delight
produced in form, action and power
so many different creatures in the world,
substance and accident mixed and pure,
giving them the most useful worthy gift of His essence:
useful, joyful, virtuous, immortal Friendship.

## Benedetto di Michele Accolti

Se mai gloria d'ingegno altri commosse,
  o amor virtüoso, a dire in rima,
  o lascivo pensier ch'al cor gli fosse;
e se mai verso alcun degno di stima,
  di memoria, compose, or si dimostri,
  per salire d'alta gloria in sulla cima;
ché materia più grata ai tempi nostri,
  o sacre Muse, a voi non si propose
  per eccitare a dire gli alunni vostri.
Né di tutte le chiare e sante cose,
  che per nostra salute a noi concesse
  son da Colui che terra e ciel dispose,
alcuna n'è che tanto esser dovesse
  illustrata di lode oneste e gravi,
  da ciaschedun che dritto senso avesse,
quanto quella che tiene ambo le chiavi
  di concordia, di pace e di salute,
  e partorisce frutti alti e soavi:
vera Amicizia, tempio di virtute,
  fonte d'amore, ostel di cortesia,
  scudo a Fortuna e sue saette acute.
E chi da tanto ben l'alma disvia
  ama poco se stesso e pare indegno
  che ricordo di lui al mondo sia.
E chi a dir lei ciascuno ingegno
  modern invita, che del sacro lume
  di Febo ha la memoria e 'l petto pregno,
veramente dimostra un largo fiume
  d'amor sempre ch'al bene acceso sia;
  e rinova fra noi gentil costume
che da' nostri maggior già si solìa
  usar; ma questo secol duro e rio
  ogni via di virtù, cieco, s'oblia.
Onde, per saddisfare al dover mio ,
  mosso sono a cantar, non perch'i' speri
  parer fra tanti fiumi un picciol rio;
ché, s'al tempo degli anni più leggeri
  quanto seppi, d' Amore in rima scrissi,
  falsa speme seguendo e van pensieri,
e gli occhi lungamente indamo fissi
  ver' lui ritenni, e mai un giorno solo
  quel fallace disio da me partissi,

## Benedetto di Michele Accolti

If ever the glory of genius were to move others—
 oh, virtuous Love—to speak in rhyme,
 oh, lascivious thought that would be in their hearts—
and if ever someone composed verses worthy of esteem,
 of memory , he would now prove
 to climb to the top of the highest glory—
for material more welcome to our times—
 oh, Sacred Muse—one does not propose
 to excite to song your students.
Nor does He who ordered earth and heaven
 concede to us for our salvation
 all enlightened and holy things,
some would merit to be as illustrated
 with honest and serious praises
 by anyone who would know right and wrong,
as well as that one who holds both the keys
 to harmony, peace and salvation—
 and bears lofty, gentle fruit:
true Friendship, temple of virtue,
 source of love, home of courtesy,
 shield of fortune and its sharp arrows.
And one who deviates the soul from so much good
 love himself little and appears unworthy
 to leave memory of himself in the world.
And one who proposes to sing of each
 modern genius has his memory and breast pregnant
 with the sacred light of Phoebus,
truly shows a large river
 of love is always excited by the good—
 and renews gentle customs among us
that used to be held by our
 elders—but this harsh, rotten and blind century
 has forgotten every virtue.
Whence, to satisfy my duty ,
 I am moved to sing, not because I expect
 to seem a little stream among many rivers—
for, if during those fickle years,
 as much as I knew about Love, I would have
 written following false hope and vain thoughts,
and I would have fixed my eyes eternally in vain
 on him, never separating myself from
 that false desire,

quanto con più fervore, al sommo Polo
rivolgendo la mente, or mi convène
d'Amicizia cantar, ch'i' seguo e colo!
Per la qual fermamente si mantène
fede, gioia, riposo e caritade,
fortezza ed onesta con giusta spene.

. . . . . . . . . . . . . . . . . . . . . . . . . . .

Oh come glorïoso, dolce e magno
frutto nasce dappoi di questa pianta
donde non esce mai vergogna e lagno!
Inde vien carità perfetta e santa,
fede, pace, sussidio della vita
che da molte fortune è spesso affranta.
E nel tempo filice ella ci aita
e conforta e diletta, e tiene 'l freno
a superchia lussuria che c'incita—
e quanto per dicordia, e per veleno
ch'inde nasce, si quasta l'universo,
tanto per questa s' orna e fa sereno .
Ed a quella amicizia el nostro verso
s' estende ancor nel suo estremo canto,
sanza la quale el mondo fora sperso:
cioè somma concordia, che per santo
proposito congiugne ei cittadini
all 'util della patria in amor tanto.
Conchiudendo: gli amici veri e fini,
mentre vivon quaggiù nel cieco mondo,
per simiglianza son fatti divini:
perché l'esser di Dio, ch'è sì profondo,
è congiunto e unito in tre persone
di Poter, di Saper, d'Amor giocondo,
come la nostra fede aperto pone.

as much as it is now necessary for me
 to sing of Friendship with more fervor,
 turning my head to God, who I follow and worship!
For whom I firmly keep
 faith, joy, calm, charity ,
 fortitude and honesty with good hope.


. . . . . . . . . . . . . . . . . . . . . . . . . . . .


Oh, how glorious, sweet and lofty
 a fruit is then born from this plant
 from which shame and grief never come!
After comes perfect and holy charity,
 faith, peace—the sustenance of life
 that is checked by many misfortunes.
And in happy times she helps,
 comforts and delights us—slowing down
 excessive luxury that excites us—
and as much as discord, venom and
 a rotten universe are born from this,
 so for her one adorns and becomes calm.
And so to her we extend our verse
 at its maximum,
 without which the world will waste away:
That is the highest concord, which by holy
 design joins in such love
 its citizens to the use of the city-state.
Concluding: true and excellent friends,
 while they live down here in the blind world,
 resemble the divine:
because the Being of God, who is so profound,
 is joined and united in the three persons
 of Power, of Knowledge, of joyful Love,
like our faith openly asserts.

## Leonardo Dati

Scelte da *Scena*

I Cantus

I' son Mercurïo, di tutto l'olympico regno          Mercurius
nuntïo, tra gli omini varïi iunctura salubre,
splendor de' saggi; porto al certamine vostro
sì cose, sì canto novo: scoltate benigni,
o circustanti che 'l canto poëtico amate,
s'i' vi son grato quanto qualunque poëta.
Ha Amore sentito, padre sommo et principe sommo
degli omini et divi, il novo qui spectaculo vostro,
et, cupido, farvi non ornamento minore
convenga, subito qua giù m'impuose venissi.
Presi e' thalari et gli abiti, vïa vènnine rapto,
et giù cala' mi su questo monte propinquo
donde sule Ytalïa, per forse ad Marte piacere,
specchiarsi in mar Tyreno et 'n quel d'Adrïa priscia.
Quivi dëe molte vidi pel colle vaganti
et nymphe seco varïe, molto inclita turba,
quali dintomo presto m ' accorsero liete.

. . . . . . . . . . . . . . . . . . . . . . . . . . . . .

II Cantus

S'egli è, Musa, maï ch'ïo da te gratia merti,          Leonardus
or me 'l dimostra; dammi sì dolce liquore,          ipse
sì claro ingegno ch'ïo quel dïadema riporti
con ver iudcïo, già non ignoblile dono.
Fa' gli omini stupidi al canto, fa' 'l tempio risulti
plaudendo meco, fa' ch'ogni spirito dica:
"Datho è el victor di tanto insigne palestra,
che coniunse piedi degni d'ornarne trïomphi."
Sento l'Amicitïa già già discende l'Olympo,
con canti et cythare resonando l'aëre seco .
Eccola: quella 'segua per me quel saphyco canto,
che con dolce lyra dilecta ingegno perito.
State voï attenti et placidi; con fronte serena
l'ascoltate, però, se consentite volerla,
sempre serà vostra iocunda et certa salute.

# Leonadro Dati

Selections from *Play*

## Canto I

I am Mercury , messenger of the entire Olympic                    Mercury
realm, healthy bond between unlike men,
splendor of the sages—I bring to your contest
such things, such new song: listen benign ones,
oh, bystanders that love poetic song ,
if I am as welcome as any other poet.
Jove, first father and loftiest prince
of men and gods, has heard your new performance here—
and, desirous to make here ornament not less than what
may be necessary , I immediately came down here to join in.
Directed with my sandals and robes, I was snatched away,
and came down on this Apennine mountain
where Italy, perhaps to please Mars,
is reflected in the Tyrrhenian Sea and that Adriatic.
Here from a little hill I saw many wandering
goddesses and different nymphs with him,
who, suddenly around, happily discovered me.

. . . . . . . . . . . . . . . . . . . . . . . . . . . .

## Canto II

If it ever happens, Muse, that I deserve mercy from you,          Leonardo
show it to me—give me such sweet liquor,                          himself
such clear genius that I would bring back that crown
as a true verdict, certainly not an unworthy gift.
Make stupid men sing, make the temple arise
applauding me, make every spirit say:
"Dato is the winner of many athletic banners,
which adds support worthy of decorating triumphs."
I truly feel Friendship descend from Olympus,
ringing the air with song and guitar.
Here it is: that which follows are my Sapphic Strophes,
that delight knowing minds with sweet lyric poetry.
Pay attention calmly—listen to them with
serene faces—however, if you agree to want it,
it will always be your happy and certain salvation.

III Cantus
(verse 1-40)

Eccomi; i'son qui dëa degli amici,                    Amicitia
  quella qual tucti gli omini solete
  mordere et, falso, fugitiva dirli;
  or la volete.
Eccomi; et già dal sollo superno
  scesa, cercavo loco tra la gente,
  prompta star con chi per amor volesse
  dame ricepto.
Vènnine primo in cas a de' patrizi
  principi, donde una maligna coppia
  fàmmisi contro, ad simili palagi
  degna famiglia.
Livor è l'uno, macilento, tristo,
  cinto con serpi et d'odïi coperto;
  Falsitas, l'altro, è dëa fraudulenta;
  gridano ver' me:
"0 dëa plebëa, animo sa troppo,
  della mortale specïe nimica,
  che vaï errando, petulante scurra ?
  donde rigiri?
Qual tüo t'ha mo' scelerato facto
  spinta dal cielo et revoluta d'indi,
  in tüa forma et varïi colori
  credula troppo?
Impreò quelli subito cadranno."
  Dixero, et, pregni gli animi minaci,
  Livor accolse brago, nel mio viso
  tutto lo volse;
l'altra malvagia et maladecta diva
  peggio mi fece: fremitando, colle
  et mani et denti la mia trezza ruppe,
  l'aurëa trezza .
Fùggomi verso il loco di coloro
  che la Fortuna ha rilevato ricchi,
  talché, veggendo gli aditi patenti,
  dentro ricórsi,
perch'ïo crési, dove si governa
  tanta vil turba, stolida, imperita,
  esser almanco dove ricrëarmi,
  diva, potessi.

Canto III
(lines 1–40)

Here I am: I am the goddess of friends,                                    Friendship
 she who all men are used
 to mocking and, falsely, calling a fugitive—
 now you want her .
Here I am: already descended from the divine
 throne, I seek a place among the people,
 ready to stay with whoever wants
 to shelter love.
I first came to the house of the noble
 princes, where a malignant couple
 acted against me, similar palaces
 of excellent families.
Hatred is the one, meager, sad,
 girded with serpents and covered with hatred—
 Falsehood, the other, is the fraudulent goddess—
 screaming at me:
"Oh, common goddess, too hostile,
 enemy of mortals,
 why are you wandering, arrogant sloth?
 Where are you deceiving?
What wicked deed moved you
 to be kicked out of heaven, fallen from there,
 too naive in your various
 form and colors?
Therefore, those will fall immediately."
 They said, and, full of threatening intentions,
 Hatred gathered slime, turning it
 in front of my face—
the other wicked and cursed goddess
 did me worse: raging, she ruined my
 hair with her hands and teeth—
 my golden tresses.
Moving quickly to the place of those
 who Fortune made rich,
 so that, seeing the certain opportunity,
 I ran inside,
for I believed—where a vile,
 stupid, raw crowd governs—
 to be where I, goddess, could at least
 rest myself.

**187**

(verse 93-120)

Dentro Paupertas, dëa molto acerba,
 come lo sceptro imperïal tenesse,
 fixa mi sgrida: "0 dëa inutile, esci,
 escine presto!
Tempo non è qui la tüa arte vagli,
 né 'l tüo sdegnoso animo potrebbe
 col dëo Mendax habitare, quale è
 nostro governo:
quel dare il victo suole, et huom bëato
 rende chi in finger segue le suo fraudi.
 Chi segue ingegno buono et arte retta
 nudo perisce."
Po'ché da tutti gli omini infugata,
 po'ché schernita ad popular tumulto
 vidimi, strinsi gli omeri et sali'nne
 donde ero scesa.
Ora, sentendo l'odïerna fama,
 torno, né fuggo ll'abitar la terra;
 sicché, se qui me rimaner volete,
 lieta rimango,
purché con meco mïa car famiglia,
 Gratïa ardente et Fede candidata,
 possino star, qual, dove son ricepte,
 portano Pace.
Da voï sol per mïo sacro censo
 Purità voglio. Rifarovi Amore,
 Gaudïo, Laude et Bene sempiterno.
 State bëati.

(lines 93–120)

Inside Poverty , a most bitter goddess,
 as she held the imperial scepter ,
 screams at me: "Oh, useless goddess, leave,
 leave now!
It isn't the time to value your art here,
 nor can your disdainful mind
 live with god Hypocrisy, who is
 our ruler:
he is used to giving the prize and making
 the blessed man deceitfully follow his fraud.
 Whoever blindly follows good ideas and
 proper art perishes."
Since I saw myself chased away by all men,
 scorned by the lowly
 mob, I shrugged my shoulders and rose
 from where I descended.
Now, feeling present-day fame,
 I return, I leave life on earth;
 so that, if you want to stay here with me,
 I remain happy,
provided my dear family is with me—
 burning Grace and purest Faith—
 may they be able to stay where I am received
 for they bring Peace.
From you I only want Purity as my
 sacred tribute. In exchange I will give
 eternal Love, Joy, Praises and Goodness.
 Bless you.

# Domenico di Giovanni, called Il Burchiello
# (1404–1449)

The oldest of eight children, Domenico di Giovanni, became a barber in Florence in 1432. His father was a carpenter and his mother a weaver of linen. With no formal education, but possessing a sharp temperament, Burchiello left Florence in 1434, writing against Cosimo de'Medici on behalf of the Albizzi family. He also engaged in a *tenzone* (an exchange of sonnets) with Leon Battista Alberti. He then settled in Siena where, in 1439, he was taken to court three times for a failure to pay his debts, with the third judgment against him leaving him in prison for several months. In 1445, he settled in Rome to lead a pauper's life until his death in 1449. Alberti considered him "unhinged and without both oars in the water." Francesco de Sanctis thought his poetry insipid. However, for as little as his work may touch upon great intellectual currents of his day, his verse demonstrates an ability to point out concrete examples of human fallibility.

## Domenico di Giovanni, detto Il Burchiello

1
Nominativi fritti e mappamondi,
e l'arca di Noè fra due colonne
cantavan tutti chirïeleisonne
per l'influenza de' taglier mal tondi.

La Luna mi dicea: "Ché non rispondi?—
E io risposi: —Io temo di Giansonne,
però ch'io odo che 'l diaquilonne
è buona cosa a fare i capei biondi."

Per questo le testuggini e i tartufi
m'hanno posto l'assedio alle calcagne,
dicendo: "Noi vogliam che tu ti stuffi."

E questo sanno tutte le castagne:
pei caldi d'oggi son sì grassi i gufi,
ch'ognun non vuol mostrar le sue magagne.

E vidi lasagne
andare a Prato a vedere il Sudario,
e ciascuna portava l'inventario.

2
La Poesia combatte col Rasoio,
e spesso hanno per me di gran quistioni,
ella dicendo a lui: "Per che cagioni
mi cavi il mio Burchiel dello scrittoio?"

E lui ringhiera fa del colatoio,
e va in bogoncia a dir le sue ragioni,
e commincia: "Io ti prego mi perdoni,
donna, s'alquanto nel parlar ti noio:

s'io non fuss'io, e l'acqua e 'l ranno caldo,
Burchiel si rimarrebbe in sul colore
d'un moccolin di cera di smeraldo."

Ed ella a lui: "Tu sei in grand'errore:
d'un tal desio porta il suo petto caldo,
ch'egli non ha 'n sì vil bassessa il core."

Ed io: "Non piú romore,
che non ci corra la secchia e 'l bacino:
ma chi meglio mi vuol, mi paghi il vino."

## Domenico di Giovanni, called Il Burchiello

1
Mixed up grammar and world maps,
and Noah's Ark between two columns
all sang Kyrie eleison
to cut off the sick fools from the evil eye.

The moon said to me: "Why don't you answer?"
And I answered: "I fear Janson,
Because I hear that the salve for abscesses
is a good thing to make hair blond."

For this the encrusted tumors and fungus
have dogged my heels,
saying: "We want to wear you out."

And all the old wives know this:
the owls are so rich from today's business
that none want to show their blemishes.

Then I saw the idiots
go to Prato to see the Holy Handkerchief
and each one carried the inventory.


2
Poetry battles the Razor
and often the two of them have big arguments about me—
she says to Him: "Why do you cause
my Burchiel to leave his writing desk?"

And, making a strainer from the filter,
he goes to the pulpit to give his reasons
by beginning: "I ask you to forgive me,
Lady, if I bother you somewhat in my speech:

if I were not myself, with water and hot lather,
Burchiel would become poor,
green from the hunger."

And she to him: "You are really wrong:
his passionate heart carries such a desire,
for he doesn't have such baseness in his heart."

And I: "No more talk!
The bucket and basin can't find middle ground:
but whoever wants me more, pays for my wine."

# Lucrezia Tornabuoni de' Medici
## (1425–1482)

Daughter of one of the great houses in Florentine history, Lucrezia Tornabuoni married Piero, son of Cosimo de' Medici, when she was 19 years old. Living with the extended family of her in-laws, Lucrezia bore six children and, as time went by, played a role in the intellectual, cultural and artistic milieu of the Medici circle as she was sought by those looking for Medici favors. Of note, she encouraged Luigi Pulci to write his *Morgante*, a famous epic poem. After Piero's death, she took a more active role in family affairs, as well as personally financing businesses, artisans, with notable aid to the needy – nuns, lower clergy, girls needing a dowry. Her verse is characterized by an admirable sincerity and intelligence that, under different circumstance, might have blossomed further.

## Lucrezia Tornabuoni de' Medici

*Ecco 'l re forte, aprite quelle porte.*

O principe infernale,
non fare risistenza,
gli è il re celestiale,
che vien con gran potenza;
fategli riverenza,
levate view le porte: ecco 'l re forte.

"Chi è questo potente,
che vien con tant'altòria?"
"Egli è 'l signor possente,
egli 'l re della vittoria,
avuto ha la vittoria,
egli ha vinto la morte: ecco 'l re forte.

"Egli ha vinto la guerra
durata già molt'anni,
e fa tremar la terra
per cavarne d'affanni,
riempier vuol gli scanni
per ristorar sua corte: ecco 'l re forte.

"E' vuole el padre antico
e la sua compagnia;
Abel vero suo amico,
Noè si mett'in via,
Moisè piú no istia,
venite alla gran corte: ecco 'l re forte.

"O Abraam patriarca
seguita 'l gran signore;
la promessa non varca,
venuto è 'l Redentore,
vengane 'l gran cantore
a far degna la corte: ecco 'l re forte.

## Lucrezia Tornabuoni de' Medici

*Behold the mighty King, open those doors.*

O infernal prince,
don't resist,
for he is the Heavenly King
who comes with great power—
give him reverence,
open the doors forever: behold the mighty King.

"Who is this potentate
who comes with arrogance?"
"He is the powerful Lord,
he is the King of Glory,
he has victory,
he has defeated death: behold the mighty King.

"He has won the war
that lasted for many years,
then he shakes the earth
to gather up our sins,
he wants to fill the seats
in order to restore his court: behold the mighty King.

"He wants Adam, the ancient father,
and his company—
his true friend Abel,
Noah he puts on the path,
Moses stays no longer,
come to the grand court: behold the mighty King.

O patriarch Abraham,
follow great Lord—
the promise isn't exaggerated,
the Redeemer has come,
may David, the great choir-leader,
deign the court: behold the mighty King.

"O Giovanni Batista
orsú sanza dimoro;
nol perdete di vista:
su nell'eterno coro,
e Simïon con loro
drieto alle fide iscorte: ecco 'l re forte.

"O parvoli innocenti,
innanzi a tutti gite:
or siate vo' contenti
dell'aúte ferite:
o gemme, o margherite,
adornate la corte: ecco 'l re forte.

"Venuti siate al regno
tanto desiderato,
ch'i' comperai in sul legno
dov'i' fui sí straziato
et ho ricomperato
tutta l'umana sorte." Ecco 'l re forte.

"O John the Baptist
Come on without delay—
don't lose sight of Him:
up high in the eternal chorus,
and Simon with them
escorts the faithful: behold the mighty King.

"O innocent children,
go before everyone else:
now you'll be happy
with your wounds:
o gems, o bread in the wine,
adorn the court: behold the mighty King

"May  you come to the much
desired Kingdom,
for I purchased it on the Cross
where I was tormented,
and I've redeemed
all humanity." Behold the mighty King.

# Lorenzo de' Medici
## (1449–1492)

Lorenzo de' Medici, the son of Piero de' Medici (1416–92) and Lucrezia Tornabuoni (1425–1482), was more than capable of assuming the mantle of power exercised in Florence by his grandfather, Cosimo the Elder (1389–1464), and his father, Piero. The Medici had been in Florence since the early Duecento, having played a part in the commerce, money lending and politics of the Commune. Although wealthy, the Medici historically drew their support from the lower class *popolani* and *popolo minuto* who constantly struggled against the aristocratic Parte Guelfa. In the *Quattrocento*, Cosimo the Elder, after suffering a ten year exile from 1424 to 1434, returned to Florence to establish a Medici political machine that created and then selectively and punitively used a progressive income tax, the *decima scalata*, to ruin those who opposed his policies. In the realm of foreign policy, Cosimo aligned Florence with the Venetians, the result of which was a military victory over Milanese forces at Anghiari in 1440. In 1450, Florence allied herself with Milan's new ruler, Francesco Sforza, against Venice and Naples. In the broad area of city life, Cosimo directly patronized and positively fostered a cultural climate in which the arts and learning were encouraged. He sponsored the first public library in Florence, promoted the teaching of Greek, aided Marsilio Ficino's Platonic academy, and encouraged the likes of Brunelleschi, Ghiberti, Alberti and Fra Angelico. Cosimo's son, Piero, who was severely limited in his activities by gout, assumed the mantle between 1464 and 1469. Upon his death, Lorenzo was asked to lead the republican government of Florence.

Lorenzo, called 'Il Magnifico,' had the perpetual advantage in life of both wealth and the immediate access to political power. However, through the actions of his mother, Lucrezia Tornabuoni, he also had a cultured upbringing. In addition to being the enlightened, sensitive and politically savvy spouse of Piero, Lucretzia was a writer who wrote *laudi*, the lives of various saints and her own lyric poetry. She was also the friend of numerous poets, encouraging Luigi Pulci to write his epic poem, *Il Morgante*. It was mainly through the influence of his mother that Lorenzo not only learned about business and politics, but also garnered a more complete picture of the human adventure through a study of history, art, literature and philosophy.

In addition to his personal charm, Lorenzo had the ambition and ability to accomplish several things during his rule, among which were various reforms of Florence's political and administrative systems. In the military realm, he subdued a rebellious Prato in 1470 and conquered Volterra in 1472. In 1478, however, tragedy struck. The Pazzi family, with the aid of Francesco Salviati, Archbishop of Pisa, and Girolamo Piario, a nephew of Pope Sixtus IV, plotted to assassinate both Lorenzo and his brother, Giuliano, while they attended mass at the Duomo. Giuliano was stabbed to death. Lorenzo was wounded, but escaped. Retribution was quick. Entire households were, after much violence, exiled from Florence. Salviati was hanged. Subsequently, the Pope excommunicated Lorenzo and had Ferdinand of Naples declare war against Florence. Lorenzo was undaunted. In late 1479, he traveled to Naples and went by himself before Ferdinand, convincing Ferdinand that if Florence and Naples went to war, the French would successfully invade Italy. Lorenzo returned to Florence in triumph, further tightened his political control over the city and was soon after reinstated in the Church by the Pope. In the area of foreign policy, he successfully maintained a balance of power between the states of Italy in order to preserve peace and minimize foreign intervention. During his later years, he envisioned a league of all Italian states to thwart any French invasion, but died before he could carry this plan out.

In addition to his regional and peninsular political brilliance, Lorenzo had a tremndous impact on the culture of Florence. Not only did he continue to support Marsilio Ficino's Platonic Academy, but he was a friend and patron of such writers as Angelo Poliziano, Luigi Pulci and Giovanni Pico della Mirandola. Among artists active in Florence during his reign were Verrocchio, Antonio and Piero del Pollaiuolo, Botticelli, Perugino and Leonardo. His inclusion of the youthful Michelangelo in his household was no small feat, either.

Lorenzo was also an accomplished poet. Three factors affected his work as a poet. First, he had an historic grasp of earlier Italian poetry, especially the work of Cavalcanti, Dante and Petrarch. No doubt this was stimulated by his conversations with Poliziano, Pulci and Pico. Second, he had an active, fertile imagination. He was able to work in many different genres of poetry, as well as imbuing his own version of a Petrarchan *Canzoniere* with his individual identity. Third, he was strongly affected by the Neoplatonism of Ficino and his Platonic Academy. Florentine Neoplatonism held that the cosmos consisted of three basic elements, hierarchically arranged. First, on the lowest level of importance was solid matter; e.g., the physical substance of the earth, plants, animals and the human body. Second, the highest level of importance was the realm of God. It was immaterial, eternal, pure goodness, consisting of pure idea (or pure soul or spirit) and containing all the ideas (or forms) of things in the material world that have existed, exist or will exist. Between these two realms is the realm of humanity, consisting of the clay of the earth formed by God's mind into the form of the human body, which, in turn, is imbued by God with a spirit that has the capacity to think and reason. Humanity, then, has two tendencies: the body wants to eat, explore its passion and acquire material possessions; the mind wants to contemplate the universe, use its reason and seek the ultimate good in God. Since the realms of the purely physical and of humanity were not eternal, but temporal, the central problem for humanity was to surmount its mortality by reuniting with the eternal in the realm of God. The Neoplatonists reasoned that since God consisted of pure idea, pure intellect, the path to reunification was, as is ably illustrated by the figure of Mercury in Botticelli's *Primavera*, through the use of the mind in learning about God's universe. Hence, for Lorenzo, his circle and his own poetry, the idea of expounding about and nurturing, in a worldly sense, the life of the mind, was a way to begin to achieve a transcendence of this world and its problems.

Neoplatonism was important in informing Lorenzo's poetry in that Lorenzo, in creating a *Canzoniere*, emulated Petrarch by writing an extended poetic sequence. The central subject of such a sequence is love. However, Lorenzo's love is neither the worldly love that Petrarch felt for Laura nor the abstract passion of the troubadors and their concept of fin' amors. Instead, Lorenzo's poetic use of love was a Neoplatonic exploration of the idea that the universe is permeated by and held together by Love, which flows from its ultimate source, God.

These are some of Lorenzo's sonnets taken from his *Canzoniere*.

## Lorenzo de' Medici

### 1

Dolci pensier', non vi partite ancora:
dove, pensier' miei dolci, mi lasciate?
Sì ben la scorta ai piè già stanchi fate
al dolce albergo, ove il mio ben dimora?

Qui non Zeffiro, qui non balla Flora,
né son le piagge d'erbe e fiori ornate:
silenzi, ombre, terror', venti e brinate,
boschi, sassi, acque il piè tardono ognora.

Voi vi partite pur, e gite a quella,
vostro antico ricetto e del mio core;
io resto nelle oscure ombre soletto.

Il cammin cieco a' piedi insegna amore,
che ho sempre in me, dell'una e l'altra stella;
né gli occhi hanno altro lume che l'obietto.

### 2

Io mi diparto dolci pensier' miei
da voi, e lascio ogni amorosa cura:
ché mia fortuna troppo iniqua e dura
mi sforza a far pur quel ch'io non vorrei.

Pianti dolci e sospir' süavi e rei,
speranze vane ed incerta paura,
che inquietavi mia fragil natura,
andate ad altri cor', lasciate lei.

O versi, o rime, ove ogni mio lamento
dolce era e quietavo tanto affanno,
mentre che in lieta servitù mi giacqqui,

lasciovi a mal mio grado, e pur consento,
come sforzato al preveduto inganno.
Ma così sia, poi che a tal sorte nacqui.

## Lorenzo de' Medici

1

Sweet thoughts, don't yet go:
where, my sweet thoughts, do leave me?
Surely you are going to escort my tired feet
to the sweet shelter where my happiness lives?

Here not Zephyr, here not Flora dance,
nor is the countryside adorned with grass and flowers:
silence, shadows, terrors, winds and frost,
trees, stones, waters constantly slow one's feet.

You leave anyway and throw her
your ancient recipe and my heart—
I'll stay in the dark shadows quite alone.

The blind walk teaches the feet love,
something I always have in me, from one and the other star—
nor do my eyes have another light as their object.

2

I abandon my every sweet thought
of you and forget every loving cure:
for my too wicked and hard fortune
forces me to do what I don't want.

Sweet tears and mild, guilty sighs,
vain hopes and uncertain fears,
that upset my fragile natures—
go to others' hearts and leave her.

Oh verses, oh rhymes, where my every lament
was sweet, I calmed every anxiety,
while I lie in happy servitude,

I leave my wretched state and even consent,
as forced against the foreseen deception.
But such it is, since I was born to such.

3

*Sonetto fatto in sul rimaggio*

Lascia l'isola tua tanto diletta,
lascia il tuo regno delicato e bello,
Ciprigna dea, e vien sopra il ruscello
che bagna la minuta e verde erbetta.

Vieni a quest'ombra, alla dolce auretta
che fa mormoreggiare ogni arbuscello,
a' canti dolci d'amoroso uccello;
questa da te per patria sia eletta.

E, se tu vien tra queste chiare linfe,
sia teco il tuo amato e caro figlio,
ché qui non si conosce il suo valore.

Togli a Dïana le sue caste ninfe,
che sciolte or vanno e senza alcun periglio,
poco prezzando la virtù d'Amore.


4

Sonetto fatto per alcuni poeticuli che
dicevano Bartolomeo Coglioni dovea fare
gran cose che in fine si risolverono in fumo

L'impio Furor nel gran tempio di Giano
orrido freme, sanguinoso e tinto:
con mille nodi relegato e vinto,
cerca disciôrsi l'una e l'altra mano.

E certamente e' s'affatica invano,
perché chi s'ha per lui la spada cinto,
già tante volte è superato e vinto,
che s'egli è vil, parer non vorrà insano.

Dunque resterà pur arido e secco,
quanto per lui, Parnaso e 'l sacro fonte,
né per ciò vincerassi il verde alloro.

Conoscesi oramai la voce d'Ecco,
né il curro più domanderà Fetonte,
ma fia quel della fata e del tesoro.

3
*Sonnet written at Rimaggio*

Leave your island pleasure,
leave your gentle and beautiful reign—
Cyprian Goddess—and come over the brook
that bathes the tiny, green grass.

Come to this shade, to the sweet breeze
that makes every tree murmur
with the sweet songs of love birds—
this is your birthright.

And, if you come among these clear waters,
bring your dear, beloved son,
for here we don't know his power.

Take Diana's chaste nymphs,
who now go free without any danger,
hardly valuing the power of Love.


4

A sonnet written for some minor poets who
Said Bartolomeo Coglioni had to do
great things that will ultimately go up in smoke

The impious Furor shudders in the great temple of
terrible Giano, bloody and stained:
        with a thousand knots retied and overcome,
with both hands he tries to untie himself.

And certainly he toils in vain—
because whoever carries a sword for him
is defeated and overcome many times over,
because if he's vile, he will not want to seem insane.

Then he will remain dry and meager—
as for him, he wouldn't win Parnassus, the
sacred fountain or the laurel.

You now know the voice of Echo—
nor will the messenger ask Phaeton any more,
but it will be that of Fate and the treasure.

5

*A Feo Belcari*

Lo spirito talora a sé redutto,
e dal mar tempestoso e travagliato
fuggito in porto tranquillo e pacato,
pensando ha dubbio e vuolne trar costrutto.

S'egli è ver che da Dio proceda tutto,
e senza lui nulla è, cioè il peccato,
per sua grazia se ci è concesso e dato
seminar qui per côrre eterno frutto,

tal grazia in quel sol fa operazione
che a riceverla è vòlto e ben disposto.
      Dunque che cosa è quella ne dispone?

Qual prima sia vorrei mi fussi esposto,
o tal grazia o la buona inclinazione.
Rispondi or tu al dubbio ch'è proposto.


6

"Come ritorni, Amor, dentro all'afflitto
cor, che pel tuo partir era tranquillo?"
"Io torno nello impresso mio sigillo
      fatto nel cor da' begli occhi trafitto."

"Lasso, io credevo che fussi prescritto,
tanto è che libertà per suo sortillo."
"Non dir così, ché 'l primo stral che aprillo,
gli occhi che 'l trasson v'han sempre relitto."

"Ben sentivo io nel cener fatto il core
pel fuoco che l'umor dagli occhi stilla,
un picciol segno dell'antico amore."

"Vedrai che quella picciola favilla
in te ecciterà eterno ardore,
colpa e disgrazia della tua pupilla."

5
*To Feo Belcari*

The spirit is sometimes reduced to
fleeing to a tranquil, peaceful port away
from the stormy, troubled sea—
thinking, it doubts and wants to learn from it.

If it's true that all proceeds from God,
and without him nothing is, that is sin,
through his grace it is admitted and given
to sow here to gather eternal fruit—

such grace only works in one
who is disposed to receive it.
So, what is it that disposes one to act?

To which one would I first want to expose myself:
grace or my natural inclinations?
Respond to the question that is proposed.


6

"How do you, Love, return to the afflicted
heart that was so calmed by your leaving?"
"I return to the print my seal
made in the heart pierced by beautiful eyes."

"Alas, I believed you were prescribed,
so good is freedom from her sorcery."
    "Don't speak so, for the first arrow that opens
the eyes always ruins them."

"I really felt my heart turned to ashes
through the fire that my humors distill from my eyes,
a small sign of old love."

"You will see that that little spark
in you will excite eternal passion,
the sin and disgrace of your pupil."

7

Se con dolce armonia due istrumenti
nella medesma voce alcun concorda,
pulsando l'una, rende l'altra corda,
per la conformità, medesmi accenti:

così par dentro al mio cor si risenti
l'imago impressa, a' nostri sospir' sorda,
se per similitudin mi ricorda
del viso, ch'è sopra l'umane menti.

Amor, in quanti modi il cor ripigli!
Ché fuggendo l'aspetto del bel viso,
d'una vana pittura il cor pascendo,

o che non vegghino altro i nostri cigli,
o che il pittor già fussi in paradiso,
lei vidi propria: or va' d'Amor fuggendo!


8

Solea già dileggiar Endimïone,
la stultizia accusar del bel Narciso,
prender ammirazion che tanto fiso
mirò l'immagin sua Pigmalïone.

Lasso! è il mio vaneggiar con men ragione,
condotto ad amar tanto un pinto viso,
che non può con parole o con un riso
quetar quel gran disio che nel cor pone.

Almen dar mi poteano qualche aita
gli occhi ch'io fuggo e le leggiadre chiome:
questo non può la vana simiglianza.

Amor, la tua potenzia è infinita:
folle è chi 'l niega: chè ho veduto or come
amar può il tristo cor senza speranza.

7

If with sweet harmony two instruments
somewhat sound in the same voice,
one throbbing, the other striking the same
chord, the same accents:

so inside my heart I hear again
the stamped image, deaf to our sighs—
if I remember her familiar
face, the human mind can't conceive it.

Love, in how many ways the heart remembers!
For fleeing the glance of that beautiful face,
the heart eating a vain picture:

Oh, that our eyes wouldn't see another!
Oh, that the painter were already in Paradise!
I truly saw her: now go fleeing Love!


8

Endymion used to ridicule
the foolish accusations of the beautiful Nacissus,
Pygmalion so strongly looked
at his statue he fell in love.

O, suffering! my wild dreaming with less reason
has led to loving a portrait
that can't calm with words or a smile
that great desire it placed in my heart.

At least the eyes and graceful tresses
I flee can give me some help:
the vain resemblance can't do this.

Love, your power is infinite:
foolish one who denies it: for I've now seen how
the sad heart can love without hope.

9

Se quando io son più presso al vago vólto
il freddo sangue si ristrigne al core,
e, se mi assale un sùbito pallore,
io so quel ch'è, ch'ogni virtù m'ha tolto.

Quel viso, in cui è ogni ben raccolto
pe' raggi del micante suo splendore,
sparge e diffonde del suo bel valore
nel cor che ad amar quello in tutto è vólto.

E tanto dentro al tristo cor soggiorna,
che l'immagine finta al tutto strugge
con la presenzia sua forma vera.

Allor quella virtù che da lei era,
qual maraviglia è se da me si fugge,
che a lei, sì come a suo principio, torna?


10

Come ti lascio, o come meco sei,
o viso, onde ogni nostra sorte move?
Come qui moro, o come vivo altrove?
Amor, dimmelo tu, ch'io nol saprei.

Chi mi sforza al partir, s'io nol vorrei?
S'io fuggo un Sol, come lo fuggo o dove?
Lasso! qual ombra fa che non ti truove,
se non è notte mai agli occhi miei?

Questo è ben ver, che se la forma vera
veggio, mi par bellissima e superba,
leggiadra oltra misura e disdegnosa;

s'io son lontan, novella primavera
riveste i prati di fioretti e d'erba:
così bella la veggio e sì pietosa.

9

If when I'm more taken by the beautiful face,
cold blood restricts my heart,
and if a sudden pallor strikes,
I know what it is, that she's taken my every power.

That face, in which every good is gathered
through her shining splendor,
spreads and diffuses her beautiful power
in the heart that is turned to totally love it.

And so much lives inside the sad heart,
that the fake image completely destroys
her true form with its presence.

Therefore, does that power that was from her—
that marvel is she who flees me—
return to her, so like its source?

10

How do I leave you or how are you with me,
oh, face, whence all of our sort moves?
How do I die here or how do I live elsewhere?
Love, tell me so I'll know.

Who will force me to leave, if I don't want to?
If I flee a Sun, how do I flee it or where?
Alas, what does shade do if it doesn't find you,
if it is never night to my eyes?

This is very true, if I see the
true form, it seems most beautiful and superb to me,
beautiful and haughty beyond measure—

if I'm far away, a new springtime
renews the fields with flowers and grass:
so beautiful and merciful I see it.

11

Superbo colle, benché in vista umìle,
più degno e più felice assai che quelli
Esquilie, Celio, Aventino e' fratelli,
benché cantati da più alto stile;

questi già vider trïonfar più vile,
d'Emili, Scipioni e di Marcelli:
tu vedi trïonfar agli occhi belli
Amor legato e ciascun cor gentile.

Vengon le Grazie catenate e scinte,
Pietà, Beltate innanzi al carro, e quelle
virtù che son in gentil cor distinte.

Liete son, ben che trïonfate e vinte,
tanto più liete quanto son più belle
nel viso della donna mia dipinte.

12

Amore in quel vittorïoso giorno,
che mi rimembra il primo dolce male,
sopra al superbo monte lieto sale:
le Grazie seco e cari frati andorno.

Lo abito gentil, di ch'era adorno,
deposto, dette a me la benda e l'ale;
a lei l'arco in la destra, e uno strale
nella sinistra, e la faretra intorno.

La candida, sottil, succinta vesta
dell'amorosa mia Dïana scuopre:
le nude membra or sopra a' panni esprime.

Febo de' raggi ornò gli occhi e la testa;
così non arti umane o mortal' opre
fù quelle benedette e dolci prime.

11

Proud hill, although humble in appearance,
more worthy and happy than those
Esquiline, Coelian, Aventine and brothers,
although celebrated in a loftier style—

More vile triumphs were seen,
of Emile, Scipione and Marcellus:
you, with beautiful eyes, see Love triumph
over every bound, noble heart.

The Graces come chained yet free,
Pity, Beauty before the chariot and those
virtues that are distinct in gently noble hearts.

They are happy, even though triumphed and conquered,
happier the more beautiful
depicted in the face of my lady.


12

Love in that victorious day
that reminds me of my first sweet sickness
rises above the proud, happy mountain:
the Graces with him and the dear brothers go forward.

The noble suit, with which he dressed,
removed, gave me his blindfold and wings—
to her, the bow in the right hand, an arrow
in the left, and his quiver and strap.

The white, delicate, sheer dress
of my amorous Diana reveals:
her nude body now speaks before her garments.

Phoebus adorned his eyes and head with rays—
and so, those blessed and sweet beginnings
were neither human arts nor mortal works.

# Angelo Poliziano
## (1454–1494)

Poet, humanist and classical scholar, Angelo Ambrogini was born to Benedetto Ambrogini, a doctor of law, and Antonia Salimbeni in Montepulciano, Tuscany. He derived his surname Poliziano from the Italian form of the Latin name of his birthplace, Mons Politianus. (The anglicized form is Politian). Poliziano's family was left in poverty after the murder of their father in 1464. Poliziano was sent to live with a cousin in Florence in 1469. To find a literary patron, he began writing epigrams in praise of different Florentines, eventually garnering the attention of Lorenzo de' Medici, to whom he dedicated the first two books of his Latin translation of Homer's *Iliad*. Sometime in 1473 he entered the Medici household. Since he had no particular duties, he was free to study at will in the Medici library. In 1474, he was given charge of educating Lorenzo's oldest son, Piero, who was then three. In 1477 he was given the priory of San Paolo as a benefice. He further educated himself while in Florence by focusing on philosophy through the lectures of Marsilio Ficino and the university courses of Cristoforo Landino. He also attended the university courses of the noted Greek masters John Argyropulus, Demetrius Chalcondyles and Andronicus Callistus.

Poliziano earned his earliest fame by translating into Latin hexameters books two through five of the *Iliad*. By 1478 he had written some of the finest humanist poetry in Latin in the form of elegies, odes and epigrams. He also aided Lorenzo de' Medici in the revaluation of vernacular poetry by helping him compile the so-called *Raccolta aragonese* (Aragon Collection), a collection of Tuscan poetry sent to Federico d'Aragona, the second son of the King of Naples. Poliziano was with Lorenzo and Giuliano during the attack of the Pazzi conspiracy on April 26, 1478. His most famous work, the *Stanze Begun for the Joust of Giuliano de' Medici*, was left unfinished due to the assasination of the poem's patron and protagonist. After a quarrel with Clarice Orsini, Lorenzo's wife, he was expelled from the Medici household in May 1479. The argument centered on whether Piero was to receive a traditional medieval religious introduction to education, Clarice's view, or a more modern humanist and secular one centered around classical literature. Soon after, Poliziano travelled to northern Italy, meeting other humanists and eventually settling at the court of the Gonzaga family in Mantua. In 1480, he wrote his dramatic piece *Favola d'Orfeo* (The Fable of Orpheus) for the Gonzaga court. During his time with the Gonzaga, he repeatedly wrote to Lorenzo for permission to return to Florence. Although Lorenzo initially said no, within a few months he invited the poet back to Florence (but not the Medici household), once again entrusting him with the education of Piero. Soon after, he was appointed Chair of Latin and Greek, delivering a series of readings in verse on Virgil's poetry, the bucolic poetry of Virgil and Hesiod, Homer and the various genres of Greek and Latin literature. He also undertook diplomatic missions to Pope Innocent VIII and went to Bologna, Padua and Venice to acquire manuscripts for the Medici library. He passed the last years of life in Florence writing a Latin translation of Epicteus' *Manual*; the *Detti piacevoli*, a collection of witty sentence; Greek epigrams; the vernacular poetry of *Canzoni a ballo* (Dance Songs) and his *Rispetti*; and, Latin letters on problems of literature and style. His most important philological work, the *Miscellanea*, is a collection of one hundred notes on classical texts that is a definitive moment in the history classical philology.

The selections from Poliziano's work presented here are from his *Stanze*, his *Rispetti spicciolati*, his *Aspettar tempo* and his *In morte del Magnifico Lorenzo de' Medici*.

## Angelo Poliziano

*Stanze scelte dalle Stanze comminciate per la giostra del Magnifico Giuliano di Piero de' Medici*


33
Ah quanto a mirar Iulio è fera cosa!
rompe la via dove il bosco è folto
per trar di macchia la bestia crucciosa,
con verde ramo intorno al capo avvolto,
con la chioma arruffata e polverosa,
e d'onesto sudor bagnato il volto.
Ivi consiglio a sua bella vendetta
prese Amor, che ben loco e tempo aspetta;


34
e con sue man di leve aer compose
la imagin d'una cervia altera e bella,
con alta fronte, con corna ramose,
candida tutta, leggiadretta e snella.
E come tra le fere paventose
al giovan cacciator si offerse quella,
lieto spronò il destrier per lei sequire,
pensando in brieve darle agro martire.


35
Ma poi che in van dal braccio el dardo scosse,
del foder trasse fuor la fida spada,
e con tanto furor il corsier mosse
che 'l bosco folto sembrava ampia strada.
La bella fera, come stanca fosse,
più lenta tuttavia par che se 'n vada;
ma, quando par che già la stringa o tocchi,
picciol campo riprende avanti agli occhi.


36
Quanto più segue in van la vana effigie,
tanto più di seguirla in van si accende:
tutta via preme sue stanche vestigie,
sempre la giugne e pur mai non la prende.
Qual fino al labro sta nell'onde stigie
Tantalo, e 'l bel giardin vicin gli pende;
ma, qualor l'acqua o il pome vuol gustare,
subito l'acqua e 'l pome via dispare.

# Angelo Poliziano

*Stanzas taken from the Lines Begun for the Joust of the Magnificent Giuliano di Piero de' Medici*

33
Oh, how fierce a thing to see Giulio
break a path where the forest is thick
in order to draw the angry beast from the bushes,
with a green laurel around his head,
with ruffled and dusty hair,
and his face bathed in honest sweat!
There, Love took counsel for his fierce vendetta;

34
and with his hands he composed from light air
the image of a lofty and beautiful doe:
with a high forehead, branching horns,
totally white, graceful and agile.
Then, as from the frightened beasts
she offered herself to the young hunter,
happily he spurred his charger to follow her,
thinking to quickly give her a bitter torment.

35
But after he tossed his spear with his arm in vain,
he drew his trusty sword from his scabbard,
and urged his charger with such great fury,
that the thick forest seemed a wide street.
The beautiful beast, as if she were tired,
appears, nonetheless, to to slow down:
but when it seemed he would grab or touch her,
she retook a little ground before his eyes.

36
The more he follows in vain the vain image,
the more he burns in vain to follow it:
he ever presses on her tired tracks,
always reaching her, then never catching her:
that brave Tantalus stands up to his lips in
the Stygian waves, the beautiful garden hanging near him,
but whenever he wants to taste water or an apple,
instantly the water or apple disappears.

37
Era già drieto alla sua disïanza
gran tratto da' compagni allontanato;
né pur d'un passo ancor la preda avanza,
e già tutto il destrier sente affannato:
me pur seguendo sua vana speranza,
pervenne in un fiorito e verde prato.
Ivi sotto un vel candido gli apparve
lieta una ninfa; e via la fera sparve.

38
La fera sparse via dalle sue ciglia;
ma il giovan della fera omai non cura;
anzi ristringe al corridor la briglia,
e lo raffrena sopra all verdura.
Ivi tutto ripien di maraviglia
pur della ninfa mira la figura;
pargli che dal bel viso e da' begli occhi
una nuova dolcezza al cor gli fiocchi.

39
Qual tigre, a cui dalla pietrosa tana
ha tolto il cacciator gli suoi car figli;
rabbiosa il segue per la selva ircana,
che tosto crede insanguinar gli artigli;
poi resta d'uno specchio all'ombra vana,
all'ombra ch' e' suo' nati par somigli;
e mentre di tal vista s'innamora
la sciocca, el predator la via divora.

40
Tosto Cupido entro a' begli occhi ascoso
al nervo adatta del suo stral la cocca,
poi tira quel col braccio poderoso
tal che raggiugne l'una all'altra cocca;
la man sinistra con l'oro focoso,
la destra poppa con la corda tocca:
né pria per l'aer ronzando uscì el quadrello,
che Iulio drento al cor sentito ha quello.

37

He was now behind his desire
a great distance from his companions,
yet he hadn't advanced a step nearer his prey,
and his charger was already exhausted;
but still following his vain hope,
he came to a flowery, green meadow:
here under a white veil appeared to him
a happy nymph and the beast disappeared.


38

The beast disappears from his eye,
but the youth no longer cared for the beast;
rather he tightens his racer's rein
and slows him on the greenery.
Here, all fills with marvel
as he looks at the figure of the nymph:
it appears to him that from her beautiful face and eyes
a new sweetness abounds in his heart.


39

That tiger, from whose rocky den
the hunter door her dear cubs,
enraged follws him in the Ircanian wood,
believing soon to bloody her claws;
then she rests at a vain reflection of the water,
at a reflection that looks like her cubs;
and while the fool is taken by such an image,
the predator devours the road.


40

Quickly Cupid, hidden in those beautiful eyes,
adjusts the notch of his arrow to his bow,
then he draws that back with his strong arm
so that both ends of the bow meet;
his left hand touches the fiery golden point,
his right breast the string:
the arrow doesn't leave hissing through the air
before Giulio has felt it inside his heart.

41

Ah qual divenne! ah come al giovinetto
corse il gran foco in tutte le midolle!
Che tremito gli scosse il cor nel petto!
Di un ghiacciato sudore era già molle;
e fatto ghiotto del suo dolce aspetto
giammai gli occhi dagli occhi levar puolle;
ma tutto preso dal vago splendore
non s'accorge il meschin che quivi è Amore.


42

Non s'accorge che amor lì drento è armato,
per sol turbar la sua lunga quïete;
non s'accorge a che nodo è già legato;
non conosce sue piaghe ancor secrete:
di piacer, di desir tutto è invescato;
e così 'l cacciator preso è alla rete.
Le braccia fra sé loda e 'l viso e 'l crino;
e 'n lei discerne un non so che divino.


43

Candida è ella, e candida la vesta,
ma pur di rose e fior dipinta e d'erba:
lo inanellato crin dell'aurea testa
scende in la fronte umilmente superba.
Ridegli attorno tutta la foresta,
e quanto può sue cure disacerba.
Nell'atto regalmente è mansueta;
e pur col ciglio le tempeste acqueta.


44

Folgoron gli occhi d'un dolce sereno,
ove sue face tien Cupido ascose:
l'aer d'intorno si fa tutto ameno,
ovunque gira le luci amorose....

41

Alas, what he became! oh, the great fire
ran through all the young man's marrow!
What trembling shook the heart in his breast!
He was completely soaked by an icy sweat;
then made ravenous for her sweet face,
by now he can't remove his eyes from hers;
but totally taken by the graceful splendor,
the wretch doesn't perceive that here is Love.

42

He doesn't see that Love is inside, armed
only to disturb his long peace;
he doesn't see he's already bound by a knot,
he doesn't know his still secret wounds;
he is totally mucked in pleasure and desire,
and thus the hunter is caught in the net.
To himself he praises her arms, face and hair—
and in her he discerns an "I-don't-know-what" divine.

43

Fair is she and white is her dress,
but decorated with roses, flowers and grass;
the curls of her golden head
fall on a forehead humbly proud.
The whole forest smiles at her
and as much as they can quiet her cares.
In her movement she is regally calm;
and even her eyes quiet storms.

44

Her eyes flash a sweet calm,
where Cupid hides his torch:
the air around her makes everything pleasing
wherever she turn those amorous lights...

*Scelte dai Rispetii Spicciolati*

*Pan ed Eco*

Che fai, tu, Eco, mentr'io ti chiamo? — Amo.
Ami tu dua o pur un solo? — Un solo.
Et io te sola e non altri amo — Altri amo.
Dunque non ami tu un solo? — Un solo.
Questo è un dirmi: Io non t'amo — Io non t'amo.
Quel che tu ami amil tu solo? — Solo.
Chi t'ha levata dal mio amore? — Amore.
Che fa quello a chi porti amore? — Ah more!

*da Bellezza*

2

Costei ha privo el ciel d'ogni bellezza
e tolti e' ben di tutto el paradiso,
privato ha il sol di lume e di chiarezza
e posto l'ha nel suo splendido viso,
al mondo ha tolto ogni suo' gentilezza
ogni atto e bel costume e dolce riso.
Amor 'ha dato il guardo e la favella
per farla sopra tutte la più bella.

*da Ammonimenti*

4

Che crudeltà sarebbe ch'i' t'amassi
e fedelmente ti donassi el core,
e tu, donna, la morte mie' cercassi
et odio mi rendessi per amore,
vorrei che qualche volta ci pensassi;
e vederesti se tu se' in errore.
Non vedi tu che la giustizia offendi,
se per fedele amore odio mi rendi?

*Selections from Dribs and Drabs of Love Poetry*

*Pan and Echo*

What were do doing, Echo, while I was calling? — I love.
Do you love two or only one? — Only one.
And I love only you and don't love others — I love others.
So you don't love only one? — Only one.
This is a response to me: I don't love you — I don't love you.
Who you love, you love alone? — Alone.
Who have you deprived by my love? — Love.
What happens to whoever loves you? — Ah, they die!

*from Beauty*

2

That one has deprived heaven of all beauty
and taken all the good from Paradise,
she's deprived the sun of light and brilliance
and placed them in her wonderful face,
she's taken all the gentle nobility from the world,
every beautiful action and custom, and sweet smiles.
Love has given her his glance and speech
to make her transcend the most beautiful.

*from Admonishments*

4

How cruel it would be were I to love you
and faithfully give you my heart,
and you, Lady, would seek my death
and give me hate for love—
I would like you sometimes to think of it
and think if you had erred.
Don't you see that you offend justice,
if you give me hate for my faithful love?

*Aspettar tempo*

1

La notte è lunga a chi non può dormire,
ma ancora è breve a chi contento giace:
se 'l giorno è grande a chi vive in sospire,
presto trapassa a chi possiede in pace:
vero è che la speranza e lo desire
più volte a ogn'un di lor torna fallace;
ma, quando l'aspettare al fin poi viene,
già mai non giunge tardi il vero bene.


2

Non sempre dura in mar grave tempesta;
né sempre folta nebbia oscura il sole:
la fredda neve al caldo poco resta,
e scuopre in terra poi rose e vïole:
so ch'ogni santo aspetta la sua festa,
e ch'ogni caso il tempo mutar suole:
però d'aspettar tempo è buon pensiero,
e chi si vince è ben degno d'impero.


3

Ogni pungente e venenosa ispina
si vede a qualche tempo esser fiorita:
crudel veneno posto in medicina
più volte torna l'uom da morte a vita:
e 'l foco che ogni cosa arde e ruina
spesso risana una mortal fedita:
così spero il mio mal mi sia salute,
ché ciò che nuoce ha pur qualche virtute.

*Patience*

1

The night is long for one who doesn't sleep,
but short for one who lies contentedly:
if the day is long for one living in sighs,
quickly it passes for one possessing peace:
it's true that hope and desire
turn false more than once;
but when waiting comes to its end,
the true good never comes late.

2

A bad storm doesn't always last at sea;
nor does thick fog obscure the sun:
cold snow hardly resists the heat,
then one finds roses and violets in the soil:
I know if every saint awaits his day (celebration),
and every case is used to changing time:
however, waiting is a good thought,
and who can conquer the self worthy of learning.

3

One sees every sharp and poisonous
thorn blossom now and then:
cruel venom placed in medicine
many time brings a person back from the dead:
and the fire the burns and ruins everything
often heals a mortal wound:
so I hope my illness is my health,
for what injures has some virtue.

*Consiglio prudente*

Chi si diletta in giovenile amore,
compera la ricolta in erba verde;
    ché sempre il frutto non risponde al fiore,
    e spesso la tempesta la disperde.
Tristo a chi si confida in bel colore,
    che dalla sera all mattina perde!
Però laudi ciascuno il mio consiglio,
s'io disprezzo le fronde e 'l frutto piglio.


*Vecchiezza*

1


Dove appariva un tratto el tuo bel viso,
dove s'udiva tuo' dolce parole,
parea che ivi fusse el paradiso;
dove tu eri, pare' fussi il sole.
Lasso! mirando nel tuo aspetto fiso,
la faccia tua non è com'esser sôle.
Dov'è fuggita tua bellezza cara?
Trist'a colui ch'alle sue spese impara!


2


Già collo sguardo facesti tremare
l'amante tuo e tutto scolorire:
non avea forza di poter guardare,
tant'era el grande amore e 'l gran disire.
Vidilo in tanti pianti un tempo stare
ch'i' dubitai assai del suo morire.
Tu ridevi del mal che s'apparecchia:
or riderai di te che sarai vecchia.

*Wise Advice*

Who delights in young love
buys the harvest in green grass;
for the fruit never corresponds to the flower,
and often the storm scatters it.
Sadness to whoever trusts in beautiful colors,
which fade from morning to night!
But may each one praise my advice,
if I belittle the leaves and pick the fruit.

*Old Age*

1

Wherever your beautiful face appeared for a moment,
wherever one heard your sweet words,
it seemed that there was paradise;
wherever you were, it would seem that you were the sun.
Weariness! looking at your fixed features,
your face is not what it used to be.
Where has your dear beauty gone?
Sadness to he who learns at his own expense!

2

In former days, with your glance you frightened
your lover and made him completely blanch:
he didn't have the strength to be able to look
so great was his love and desire.
One time I saw him in so many tears
that I doubted death would be enough.
You laughed at the pain that was prepared for him:
Now I will laugh at you—that you are old.

*Preso da In morte del Magnifico Lorenzo de' Medici*

1

Morte, per tôrre il più ricco tesauro
che fussi sotto il ciel, superba svelse
un sì famoso e prezïoso lauro.
 Ben fra tutti e' mortali il fiore scelse,
per riportar le più onorate spoglie
che mai fussino in terra e più eccelse;
 e non pensò lasciare in pianto e doglie
la sua città dolente, per tôr quello
che 'n ciel di sua bontà buon frutto coglie;
 ché forse per pietà l'aspro coltello
arìa rimesso o la falce affilata
per far sempre di noi crudel macello.
 Ma qual vita fu mai tanto onorata?
Qual glorïosa prole ornata e franca?
D'onde è ogni virtù nutrita e nata?
 Ogni lingua ogn'ingegno ogni stil manca
a cantar di suo' laude senza fine,
dove ogni tuba risonante è stanca.
 Tutte le grazie immortali e divine
sempre drento a quel petto albergo ferno
di mille arti e infinte discipline;
 della sua patria uno amor, e un governo
di carità di zelo inestimabile,
che han fatto il nome suo sempre eterno.
 Mentre fie 'l mondo agli animali durabile
mentre del ciel le stelle luceranno,
durerà tanta fama invïolabile....

*Taken from Upon the Death of the Magnificent Lorenzo de' Medici*

1

Rough death, in taking the richest treasure
that was under the sky, uproots
such a famous and precious laurel.
The flower chose well from all mortals
to bring back the most honored and lofty
rewards that were ever on earth;
and he didn't think to leave his sorrowing
city suffering in tears, in order to take his
goodness took his goodness from heaven;
because, perhaps for pity, the bitter knife
remained unused or was falsely sharpened
in order to give to us the cruel slaughter.
But what life was ever so honored?
What glorious offspring so ornate and privileged?
From whence is every virtue born and nourished?
every language, every genius, every style lacks
the ability to sing of his endless praises,
where every resounding trumpet is tired.
All the immortal and divine graces
always make home inside that warm dwelling
of a thousand arts and infinite disciplines;
one love of his homeland and one government
of mercy and inestimable zeal,
that have made his name forever eternal.
While the world will be for earthly animals,
while the stars will shine in heaven,
his inviolable fame will last....

2

Trofei colossi templi a Roma a Jove,
aquedutti colonne anfiteatri,
e stagni e terme non più visti altrove,
 e simulacri statue e teatri
non han potuto conservare in fine
la priscia fama degli antiqui patri.
 Tutte cose alte immortale e divine,
ciò che mai fatto fu ne' sette monti,
pur è converso in cenere e ruine.
 Ma chi le Muse esaltano a' lor fonti
florisce sempre pollutante e verde;
e manca porti scetri ostri archi e ponti.
 Vedi: il lauro tuo sempre rinverde
al monte ove tu ancor potrai ascendere:
ché chi crede altrimenti il tempo perde.
 Io ti potrei con mille esempi accendere;
ma, perch'io ti chiamai piropo ardente,
so che tu ardi ancor tuo conio spendere.
 Altro già non sperava questa gente
di te. Dimostra dunque tanto ardore
di superar di fama il tuo parente.
 La terra e 'l mare e 'l ciel ti dan favore.


3

 Morte crudel che in questo corpo venne!
Che dopo morto, il mondo andò sossopra:
mentre che visse, tutto in pace tenne.

## 2

Trophies, colossi, temples to Jove in Rome,
aqueducts, columns, amphitheaters,
and pewter and baths no longer seen elsewhere—
 portrait busts, statues and theaters
are not, in the end, able to preserve
the former fame of the ancient fathers.
 All lofty things immortal and divine,
those which were made in the seven hills,
are now turned into ashes and ruins.
 But whoever the Muses exalt at their spring
always flourishes budding and green—
and doors, sceptres, purples, arches and bridges are lacking.
 You see: your laurel always renews
on the mountain where you can still climb:
anyone who believes otherwise, wastes time.
 I could inspire you with a thousand examples;
but, because I called you a burning ruby,
I know that you burn to spend your money.
 These people expect nothing else
from you. Your kinsman demonstrated such
ardor in transcending fame.
 The earth, sea and heaven smile upon you.


## 3

 Cruel death that came in this body!
For after death, the world went topsy-turvy:
while he was alive, he kept all at peace.

# Luigi Pulci
# (1432–1484)

Luigi Pulci, free thinker and religious nonconformist, saw life in Medicean Florence from both the bottom and the top. He was born to an old, noble Florentine family that had fallen on hard times. The bottom came early when Luigi's father, Iacopo di Francesco, died in 1451, leaving his wife, Brigida de' Bardi, with, in addition to three sons and two daughters, considerable debts to pay. Luigi and his brothers were unsuccessful in their sincere attempts to pay off these debts. Promising venture after promising venture failed. In 1464, Luigi and his brother, Bernardo, were expelled from Florence for non-payment of debt, only to return to the commune after Lorenzo de' Medici intervened on their behalf. His other brother, Luca, would die in debtors prison in 1470. Yet, because of his talent as a poet, he also saw life from the top, as a confidant and intellectual of the Medici household and as a close personal friend of Lorenzo. He was even encouraged by Lorenzo's mother, Lucretia Tornabuoni, to write his *Morgante*, one of the Italian Renaissance's most famous epic poems. After having left Florence and serving a northern condottiere, Roberto Sanseverino, for many years, Pulci died in 1484 in Padua. Because of his belief in magic, his skepticism toward Christian doctrine and the glorification of non-Christian religion in his poetry, he was buried as a heretic on unconsecrated ground.

Pulci was fully a part of that strand of Renaissance thought that took nothing on authority and attempted to view the world anew and discover nature afresh – in short, to analyze all things in an attempt to discover both their constituent parts and their overall design. This attitude comes to the fore in his *Morgante*, a narrative poem that Pulci originally composed with 23 cantos but later expanded to 28. The poem is literally a narrative of the exploits of Roland and Morgante, a giant converted to Christianity by Roland, who then serves as his squire. However, the implications of the text go far beyond the legend of Charlemagne. The poem poses such sharp social dilemmas as the compatibility of Christian ideals and rapacious capitalism, the conflict between the chivalric ideal of honesty and the political necessity of treachery and deceit, and the adherence to Biblical explanation in the face of the intellectual liberty that was supposedly a core value of the Florentine Republic.

The passage presented here from Pulci's *Morgante* is an episode dealing with the demon Astarotte. On the one hand, Rinaldo is a good Christian. On the other hand, he needs to use Astarotte's black magic to get to Roncesvalles to help Roland. As Francesco de Sanctis writes of Pulci's creation of Astarotte, "This conception is one of the most serious of our literature and one of the best inventions of the *Morgante*. Here is the century in its innermost tendencies not yet clarified, a century that is turning its back on scholasticism and ascetic contemplation. In favor of abstract reasoning, it throws itself avidly into the exploration of nature and humanity. The world expands hereafter, and while some follow a historic path and recreate Athens and Rome, others leave behind theology, philosophy astrology and other 'blind ideas'…to go with their imaginations over the expanses of the ocean. The century begins to take possession of the earth: natural history, physics, seamanship, geography take the place of general questions about being and existence. Facts and experience occupy people's minds more than splitting hairs with words alone (De Sanctis, 464)." Astarotte has been likened to Pulci himself or the brilliant Florentine scientist, Paolo Toscanelli. Above all, with his questioning of religious authority, he at once harkens back to Prometheus, points toward Luther and Protestantism, and empowers the individual to think for himself.

## Luigi Pulci

Dal *Morgante* – *La battaglia*

E' si vedeva tante spade e mane,
tante lance cader sopra la resta;
e' si sentia tante urle e cose strane,
che si poteva il mar dire in tempesta:
tutto il dí tempelloron le campane,
sanza saper chi suoni a morto o festa:
sempre sordi con baleni a secco,
e per le selve rimbombar poi Ecco.

E' si sentiva in terra e in aria zuffa,
perché Astarotte, non ti dico come,
e Farfarello, ognun l'anime ciuffa,
e n'avean sempre un mazzo per le chiome,
e facean pur la piú strana baruffa,
e spesso fu d'alcun sentito il nome:
—Lascia a me il tale! a Belsebú lo porto—.
L'altro diceva: —E Marsilio ancor morto?

—E' ci farà stentar prima che muoia:
non gli ha Rinaldo ancor forbito il muso,
che noi portian giú l'anima e le cuoia—.
O ciel, tu par questa volta confuso!
O battaglia crudel, qual Roma o Troia!
Questa è certo piú là ch'al mondano uso.
Il sol pareva di fuoco sanguigno,
e cosí l'aria d'un color maligno.

Credo ch'egli era piú bello a vedere
certo gli abissi il dí, che Roncisvalle:
ché i Saracin cadevon come pere,
e Squarciaferro gli portava a balle;
tanto che tutte le infernal bufere
occupan questi, ogni roccia, ogni calle,
e le bolge e gli spaldi e le meschite,
e tutta in festa è la città di Dite.

Lucifero avea aperte tante bocche,
che pareva quel giorno i corbacchini
all'imbeccata, e trangugiava a ciocche
l'anime che piovean de' Saracini,
che par che neve monachnia fiocche,
come cade la manna a' pesciolini:
non domandar se raccoglieva i biocoli,
e se ne fece gozzi d'anitroccoli!

# Luigi Pulci

*From Il Morgante  – The Battle*

....and you could see many swords and fists,
many lances lowered on target,
and you could hear many screams and strange things,
that one might say the sea was at storm:
all the day the bells rang,
without knowing whether they were to mourn or cheer—
always empty thunder with cloudless lightening,
then in the woods, Echo resounded.

You could see hand-to-hand combat on the ground and in the air,
because the devils Astarote—I won't tell you how—
and Farfarelle, each seizing manic souls
by their hair,
carrying on the strangest quarrel,
often hearing from them the name:
"Leave me that one! I'll take him to Beelzebub."
The other would say, "Is Marsilio dead yet?"

"And he will make us suffer before he dies:
he made Rinaldo clean his face
before carried his soul below and cooked it."
Oh Heaven, you seemed confused this time!
Oh cruel battle—what of Rome, what of Troy!
This is certainly more there than here on earth.
The sun appeared bloody fire
and the air a spiteful color.

I believe it was certainly more beautiful to see
the abysses that day than Roncevalles:
for the Saracens feel like pears
and Squarciaferro carried them in abundance;
so much so that the entire infernal hurricane
occupied every rock, every path,
and the Circles of Hell, the balconies and mosques—
putting the entire city of Dix in celebration.

Lucifer opened so many mouths
on that day that it seemed the crows
were feeding and swallowing up the clusters of
souls that rained with Saracens—
and it seemed it was snowing plums,
like manna falling to the fish:
don't ask if they picked up the crumbs,
and made like the throats of young ducks!

E' si faceva tante chiarentane,
che ciò ch'io dico è disopra una zacchera:
e non dura la festa mademane,
crai e postcrai e poscrigno e postacchera,
come spesso all vigna le Romane;
e chi sonava tamburo, e chi nacchera,
baldosa e cicutrenna e zufoletti,
e tutti affusolati gli scambietti.

E Roncisvalle pareva un tegame
dove fusse di sangue un gran mortito,
di capi e di peducci e d'altro ossame,
un certo guazzabuglio ribollito,
che pareva d'inferno il bulicame,
che innanzi a Nesso non fusse sparito:
il vento par certi sprazzi avviluppi
di sangue in aria con nodi e con gruppi.

La battaglia era tutta paonazza,
sicché il Mar Rosso pareva in travaglio,
ché ognun, per parer vivo, si diguazza:
e' so poteva gittar lo scandaglio
per tutto, in modo nel sangue si guazza,
e poi guardar, come e' suol l'ammiraglio,
ovver nocchier, se conosce la fonda,
ché della valle trabocca ogni sponda.

Orlando aveva il marchese sentito,
e, come il veltro, alle grida si mosse:
Ulivier tanto sangue gli era uscito,
che non vedeva in che luogo e' si fosse:
tanto ch'Orlando in sull'elmo ha ferito,
che non sentí mai piú simil percosse;
e disse —Che fai tu, cognato mio?
Or hai tu rinnegato il nostro Iddio?—

Disse Ulivier: —Perdonanza ti chieggo,
s'io t'ho ferito, o mio signore Orlando;
sappi che piú nïente lume veggio,
sí ch'io non so dove mi meni il brando,
se non che presso all morte vaneggio,
tanto sangue ho versato e vo versando;
ché Arcaliffa m'ha ferito a torto,
quel tradito; ma di mia man l'ho morto!—

They danced and danced,
so that what I tell you above is a mere trifle:
and the festival did not last just today,
but tomorrow, the day after, the next day, and on—
like the Romans often at the grape harvest—
and one played the drum, another the castanets,
the baldosa, the cicutrenna and whistles,
with all exchanging them nimbly.

And Roncevalles appeared a frying pan
with a great meat dish of blood,
with heads and legs and other such bones,
a certain boiled up mixture
that seemed bubbling up from Hell,
that did not disappear before Nesso:
the wind appeared a certain confusion of sprinkles
of blood in the air, swirling and clumping.

The battle was totally violet,
so that the Red Sea appeared troubled—
for each one, in order to seem alive, paddled about:
having to throw out the sounding line
all around in such a way that they waded in blood
and then looked—like they were used to being admirals—
where to navigate, as if they knew the depths,
for the valley overflowed from every side.

Roland heard the Marquis
and, like the greyhound, moved himself to shriek:
Oliver had lost a lot of blood
and he couldn't see where he was:
so, he wounded Roland's head—
Roland, who never felt such blows,
asked: "What are you doing, my brother-in-law?
Have you now denied our god?"

Oliver said: "I ask your mercy,
if I injured you, Roland, my lord—
you know that I no longer see any light,
so I don't know where my sword leads me,
but I go raving as if near death—
so I've lost so much blood and continue to bleed—
for Arcaliffe wrongly wounded me,
that traitor, but I killed him with my own hand!"

Gran pianto Orlando di questo facea,
perché molto Ulivier gli era nel core,
e la battaglia perduta vedea,
e maladiva il Pagan traditore:
e Ulivier, cosí orbo, dicea:
—Se tu mi porti, come suoli, amore,
menami ancor tra la gente più stretta:
non mi lasciar morir sanza vendetta—.

Rispose Orlando: —Sanza te non voglio
viver quel poco che di vita avanza:
io ho perduto ogni ardire, ogni orgoglio,
sí ch'io non ho piú nulla speranza;
e perch'io t'amo, Ulivier, com'i'soglio,
vienne con meco a mostrar tua possanza;
una morte, una fede, un voler solo—.
Poi lo menò nel mezzo dello stuolo.

Ulivier, sendo nella pressa entrato,
come e' soleva, la gente rincalcia,
e par che tagli dell'erba del prato,
da ogni parte menando la falcia,
ché combatteva come disperato,
e pota e tonda e scapezzava e stralcia.
E, in ogni luogo faceva una piazza,
ché come gli orbi girava la mazza.

This made Roland cry a good deal
for Oliver was dear to his heart
and the battle seemed lost,
so he cursed the Pagan traitor:
and Oliver, blind, said:
"If you carry me, like you used to, beloved friend,
take me to the thick of the battle:
don't let me die without vengeance."

Roland resounded: "I don't want
to live what little life is left without you:
I've lost all my courage, all my pride,
so that I've no hope left:
and because I love you, Oliver, like I used to,
come to me to show your strength—
a death, a prayer, a single wish."
Then he led him to the middle of the battle.

Oliver, feeling himself in the middle of the fight,
reinforced his troops just like he used to,
like cutting the grass of the field,
everywhere like a mower—
he fought like one without hope—
trimming, pruning, lopping off and finishing.
And, in every place, he made a clearing,
for he swung his mace like the planets.

# Giovanni Pico della Mirandola
## (1463–1494)

Count Giovanni Pico della Mirandola, philosopher, scholar and poet, was born February 24, 1463 to Gianfrancesco Pico, Prince of Mirandola, a small territory near Ferrara, and Giulia Boiardo. At fourteen, he was sent to study canon law in Bologna. In 1479, he studied in Ferrara, while the next year he was sent to Padua, where he studied Aristotelian philosophy for two years. He then went to Pavia, Mirandola and Carpi, finally settling in Florence in the spring of 1484, when he became a close friend of Marsilio Ficino, the major proponent of Neoplatonic philosophy at the time. By his early twenties, he had learned not only Latin and Greek, but also Hebrew, Aramaic and Arabic. His studies in language and philosophy, as well as his own personality and original intellectual orientation, led him to seek the similarities between different philosophical systems and religions. This practice, known as syncretism, is one of the hallmarks of Pico's thought and one of the primary examples of the tolerance and intellectual openness of the Medici circle. Needless to say, when he attempted to practice his philosophy by publicly defending 900 theses taken from different Greek, Hebrew, Arabic and Latin thinkers, thirteen of these theses were declared heretical by a papal commission and his public presentation was forbidden by Pope Innocent VIII. After attempting to defend these theses in an *Apologia*, he fled to France, but was allowed to return to Florence after Lorenzo intervened on his behalf. Pope Alexander VI absolved him from any suspicion of heresy in 1493. Pico died at the young age of 31 on November 17, 1494.

Among his writings were his *Heptaplus,* an exposition of Genesis; his treatise *De Ente et Uno*, which in part seeks a harmony between Plato and Aristotle; his famous *Oration on the Dignity of Man*; and, an unfinished work on the enemies of the Church, part of which was his attack against astrologers, which influenced Johannes Kepler in the 17th century. Not generally known, Pico also wrote around 100 sonnets, several of which are presented in this volume. Clearly influenced by the older Lorenzo de' Medici's fascination with the poetry of both Petrarch and Cavalcanti, Pico is able to transform Petrarch's suavity and Cavalcanti's subtle embodiments of suffering into his own original voice, giving a sharp, direct form to a sustained sense of loss about love, relationships, society and politics.

## Giovanni Pico della Mirandola

1
Amor, focoso giacio e fredda face:
Amor, mal dilectoso e dolce affanno;
Amore, pena suave et util danno;
Amor, eterna guerra senza pace.

Amor, tetro timor, speme fallace;
Amor, bugïa, fraude, sdegno e inganno;
Amor, false promesse, che l'uom fanno
gioir del mal come d'un ben verace.

Amore, amaro felle, amaro asenzio;
Amore, vane speranze e van desiri;
Amor, roco parlar, longo silenzio.

Amor, faville, lacrime e sospiri;
Amore, segnor crudel più che Mezenzio,
che gode sempre de gli altrui martiri.


2
Quando del sol la corruscante lampa
risplende, e quando a noi la nocte viene;
quando di neve son le spiage piene,
quando Zefir di fior le pinge e stampa,

quel mio nimico da cui uom mai non scampa,
per farme viver sempre in doglia e in pene,
cun lumi, laci, stral, fiamme e catene
mi piglia, punge, lega, abaglia, avampa.

E se talor di quei pensier io m'armo,
che sì forte mi fan, ch'io giurerei
d'esser piú forte che mai petra o marmo,

súbito poi, né come dir saprei,
ardo qual cera e me stesso disarmo,
in soccorso d'Amore e danni mei.

## Giovanni Pico della Mirandola

1
Love, fiery ice, cold torch;
Love, delightful sickness, sweet anguish;
Love, pleasant pain, gainful harm;
Love, eternal war without peace.

Love, gloomy fear, false hope;
Love, lie, fraud, disdain and deceit;
Love, false promises that make a man
celebrate evil as a true good.

Love, bitter gall, bitter wormwood;
Love, vain hopes, vain desires;
Love, rocky speech, long silence.

Love, sparks, tears and sighs;
Love, master more cruel than Mezenzio,
who always enjoys the suffering of others.


2
When the flashing light shines
from the sun and when night comes to us,
when the beaches are covered with snow,
when Zephyr paints and engraves them with flowers,

that enemy of mine no one ever escapes—
in order to make me live in suffering and pain—
crushes, pricks, binds, beguiles and burns me
with lights, leather, arrows, flames and chains.

And if sometimes I arm myself with those thoughts
that make me so strong that I would swear
to be ever stronger than stone or marble—

suddenly then, like I would know how to speak of them,
I dare that countenance and disarm myself
to the care of Love and my wounds.

3

Un sguardo altero e vergognoso e vago,
un minio che uno avorio bianco pinge,
gli ochi mei stanchi a lacrimar suspinge
mutandoli in um rivo, un fiume, un lago.

E mentre lor contemplan l'altrui imago,
perdo la propria, e for di me mi spinge
el vigor di quei lumi ch'Amor tinge
e 'l stral contra cui mai valse erba né mago.

Cosí mentre si scorda la ragione
di sé, vincta dal cieco et amoroso
desio, qual uom rimango che non sente;

e ben che 'l cor per ciò provi un noioso
stato, ben se ne dol, ma non se 'n pente,
quasi che goda de la sua pregione.


4

Ecco doppo la nebia el cel sereno
che invita li uccelletti andare a schera;
ecco la luce che resplende ove era
di caligine opaca dianci pieno.

Afligice mo, Invidia, aspro veneno
a cui t'alberga! abassa la tua altera
testa, ché chiunque alfine in Dio non spera,
presto ne veni ogni sua forza al meno!

Carità cun Iustizia e intera Fede,
che sempre furono a me fide compagne,
secur mi fan de chi fra via m'assale;

e mentre el cor, ch'è in me, da lor se vede
accompagnato andar, poco gli cale
di che altrui rida, o di che alcun si lagne.

3
A glance lofty, modest and graceful,
a red that paints a white ivory,
it forces my tired eyes to cry,
changing them into a brook, a river, a lake.

And while they contemplate other people's image,
I lose my own—and the power of those lights
that Love tinges and the arrow against which
neither herb nor magic work pushes me outside myself.

so while my reason untunes
itself, defeated by the blind and loving
desire, I remain that man who doesn't feel;

and well that my heart—for which reason proves a troubling
state—well that it suffers, but does not repent,
almost enjoying its prison.


4
Here after the fog, the calm sky
invites the birds to flock together;
here is the light that shines where it was
full of opaque mist a little while ago.

Afflict me, Jealousy, harsh venom
that lives in you! lower your proud
head, for whoever doesn't ultimately believe in God
quickly loses his power!

Chastity with Justice and perfect Faith,
always were my faithful companions,
making me safe from whoever assailed me;

and while my heart—that is in me—seen
accompanied by them, cares little
for those who mock or others who complain.

5

Che fai, alma? che pensi? Ragion, desta
lo spirito, ché la voglia è già trascorsa
là dove ogni salute nostra è in forsa,
se la diffesa tua non sarà presta;

aluma el core; el penser vago aresta;
cosí fa' el senso, che punto lo smorsa.
O scogli, o mar falace, ove era corsa
la debil barca mia in sí atra tempesta!

Da ora inanci fia piú l'ochio interno
acorto; ogni desir men bono è spento;
la mente accesa al ben, presta e gagliarda.

E se puncto te offesi, o Patre eterno,
perdoname, sí come io me ne pento:
sai che da' primi assalti om mal si guarda.


6

Che bisogna che piú nel mar si raspe,
fra tante frode e fra sí falsi inganni?
Parca, depone el fin a tanti affanni,
qual si sia quella che 'l mio fato inaspe!

Da l'erculëo freto al fiume Idaspe
si sa como abia perso i mei verdi anni
in adorar colei, che nei mei danni
si gloria, a mie pregher' sorda qual aspe.

Sino gli ucelli, i fiummi, i monti e i campi
san como suspirando si distempre
il pecto stanco e como il cor avampi;

san como Amor e in che diverse tempre
senza pietá me incenda con doi lampi:
donque meglio è morir che languir sempre.

5

What do you do, soul? what do you think? Reason, wake
the spirit, for the will has run
where every salvation of ours is in doubt,
if your defense be not ready.

The heart kindles, the eager thought stops,
so do the senses, whose limit unbridles it.
Oh rocky shoals, oh deceitful sea where my weak
boat ran in such a black storm!

Since then the prudent inner eye will be
more, every less good desire is dead,
the mind inflamed with the good—quick and strong.

And if the condition offends you, oh eternal Father,
forgive me as I repent:
you know from the onset man is aware of evil.


6

What good is it to paw more in the sea
between so much fraud and such false illusions?
Sparse—the end speaks to so many anxieties—
that which winds my fate!

From the Straits of Hercules to the River Ydaspe
one knows how I lost my youth
in adoring her, who glories in
my suffering—that asp—deaf to my pleas.

Until the birds, rivers, mountains and fields
know how, sighing, my tired breast
softens and my heart burns.

They know how Love—and in those strange moods
without pity—inflames me with his lightening:
therefore, it's better to die than languish forever.

7

Se 'l basso dir di mei suspir in rima,
i quali Amor ne la età mia aprile,
per segregarme dal vulgo più vile,
tra' da parte del cor secreta et ima;

e se la nostra inculta e roza lima,
se 'l mio cantare e 'l mio debile stile
può meritar, ben che inornato e umile,
nome fra quei di che fa el mondo stima,

non vo' mi guidi di Latona il fio
a' fonti aganippei, o di sua insegna
Callïopè m'adorni, Euterpe o Clio.

Ché nulla Musa e d'ogn'altra piú degna
in piú fresche aque e in piú onorato rio
mi bagna, e su nel ciel salir m'insegna.


8

Se ellecto m'hai nel cel per tuo consorte,
Segnor, fa' non mi tenga Amor piú a bada,
né per me indarno aperta sia la strada
del cel e de Pluton rotte le porte.

Sai come sopra noi regna la Morte,
come el dí sette volte el iusto cada,
come un piacer terreno ai sensi agrada,
come io son fral, come 'l nemico è forte.

Tu sai, Signor, che me su la tua stampa
formasti con mirabil magistero
e spirasti nel volto a me la vita;

donque d'amor, di fé el mio core avampa
e cercami, s'i' vo fuor del sentero,
come un pastor la peccora smarita.

7

If my lowly poems sigh in rhyme,
which Love in the April of my life—
in order to set me apart from the vile mob—
draws from the secret and lowly part of my heart;

and if our unfinished and rough file,
if my song and my weak style
are able to merit—well that unadorned and humble—
a name among those that the world makes worthy,

I don't want the son of Latona to guide me
to the Spring of Aganippe or Calliope,
Euterpe or Clio to adorn me with their signs.

For no Muse, nor any other worthy,
bathes me in fresher waters and in more
honored streams, teaching me to ascend to the heavens.


8

If you've chosen me as your companion in heaven,
Lord, make Love not delay me any longer—
for me, the path to heaven was not
opened and Pluto's doors smashed in vain.

You know how Death rules over us,
like the just fall seven times a day,
like an earthly pleasure pleases the senses,
like I'm frail—like the enemy is strong.

You know, Lord, that you formed me
in your image and breathed life
in my face with admirable ability;

therefore, of love, kindle my heart with faith
and search for me if I go outside my path,
like a shepherd the lost sheep.

9

Sí como del mondo umbra senza luce,
posta del mondo alle piú inferne parte,
cosí riman tu, Italia: ecco si parte
el tuo vivo splendor ch'altrove or luce.

De' soi bei raggi aviva le tue luce
mentre che a' Galli e a noi suo lume parte,
che quando tutta vòlta in altre parte
serà, rimanga in te la impresa luce.

Alor me parerai como del cieco
regno di Dite stano i spiriti bui,
ché si cognosce un ben quando è perduto.

E quando il danno tuo fie cognosciuto,
intenderai s'avia da pianger teco,
dicendo: —Io non son piú quella ch'i' fui.—


10

Chiara alma, chaira luce, chiaro onore,
chiara virtú, chiari costumi alteri,
chiaro intellecto, chiari desideri,
chiara nova beltà, chiaro splendore,

chiaro albergo di senno e di valore,
chiari, canuti e leggiadri penseri,
chiaro spirito e chiari magisteri,
chiara rosa vermeglia, chiaro fiore,

chiara gemma piú assai che un chiaro sole
quando apre l'anno verde, e rivi, colli
orna de fresche e palide vïole:

questi doni fe' Giove, e a ti donolli
per monstrar che lui può quanto che vòle;
per farne fede poi qua giú mandolli.

9

So like darkness without the light of the world,
the most infernal part of the world,
so you remain, Italy: here your living
splendor now leaves the light for somewhere else.

May you enliven the light of your beautiful rays
while its light divides the Gauls and us—
so that when all is twisted to another
part, may the known light remain in you.

Then, you will appear to me like the dark spirits
of the blind kingdom of Dis—
for one knows a good thing when it is lost.

And when your loss is known,
I would understand I had to cry with you,
saying: "I am no longer what I was."


10

Bright soul, bright light, bright honor,
bright virtue, bright conduct,
bright intellect, bright desires,
bright and fresh beauty, bright splendor,

bright inn of judgment and power,
bright, mature and graceful thoughts,
bright spirit and bright abilities,
bright red rose, bright flower,

gem brighter than a bright sun
when it opens the green season—and streams, hills,
adorned with fresh, pale violets:

Jove made them gifts and I give them to you
to show he can do what he wants:
I send them to bear witness to him.

11

Io me sento da quel che era en pria
mutato da una piaga alta e suave,
e vidi Amore del cor tôrme le chiave
e porle in man a la nemica mia.

E lei vid'io acceptarle altera e pia
e d'una servitú legera e grave
legarme, e da man manca in vie piú prave
guidarme occultamente Gelosia.

Vidi andarne in exilio la Ragione,
e desiderii informi e voglie nove
rate a venir ad alogiar con meco.

E vidi da l'antica sua pregione
l'alma partir per abitare altrove,
e vidi inanti a lei per guida un cieco.


12

Misera Italia e tutta Europa intorno,
che 'l tuo gran padre Papa iace e vende,
Marzoco a palla gioca e l'onge stende,
la Bissa è pregna et ha sul capo un corno.

Ferrando inferra e vendica el gran scorno,
San Marco bada, pesca a puoco prende,
La vincta Bissa ora San Giorgio offende,
la Lupa a scampo veglia nocte e giorno.

Sega la grassa stracia in Mal avezi
e la Pantiera circondata crida,
femine e puti tien Romagna in pezi.

Da Aquile e Griffi al ciel ne va le strida,
e 'l ciel non ode, e regna Mori egipzi,
Tarquin, Sardanapal, Crasso e Mida.

11

I feel myself changed from what I was before
by a lofty and sweet wound,
for I saw Love turn the keys of my heart
and put them in my enemy's hand.

Then I saw her, proud and pure, accept them
and Jealousy bound me to a fickle, serious servitude
and secretly guided me by hand through
the most depraved streets.

I saw Reason go in exile,
and unshaped desires with new, certain
ones come to live with me.

And from her ancient prison I saw
my soul leave to live elsewhere,
and I looked to her judgment to guide a blind man.


12

Miserable Italy and all of Europe
that your great Pope lays out and sells,
Marzocco plays with the balls and stretches his claws,
the Serpent is pregnant and has a horn on its head.

Ferdinand shackles and avenges the shame,
St. Mark bides, fishes and catches little,
the defeated serpent now offends St. George,
the She-wolf stays up night and day for safety.

The Saw shreds
and the surrounded Panther cries,
Romagna rips women and babies to pieces.

From Eagles and Griffons the screams reach Heaven,
and Heaven doesn't hear—and the Egyptian Moor,
Tarquin, Sardanopolous, Crasso and Midas reign.

# Matteo Maria Boiardo
## (1441–1494)

Matteo Maria Boiardo was born in 1441 to Giovanni Boiardo and Lucia Strozzi in Scandiano, a small fief his family was invested with by Marquis Nicholas III. Soon after his birth, Matteomaria's family moved to Ferrara where he began his early education. After his father's death in 1451, the family moved back to Scandiano. Matteomaria continued his education, studying religion, poetry and life under the tutelege of his paternal grandfather Feltrino and after the example of his maternal uncle Tito Vespasiano Strozzi, a humanist. In 1456 Feltrino died and a few years later his paternal uncle Giulio Ascanio died, leaving the nineteen year old as head of the fief. From his home in his family's lovely palace in Scandiano, Matteomaria spent the next few years studying poetry and literature, hunting in the nearby valleys, entertaining various guests, traveling to Modena and Reggio, and even serving as the governor of Reggio in 1462 for the Borso family, protectors and overlords of the Boiardo family. In 1469 he was part of the official greeting party for the entrance of Emperor Frederick III into Ferrara. In 1471 he went to Rome where he attended the crowning of one of the Borso duke by Paul II. In 1473 he participated in the cavalcade that escorted Eleonora d'Aragona. On this trip he met Poliziano in Florence. In 1476 he moved to the ducal court in Ferrara and in 1479, he married Taddea dei conti Gonzaga di Novellara. In 1474, he avoided being poisoned by two relatives who wanted their own way with the fief. Shortly thereafter the fief was divided into two by the Duke, with the division doing little to end the acrimony of a long-standing family feud. From 1480-82 Matteomaria was the captain of the ducal forces in Modena and from 1487 to his death, captain of those in Reggio. He was sincerely mourned by the citizens of Reggio, not simply as a poet and scholar, but as a virtuous man and model ruler. His letters written as the captain of ducal forces in Reggio revealed him to be knowledgeable about administrative affairs, economic conditions in the region, the dispensation of justice and the defense of his powers in the face of other magistrates. Boiardo was a man with a strong sense of duty, a strong respect for the law and strong desire to live a life filled with peace and love.

As a writer Matteomaria wrote in both Latin and Italian. His earliest poems were in Latin: *De laudibus Estensium*, praises of the Este; and, ten pastoral eclogues in the manner of Virgil. He also translated several works from Latin into Italian, among which was *The Golden Ass of Apuleius*. His masterpiece is the *Orlando innamorato*, an unfinished epic poem in Italian. Matteomaria had planned three parts to the poem, but had only finished the first two and nine books of the third before his death. The poem combines the Arthurian cycle of chivalrous adventures in love with the myth of Charlemagne that glorifies military power.

The selections for this volume are from the third book of his Petrarchan poetic sequence *Amorum libri tres* (Three Books of Love), orginally published in 1499. The *Libri* relate his feelings about his love for Antonia Caprara, which lasted from 1469-71. Although the *Libri* appears to mimic the *Canzoniere* of Petrarch, Vittorio Rossi, a 20th critic, writes Boiardo's "songbook is a marvel. Rich in thought and sentiment, it contains a large amount of true poetry that is not found in any of the other songbooks of the Quattrocento and in few of the 16th century...Boiardo is Petrarchan, but he imitates his style and rhythm with a parsimony...he is Petrarchan only at first glance, for his work renews itself with new offshoots no less alive than the original. His inspiration comes from within, from the motions of a soul that loves, that suffers jealousy, that cannot renounce an ideal long sought (Rossi, 674)." In the first book, Matteomaria is happy. In the second he is sad because he has discovered that Antonia has given her love to others. In the third book, Boiardo's passions are rekindled and he momentarily deludes himself. No doubt the memory of the ruins of Rome intermingled with his broken heart were a central part of the last poem of this anthology.

## Matteo Maria Boiardo

Scelte dal Terzo libro dei *Amorum libri*

1

Quella nemica mia che tanto amai,
ed amo tanto ancor, contro a mia voglia,
sì de drito voler il cor me spoglia,
che a seguirla son vòlto più che mai.

Così avesse io, dal dì che il comminciai,
disposto quel desir che oggi me invoglia,
con tempo a poco a poco a soffrir doglia:
ché a l'assueto è il dôl minor assai.

Tratto fui gioveneto in questa schiera,
de lo incarco d'Amor sì male accorto
che ogni gran salma mi parea ligiera.

Ora sostengo tanto peso a torto,
che maraviglia non è già ch'io pèra,
ma da maravigliar che io non sia morto.

2

Quel fiamegiante guardo che me incese
e l'osse e le medole,
quelle dolce parole
che preson l'alma che non se diffese:

Vòlto han le spalle; e me co 'l foco intorno,
anci dentro dal petto, han qui lasciato
a le insegne d'Amor preso e legato,
né speranza mi dan di suo ritorno.

Così stando captivo, il lungo giorno
tutto spendo in preghiera;
così la notte nera,
mercè chiamando a quella che mi prese.

# Matteo Maria Boiardo

Selections for the Third Book of *Books of Love*

1

That enemy of mine I loved so much
and still very much love against my will,
so my heart robs me of right reason—
for I'm bent to follow her more than ever.

So I am, from the day I began,
disposed to that desire that today encircles me,
with the time, little by little, to suffer pain:
for the lesser pain, as usual, is enough.

As innocent youth I was drawn into this battle
of the so unwise burden of Love
because every great burden seemed light.

Today I wrongly carry so much weight
it isn't a marvel that I've weakened,
but to marvel I haven't died.

2

That flaming glance that ignited me,
my bones to the marrow—
those sweet words
that presumed my soul is defenseless:

She turned and left, with fire all around me,
or rather, from within my heart—she left here
taken and bound to the sign of Love—
and gave me no hope of her return.

So I remain a captive, spending the long
day in prayer—
and thus the black night,
calling for mercy from she who took me.

3

Se passati a quel ponte, alma gentile,
che in bianco marmo varca la rivera,
fiorir vedreti eternamente aprile,
e una aura sospirar dolce e ligera.

Ben si scorgo sin or che v'è una fiera
che abbatte e lega ogni pensier virile,
e qualunqua alma è più superba e altera,
persa la libertà, ritorna umìle.

Ite, s'el v'è un piacer, là dove odeti
cantar li augèi ne l'aria più serena
tra ombrosi mirti e pini e fagi e abeti.

Ite, là voi, che io son fugito a pena:
libero non, ché pur, come vedeti,
porto con meco ancora la catena.


4

Tu te ne vai, e teco vene Amore,
e teco la mia vita e ogni mio bene;
ed io soletto resto in tante pene,
soletto, sancia spirito e sanza core.

Debbio, forsi soffrir questo dolore
ch'io non venga con teco? E chi me tene?
Ahi, lasso, me! che con tante catene
me legò sempre e lega il nostro onore.

Oh, se io credesse pur che alcuna volta
di me te sovenisse, anima mia,
quanto minor sarebbe il mio martìre!

Ma quando io penso che me sarai tolta
oggi, e sì presso è la partita ria,
campar non posso, o di dolor morire.

3

If you cross that bridge, gently noble soul,
that crosses the river in white marble,
you will see flowers eternally April,
and a sweet and graceful aura so to sigh.

Well do I guide you until a wild beast
beats down and binds every manly thought,
and as a soul is more proud and haughty,
it loses its liberty and becomes humble.

Go—if there's pleasure there—there where you hear
the birds sing in the calmest air,
among the dark myrtle, pines, beeches and firs.

Go there, what I've fled in pain:
free no—for even, as you see,
I still carry chains with me.


4

You go away and with you goes Love,
and with you my life and every pleasure—
and I quite alone in great pain,
quite alone, without spirit, without heart.

Must I, then, suffer this pain
that I don't come with you? And who keeps me?
Alas, suffering me! For with many chains
she always binds me and binds our honor.

Oh, if I were to believe that some time
you would remember me, my soul,
how much less would be my martyrdom!

But when I think that you will be taken from me
today—and so close is the parted criminal—
I can neither live nor die from suffering.

5

Sperando, amando, in un sol giorno ariva
la nostra etade a l'ultima vechieza;
quella speranza, che sì ben fioriva,
come caduta è mo di tanta alteza!

Come fa mal colei che me ne priva:
ché il nostro amore e l'alta sua bellezza
farebbe odir in voce tanto viva,
che se apririan le pietre per dolcezza.

Sperai con tal desir, e fui sì presso
al fin del mio sperar, che io vo' morire
pensando ora che fui, che sono adesso.

Copri dentro, dolor, non mi far dire;
ma pur questo dirò: non venga spesso
sì bella pressa a chi non sa tenire.


6

Io son tornato a la mia vita antica,
a paigner notte e giorno, a sospirare,
dove già non credea più ritornare,
ché pur sperava al fin pietade amica.

Ahi lasso! che io non so quel che io me dica,
tanto mia doglia mi fa vanegiare;
non spero, e non potei già mai sperare
in questa fera di mercè nemica.

Ben fu tradito il misero mio core,
ché un poco il viso li mostrò ventura,
perché sua doglia poi fosse magiore.

Sempre la bianca sorte con la scura
di tempo in tempo va cangiando Amore:
ma l'una poco, e l'altra molto dura.

5

Hoping, loving , in a single day our
summer reaches its final old age—
that hope, so well flowered,
how it has now fallen from such heights!

What evil she does who deprives me:
because I would hear, in such a spirited
voice, our love and her lofty beauty,
which would open the stones with their sweetness.

I hoped with such desire—and was so taken
to the end of my hope—that wanted to di,
thinking now that I was, that now I am.

Hide inside, suffering—don't make me speak—
but still I say this: such beautiful desire
doesn't often come to one who doesn't know how to keep it.


6

I've returned to my ancient life
to cry night and day, to sigh,
to where she believed I would no longer return,
for, in the end, even she hoped pity a friend.

Oh, misery! I don't know what I said to myself,
my suffering makes me rave—
I don't now hope and could never before hope
in this fierce enemy of mercy.

My miserable heart was completely betrayed
because my face showed it a little trick,
that its pain was greater.

Love always changes the
light sort with the dark:
but one lasts a little and the other a lot.

7

Il terzo libro è già di mei sospiri,
e il sole e l'anno ancor non è il secondo:
tanto di pianti e di lamenti abondo,
che il tempo han trapassato e mei martìri.

In sensato voler, dove mi tiri
a lamentar del mio stato giocondo?
Qual più diletto me paregia al monso.
Se avien che gli ochi nel bel viso agiri?

Ben muta ancor dureza questa voglia,
a cui non basta che una volta pèra,
ma vôl che io mi consumi in foco e in gielo.

Qual fia quella pietà che mi disoglia
e doni l'ale a l'anima ligera,
che quindi se sveluppi e voli al celo?

8

*In prosectu Romae*

Ecco l'alma città che fu regina
da l'unde Caspe a la terra Sabèa,
la trionfal città che impero avea
dove il sol se alza insin là dove inchina.

Or levo fato e sentenzia divina
sì l'han mutata a quel ch'esser solea,
che, dove quasi al ciel equal surgea,
sua grande alteza copre ogni ruina.

Quando fi adunque più cosa terrena
stabile e ferma, poi che tanta altura
il tempo e la fortuna a terra mena?

Come posso io sperar già mai sicura
la mia promessa? Ché io non credo a pena
che un giorno intiero amore in donna dura.

7

The third book is already about my moaning
and the sun and the year are not the second:
I abound in so many tears and laments
that my sufferings have surpassed the occasion.

Foolish desire, where do you pull me
to lament my happy state?
If only other pleasures in the world would appear to me.
If the eyes of that beautiful face would turn?

Hardness really changes this desire
to which it's not enough it dies just once,
but demands that I consume myself in fire and ice.

Which will be that mercy that dissolves me
and gives wings to my happy soul,
that then grow and fly to heaven?

8

*In Light of Ancient Rome*

Here is the sacred city that was queen
from the Caspian waves to the Sabian desert,
the triumphal city that had an empire
from where the sun rose to where it set.

Now I raise fact and divine judgment
that they've changed from what they were—
that, where the sun rose equal to the heaven,
its greatest height covers every ruin.

When will there be a more stable and
solid earthly thing, seeing time
and fortune leading such loftiness to earth?

How can I ever expect certain
security? For I don't hardly believe
love in a woman lasts an entire day?

9

*Moralis allegoria cantu tetrametro*

1. Zefiro torna, che de amore aspira
   naturalmente, desïoso instinto,
   e la sua moglie co il viso dipinto
   piglia qualunche e soi bei fiori amira.
   Ma chi riguarda il ciel sopra agira,
   non teme e laci de la falsa amante,
   ché la sua rete, che a morte ne tira.
   lo ochio sol prende cupido e vagante.
   Ecco l'aria roseggia al sol levante;
   dirciamo il viso a la chiara lumera,
   che 'lanima non pèra
   per volger li ochi al loco de le piante.

2. Che riguardati, o spiriti perregrini?
   Il color vago de la bella rosa?
   Fugiti via, figiti, ché nascosa
   E' la loncia crudel ne' verdi spini.
   Non aspettati che la luce inchini
   verso lo occaso, ché la fera allora
   esce sicura ne' campi vicini,
   e li dormenti ne l'ombra divora.
   Per Dio, non aspettati a l'ultima ora!
   Credeti a me che giaqui sopra al prato,
   e ben che io sia campato,
   mercè n'ha il Ciel, che vôl che io viva ancora.

3. Se ve colcati ne' suavi odori
   che surgon quinci a la terra fiorita,
   in brivi giorni avreti dolce vita,
   in lunga notte morte con dolori.
   Uno angue ascoso sta tra l'erbe e' fiori,
   che il verde dosso al prato rasumiglia:
   nulla se vede, sì poco par fôri,
   né pria si sente, se non morde o piglia.
   Forsi il mio dir torreti a maraviglia,
   ma salir vi convien quel col fronzuto.
   Né si trova altro aiuto;
   chi provato ha ogni schermo, vi consiglia.

9

*Moral Allegory in Tetrameter*

1. Zephyr returns, naturally breathing
the amorous impulse of love,
and his wife, Springtime, with face beautiful,
picks some flowers and looks at them.
But he who looks at the sky rambling above
isn't there afraid of a false lover,
for her net—which will pull you to your death—
only takes the greedy, wandering eye.
Here is the rosy sky of the rising sun:
we will direct his face to the white light,
so his soul won't die
by turning his eyes down to the plants.

2. Wandering spirits, what are you seeking?
The fascinating color of the beautiful rose?
Run away, run, for hidden in its
thorns is the cruel panther.
Don't expect the light to bend
to the west, for the beast
comes out unafraid in the nearby fields
and devours the sleeping in the dark.
For God's sake, don't wait until the last minute!
Believe me that it waits in the field
and that I escaped—
Heaven has mercy and wanted me to live longer.

3. If you lay down in the sweet aromas
rise from the flowered earth,
in a short time you'll have the sweet life,
death with pain in the long night.
    A hidden serpent is among the grass and flowers,
with his green back blending into the green field:
no one sees him, he seems out of range,
nor can you feel him if he doesn't bite or strike.
Perhaps my poem will take the spell away,
but you must rise with those stalks.
And you won't find other help—
I tell you—you who've tried every defense.

4.　Quel dolce mormorar de le chiare onde,
　　ove Amor nudo a la ripa se posa,
　　là giuso ad immo, tien la morte ascosa;
　　ché una sirena dentro vi nasconde,
　　con li ochi arguti e con le chimoe bionde,
　　co 'l bianco petto e con lo adorno voloto;
　　canta sì dolce, che il spirito confonde,
　　e poi lo occide che a dormir l'ha còlto.
　　Fugeti, mentre il senso non vi è tolto,
　　ché il partir doppo il canto è grave affanno;
　　ed io, che so lo inganno,
　　quasi contro a mia voglia ancor l'ascolto.

5.　Non ve spechiati a questa fonte il viso,
　　ché morte occulta vi darà di piglio;
　　in quel fioreto candido e vermiglio,
　　sol per mirarsi, se cangiò Narciso.
　　Legeti il verso a lettere d'oro inciso
　　nel verde marmo di sua sepultura,
　　che dice: "Lasso chi è di sé conquiso,
　　ché mortal cosa piccol tempo dura."
　　Lassati adunque al basso ogni vil cura,
　　driciati ad erto la animosa fronte;
　　avanti aveti il monte
　　che ne la cima tien vita secura.

　　Canzone, se alcun te lege e non intende
　　dentro a la scorza, di' lui chiaro e piano,
　　che in tutto è pazo e vano
　　qualunque aver diletto in terra attende.

4.  That sweet murmuring of the clear waves,
    where nude Love rest on the shore,
    there down below, death is hidden—
    with a siren hidden inside,
    with provocative eyes and blond tresses,
    a fair breast and adorned face;
    she sings so sweetly your spirit is confused,
    then she kills the one she's taken to bed.
    Flee, before your sense is taken,
    for leaving after she sings brings great pain—
    and I, who know the game,
    listen almost against my will.

5.  Don't become obsessed with this source,
    for hidden death will take you—
    in that pure and red tiny blossom,
    only to look at himself, Narcissus was changed.
    Read the verse written in gold letters
        in the green marble of his tomb—
    it says: "Suffering to one so conquered.
    for mortal things last a short time."
    Leave every vile desire at the bottom,
    focus your courageous mind on the steep climb—
    ahead you have the mountain
    that has certain life at the top.

    Poem, if someone reads you and doesn't understand,
    tell their inner selves clearly and simply
    that it's totally crazy and vain
    to expect pleasure in earthly things.

# Jacopo Sannazzaro
# (1457–1530)

Jacopo Sannazzaro's family took its name from a small village in Lomellina in the Kingdom of Naples. Among his ancestors was a certain Rosso, a man of arms, who possessed castles and minor territories in the region. Jacopo was the son of Nicolò (nicknamed Cola), a grandson of Rosso, and Masella di Santo Mango, who came from an old family in Salerno. As a baby, Jacopo was taken by his mother to San Cipriano Picentino. His father died c.1470. In 1475 Jacopo returned to Naples where he began lessons in rhetoric and poetry with Giuniano Maio and Lucio Crasso. Of note is the fact that Giovanni Pontano, head of the Academy, dubbed Jacopo "Actius Syncerus," a Latin name which, given the context, translates roughly as "pure creation." *Actius*, or 'action,' is a play both on the idea that Jacopo had already undertaken 'action' by having written some fishing eclogues and on the notion that such eclogues are set on the beach, the Latin word for which is *acta*. Syncerus might have been derived from the Hebrew etymology for the saint his surname is taken from, San Nazzaro, with Nazzaro meaning 'pure,' 'uncorrupted' or 'sincere.' During the time of his studies Jacopo was accepted by the House of Aragon, the rulers of the Kingdom, and by 1481, the Duke of Calabria listed him among his "officiali de casa." In 1501, the last king of the Aragon dynasty, Frederic, lost his throne and Jacopo accompanied him to France, where he discovered several lost Latin works from Antiquity: Ovid's *Halieutica* and Nemesianus' *Cynegetica*.

Sannazzaro wrote in both Latin and Italian. Among his Latin works are his *Eclogae piscatoriae*, his fishing eclogues; the *De partu virginis* (On the Virgin Birth), a celebration of the birth of Christ; and, his *Elegiae* and his *Epigrammata*, both of which reveal his sensitive personality. In Italian, Jacopo wrote a Petrarchan canzoniere and his most famous work, *Arcadia*, a pastoral poem consisting of prose narrative and poetic eclogues. He initially wrote *Arcadia* in ten books, each with a prose introduction to an eclogue that consisted of dialogue between several shepherds. Soon after, however, Sannazzaro added two more books. The story of the *Arcadia* is a simple one. Sincero, wanting to forget his troubles with love, leaves Naples and joins the shepherds in *Arcadia*, where he joins their poetry contexts and festivals. However, he decides to return to civilization since he cannot find peace of mind in *Arcadia*. He returns through underground caves guided by a nymph.

The selection in this volume is the poetry from *Eclogue Ten* of *Arcadia*. In it Selvaggio and Fronomio go beyond a superficial *laudatores temporis acti* ('praises of times past') in comparing the ancients and moderns, delving into deep causes for the success of the former. To begin, Fronomio complains that the ancients are forgotten, that people are now ignorant and the world is in danger of being destroyed. Selvaggio then explains that while he was wandering, sick from unrequited love, the Fates told him to seek the lofty city of the ancient Chalcydeans. He did not know what they meant, but the shepherds explained it to him. They then taught him art and science. He then hears Caracciol's apocalyptic song, which tells of the collapse of ancient civilization and the death of nature because the gods lost their virtue and could no longer cooperate with each other. Carraciol warns Selvaggio that the moderns should not repeat their mistake.

## Jacopo Sannazzaro

*Ecloque 10 da Arcadia – Selvaggio e Fronimo*

Sel.     Non son, Fronimo mio, del tutto mutole,
com'uom crede, le selve; anzi risonano,
tal che quasi all'antiche egual riputole.

Fron.    Selvaggio, oggi i pastor più non ragionano
de l'alme Muse, e più non pregian naccari,
perché, per ben cantar, non si coronano.
   E sì del fango ognun s'asconde i zaccari,
che tal più pute che ebuli et abrotano
e par che odore più che ambrosia e baccari.
   Ond'io temo gli Dii non si riscotano
dal sonno, e con vendetta ai boni insegnino
sì come i falli de' malvagi notano.
   E s'una volta avvien che si disdegnino,
non fia mai poi balen né tempo pluvio,
che di tornar al ben pur non si ingegnino.

Selv.    Amico, io fui tra Baie e 'i gran Vesuvio
nel lieto piano, ove col mar congiungesi,
il bel Sebeto, accolto in picciol fluvio.
   Amor, che mai dal cor mio non disgiungesi
mi fe' cercar un tempo strane fiumora,
ove l'alma, pensando, ancor compungesi.
   E s'io passai per pruni, urtiche e dumora,
le gambe il sanno; e se timor mi pusero
crudi orsi, duri genti, aspre costumora!
   Al fin le dubbie sorti mi ripusero:
—Cerca l'alta cittade ove i Caldici
sopra 'l vecchio sepolcro si confusero.—
   Questo non intens'io; ma quei fatidici
pastor mel fer poi chiaro e mel mostrarono,
tal ch'io gli vidi nel mio ben veridici.
   Indi incantar la luna m'insegnarono,
e ciò che in arte maga al tempo nobile
Alfesibo e Meri si vantarono.
   Né nasce erbetta sì silvestra ignobile,
che 'n quelle dotte selve non conoscasi;
e quale stella è fissa, e quale è mobile.
   Quivi la sera, poi che 'l ciel rinfoscasi,
certa l'arte febea con la pallidia,
che non c'altri, ma Fauno a udir rimboscasi.
   Ma a guisa d'un bel sol fra tutti radia
Caracciol, che 'n sonar sampogne o cetere
non troverebbe il pari in tutta Arcadia.

# Jacopo Sannazzaro

*Ecloque 10 from Arcadia – Selvaggio and Fronimo*

Sel.     The woods are, my Fronimo, not completely mute
as men believe—rather they echo
in such a way I believe them equal to the ancients.

Fron.    Selvaggio, today the shepherds don't discuss
the immortal Muses and don't value the castanets,
because they aren't crowned for singing well.
And each of them so hides his muddy stains
that such men stink more than dwarf-elder and southern
wood and seem to smell more than ambrosia and spilkenard.
Whence I fear the Gods don't wake themselves
from sleep and, with vengeance, teach the good
how they note the sins of the wicked.
And if it sometimes happens that they are disdainful,
there will never again be lightening or time or rain,
if they don't strive to turn to the good.

Selv.    Friend, I was between Baiae and great Vesuvius,
in that happy plain where the beautiful Sebeto,
gathered into a little river, joins himself with the sea.
Love, never leaving my heart,
was once making me seek a strange river place
where my soul, thinking, was then pierced.
And if I walked through thorns, nettles and briars,
my legs know it as if I'm frightened
by cruel bears, rough people and harsh manners!
Finally, the doubtful fates replied to me:
"Seek the lofty city where the Chalcedeans
fled for refuge over the ancient sepulcher.
I didn't understand this, but those prophetic
shepherds made it clear to me,
so that I saw them speak the truth about my welfare.
Then, they taught me to enchant the moon
and the art of sorcery from that noble age
when Alphesiboeus and Moeris were boasting.
Nor does any wild herb grow
in those learned woods that is not known—
which star is fixed and which moves.
Here in the evening, when the sky darkens,
the Phoebean art fights with the Pallasian
so none other than Faunus hides in the bush to hear.
But Caracciol shines among them all like
a beautiful sun, who in playing the zampogna or lyre
could not find his equal in all of Arcadia.

Costui non imparò putaro o metere,
ma curar greggi da la infetta scabbia
e passïon sanar maligne e vetere.
   Il qual un dì, per isfogar la rabbia,
così prese a cantar sotto un bel frassino,
io fiscelle tessendo, egli una gabbia:
   —Proveda il ciel che qui vèr noi non passino
malvage lingue; e le benigne fatora
fra questi armenti respirar mi lassino.
   Itene, vaccarelle, in quelle pratora,
acciò che quando i boschi e i monti imbrunano,
ciascuna a casa ne ritorne satora.
   Quanti greggi et armenti, oimè, digiunano,
per non trovar pastura, e de le pampane
si van nudrendo, che per terra adunano!
   Lasso, c'appena di mill'una càmpane;
e ciascun vive in tanto estrema inopia,
che 'l cor per doglia sospirando avampane.
   Ringrazie dunque il ciel qualunque ha copia
d'alcun suo bene in questa vil miseria,
che ciascun caccia da la mandra propria.
   I bifolci e i pastor lascian Esperia,
le selve usate e le fontane amabili;
ché 'l duro tempo glie ne dà materia.
   Erran per alpe incolte inabitabili,
per non veder oppresso il lor peculio
da genti strane, inique, inesorabili.
   Le qua' per povertà d'ogni altro edulio,
non già per aurea età, ghiande pascevano
per lor grotte da l'agosto al giulio.
   Viven di preda qui, come solevano
fra quei primi pastor nei boschi etrurii.
Deh c'or non mi sovien qual nome avevano!
   So ben che l'un da più felici augurii
fu vinto e morto—or mi ricorda, Remo—
in su l'edificar de' lor tugurii.
   Lasso, che'n un momento io sudo e tremo
e veramente temo     d'altro male;
ché si de' aver del sale         in questo stato,
perché 'l comanda il Fato     e la Fortuna.
Non vedete la luna         ineclissata?
La fera stella armata    di Orïone?
Mutata è la stagione  e 'l tempo è duro,
e già s'atuffa Arcturo     in mezzo l'onde;
e 'l sol, c'a noi s'asconde,     ha i raggi spenti,
e van per l'aria i vènti          mormorando,

He did not teach pruning or reaping,
but curing the flocks of infected scabs
and healing old, spiteful feelings.
  One day, to vent his rage,
he was taken to sing under a large ash,
I weaving little baskets, he a cage:
  "May heaven provide that no wicked tongues
speak here and the benign fates
let me breathe among these herds.
  Go, cattle, to those pastures,
so that when the woods and mountains grow dark,
each of you may return home satisfied.
  How many flocks and herds—alas—don't eat
for lack of finding pastures and nourish themselves
on vine leaves as they gather from the land!
  Alas, hardly one of a thousand lives through it—
and each one lives in extreme poverty,
while their hearts, sighing from pain, burn from it.
  Therefore, he should thank heaven
if he has enough in this vile misery,
a misery that drives each one from his own herd.
  The cowherds and shepherds leave Hesperia,
the familiar woods and friendly springs,
because the hard time gives them reason.
  They wander among the uncultivated, uninhabitable
mountains in order not to see their flock oppressed
by foreigners, wicked, unrelenting.
  They, through the lack of any other food,
not certainly because of the Golden Age, eat acorns
in their caves from August to July.
  Here they live on their hunting, like the
first shepherds did in the Etruscan woods.
Alas, for the moment, their name escapes me.
  I well know that was killed by one of
the happiest diviners—now I remember, Remus—
while building their huts.
  Alas, for in one instant I sweat and shiver
and I fear another evil—
for you have to have your wits       in this condition—
because Fate and Fortune     command it.
Don't you see the moon                 eclipsed?
The fierce armed star            of Orion?
The season is changed                 and the weather is harsh,
and Arcturus already dives    in the middle of the waves—
    and the sun, who hides from us, extinguished its rays,
and go through the air                 murmuring,

né so pur come o quando     torne estate.
E le nubi spezzate     fan gran suoni;
tanti baleni e tuoni    han 'aria involta,
ch'io temo un'altra volta    il mondo pera.
O dolce primavera,   o fior novelli,
o aure, o arboscelli,  o fresche erbette,
o piagge benedette,    o colli, o monti,
o valli, o fiumi, o fonti,    o verdi rive,
palme, lauri et olive,     edere e mirti;
o glorïosi spiriti    degli boschi;
o Eco, o antri foschi,     o chiare linfe,
o faretrate Ninfe,   o agresti Pani,
o Satiri e Silvani,    o Fauni e Driadi,
Naiadi et Amadriadi,    o semidee,
Oreadi e Napee,    or sète sole;
secche son le vïole    in ogni piaggia:
ogni fiera selvaggia,  ogni ucelletto
che vi sgombrava il petto,    or vi vien meno.
E 'l misero Sileno    vecchiarello
non trova l'asinello  ov'ei cavalca.
Dafni, Mopso e Menalca,    oimè, son morti.
Priapo è fuor degli orti     senza falce,
né genebro né salce    è che 'l ricopra.
Vertunno non s'adopra     in transformarse,
Pomona ha rotte e sparse     le sue piante,
né vòl che le man sante    puten legni.
E tu, Pale, ti sdegni   per l'oltraggio,
ché di april né di maggio    ha sacrificio.
Ma s'un commette il vicio,  e tu nol reggi,
che colpa n'hanno i greggi   de' vicini?
Che sotto gli alti pini     e i dritti abeti
si stavan mansüeti   a prender festa
per la verde foresta  a suon d'avena;
quando, per nostra pena,    il cieco error
entrò nel fiero core  al neghittoso.
E già Pan furïoso    con la sanna
spezzò l'amata canna;    ond'or piangendo,
se stesso riprendendo,    Amor Losinga,
ché de la sua Siringa    si ricorda.
La saette, la corda,   l'arco e 'l dardo,
c'ogni animal fea tardo,    omai Dïana
dispregia, e la fontana    ove il protervo
Atteon divenne cervo;    e per campagne
lassa le sue compagne    senza guida;
cotanto si disfida    omai del mondo,
che vede ognor al fonso   gir le stelle.

I don't know how or when          summer returns.
And the broken clouds        make great noises—
so much thunder and lightening        envelops the air,
that I fear one more time      the world will vanish.
O sweet Spring                  o fresh flowers
o breezes, o bushes, o fresh grasses,
o blessed shores,        o hills, o mountains,
o valleys, o rivers, o springs,            o green banks,
pals, laurels and olives,          ivy and myrtle—
o glorious spirits        of the forests—
o Echo, o dark caves,            o clear waters,
o Quivered Nymphs,              o rustic Pans,
o Satyrs and Sylvans,            o Fauns and Dryads,
Maiads and Hamadryads,        o Demigods,
Oreads and Napeans,                  now you are alone—
dried are the violets   on every hillside:
every wild beast        every bird
that used to cleanse its breast            faints away.
And wretched Silenus        little old man
doesn't find the ass    he can ride.
Daphne, Mopsus and Menaclas,          alas! are dead.
Priapus is outside his orchards          without his scythe,
neither juniper nor willow    occupies him.
Vertumnus doesn't endeavor          to transform,
Pomona has broken and scattered      her plants,
nor does she want her sainted hands    to trim the branches.
And you, Pales, get angry      at the outrage—
for in neither April nor May    have you had a sacrifice—
But if one commits the sin,    and you don't oppose it,
what fault do the neighboring flocks          have for it?
That under the tall pines      and straight firs
they were used                to having festivals
in the green forest        with music of the shepherd's pipe—
when, for our pains,            the blind mistake
entered the heart      of the lazy one.
Then furious Pan      ripped his beloved reed
with the boar's tusk—          whence now crying,
correcting himself,          he flatters Love,
for he remembers      his Syrinx.
The arrows, the string,        the bow and the dart,
which slow every animal,      Diana now
scorns—and the fountain              where the arrogant
Actaeon became a stag—        then in the countryside
she leaves her companions    alone and lost—
so does she now mistrust            the world,
that she the stars    turn to the depths.

Marsïa senza pelle    ha guasto il bosso,
per cui la carne e l'osso    or porta ignudo;
Minerva il fiero scudo    irata vibra;
Apollo in Tauro o in Libra    non alberga,
ma con l'usata verga    al fiume Anfriso
si sta dolente, assiso    in una pietra,
e tien la sua faretra    sotto ai piedi.
Ahi, giove, e tu tel vedi?    E non ha lira
da pianger, ma sospira,    e brama il giorno
che 'l mondo intorno intorno    si disfaccia
e prenda un'altra faccia    più leggiadra.
Bacco con la sua squadra    senza tirsi
vede incontro venirsi    il fiero Marte
armato, e 'n ogni parte    farsi strada
con la crüenta spada.    Ahi vita trista!
Non è chi gli resista.    Ahi fato acerbo!
ahi ciel crudo e superbo!    Ecco che 'l mare
si comincia a turbare,    e 'ntorno ai liti
stan tutti sbigottiti    i Dii dell'acque,
perché a Nettuno piacque    esilio darli
e col tridente urtarli in su la guancia.
La donna e la bilancia    è gita al cielo.
Gran cose in picciol velo    oggi restringo.
Io ne l'aria dipingo, e tal si stende,
che forse non intende    il mio dir fosco.
Dormasi fuor del bosco.    Or quando mai
ne pensàr tanti guai bestemmie antiche?

Gli ucelli e le formiche    si ricolgono
de' nostri compi il desïato tritico;
così gli Dii la libertà ne tolgono.
  Tal che assai meglio nel paese scitico
veven color sotto Boote et Elice,
benché con cibi alpestri e vin sorbitico.
  Già mi rimembra che da cima un'élice
la sinestra cornice, oimè, predisselo;
ché 'l petto mi si fe' quasi una selice.
  Lasso, che la temenza al mio cor fisselo,
pensando al mal che avvenne; e non è dubbio
che la Sibilla ne le foglie scrisselo.
  Un'orsa, un tigre han fatto il fier connubbio.
Deh, perché non troncate, o Parche rigide,
mia tela breve al dispietato subbio?
  Pastor, la noce che con l'ombre frigide
nòce a le biade, or ch'è ben tempo, trunchesi,
pria che per anni il sangue si rinfrigide.
  Non aspettate che la terra ingiunchesi

Marsyas without skin      has broken the boxwood,
which he now wears nude    for skin and bones—
angry Minerva shakes      her fierce shield—
Apollo doesn't live     in Taurus or Libra,
but with the usual scepter   is crying
by the river Amphrysus,      seated on a rock,
with his quiver     under his feet.
Alas, Jove, do you see it?    And he has no lyre
for crying, but sighs  and longs for the day
when the world everywhere   destroys itself
and takes on another,      happier face.
Bacchus with his troops     without the thrysis
sees fierce Mars coming     against them,
armed, everywhere making    a path
with his bloody sword.     Alas, cruel life!
No one can resist it.      Alas, bitter fate!
Alas, harsh and rough heaven!     Here is how the sea
begins to churn,     and on the shores
stand the Gods of the waters   completely terrified,
for Neptune liked        to exile them
and cut their cheeks with his trident.
The lady and the scales      have gone to heaven.
Today I wrap great things   in thin veil.
I paint in the air      and so stretch it
that perhaps my darkened rhyme   doesn't express.
May it sleep outside the woods.   Now, whenever
did the ancient blasphemies  think of such troubles?

   The bird and ants gather
the desired grain from our fields—
thus the Gods take liberty from us.
   So that they live better in atheistic countries
under Boötes and Helice,
although with mountain food and hard cider.
   Suddenly I remember that from atop an oak
an evil crow—alas—predicted it—
so my breast was hardened almost to flint.
   Alas, how fear fixed itself to my heart,
thinking of the evil that would happen—and there is no
doubt the Sibyl wrote in in her pages.
   A bear, a tiger have made a fierce marriage.
Alas, why don't you sever, o rigid Parcae,
my short fabric from the cruel loom?
   Shepherd, it's well time to cut the nut
tree with its freezing shade ruining the grain
before the blood grows cold for years.
Don't wait for the earth to be bound

di male piante, e non tardate a svellere,
fin che ogni ferro poi per forza adunchesi.
   Tagliate tosto le radici all'ellere;
ché se col tempo e col poder s'aggravano,
non lasseranno i pini in alto eccellere."

   Così cantava, e i boschi rintonavano
con note, quai non so s'un tempo im Menalo,
in Parnaso o in Eurota s'ascoltavano.
   E se non fusse che 'l suo gregge affrenalo
e tienlo a forza ne l'ingrata patria,
che a morte desïar spesso rimenalo,
   verrebbe a noi, lassando l'idolatria
e gli ombrati cosutmi al guasto secolo,
fuor già d'ogni natia carità patria.
   Et è sol di vertuù sì chiaro specolo,
che adorna il mondo col suo dritto vivere;
degno assai più ch'io col mio dir non recolo.
   Beata terra che 'l produsse a scrivere,
e i boschi, ai quai sì spesso è dato intendere
rime, a chi 'l ciel non pòte il fin prescrivere!
   Ma l'empie stelle ne vorrei riprendere,
né curo io già, se col parlar mio crucciole;
sì ratto fer dal ciel la notte scendere,
   che sperando udir più, vidi le lucciole.

with weeds—and don't wait to tear them out
until every tool is twisted from work.
   Immediately cut the roots of ivy—
for they will grow with time and strength,
and not let the pines excel in height."

   Thus he sang and the woods resounded
with notes, which I don't know if were ever
heard on Menalus or Parnassus or Eurotas.
   And if it weren't that his flock slowed him
and kept him by force in his ungrateful country—
that often leads him to desiring death—
   he would come to us, leaving idolatry
and dark habits to a broken age,
a country beyond every natural courtesy.
   Then he alone is the only mirror of virtue
who adorns the world with his right living—
more worthy than I achieve with my song.
   Blessed be the earth that made him write
and the woods, to whom he often aimed
verse, which the heavens could not end!
   But I would like to scold the inhuman stars—
and I don't care if I torment them with my speech—
they made the night so suddenly to descend from heaven—
that hoping to hear more, I saw the fireflies.

# Girolamo Savonarola
## (1452–1498)

Religious reformer, mystic and political firebrand, Girolamo Savonarola was born in Ferrara to Niccoló Savonarola and Elena Bonaccorsi. Educated by his paternal grandfather, Michele, who was a doctor and man of strong religious sentiment, Savonarola received his earliest education, one colored by medieval ideas on sin, the evils of material acquisition and obedience to God. This attitude would soon manifest itself both in the young Savonarola's general condemnation of the 'blind wickedness' of the Italian people and in his rejection of the humanistic paganism found in much of the art, literature and culture of the time. Savonarola would eventually come to level his febrile criticism at not only the clergy, but the papacy itself.

In 1475 Girolamo left both his family home and medical studies to enter the Domincan order in Bologna. He returned to Ferrara in 1479 to teach scripture at the Convento degli Angeli. In 1482 he was sent to Florence where he lectured at San Marco, developing a reputation for both his learning and his asceticism. However, he was relatively unsuccessful as a preacher until he had a sudden revelation to deliver prophetic sermons. He explained the basis of his prophecy in San Gimignano, a small town near Florence, at Lent in 1485 and 1486. His message was simple. The Church needed reform. First it would be scourged and then it would be renewed. In 1487, Savonarola went to Bologna where he became the master of the *studium generale* for a year. After that he went to different cities to preach until Lorenzo de' Medici had him asked back to Florence.

Soon after his return to Florence, Savonarola took to the pulpit to damn what he perceived as the tyranny of the Florentine government and the Medici. As Savonarola's preachings gained popular support, Lorenzo de' Medici, suffering the decline of health, was unable to successfully quell the Dominican's growing support. As Lorenzo lay dying, Savonarola absolved him of his sins. Two years later Charles VIII, King of France, invaded Italy and Florence, making Savonarola's prophecies appear to come true. The Medici were expelled from Florence and Savonarola introduced democratic government to the commune. Although Savonarola did not directly intervene in politics, his long-term goal after reforming Florence, was to use that as a springboard to do the same for Italy, Rome and the Church. Needless to say, such a sweeping agenda, regardless of its honest motivation, brought opposition, specifically in the form of a newly formed Florentine political party known as the *Arrabbiati* (The Angry Ones). The *Arrabbiati* quickly formed an alliance with Milan and the Pope. As Savonarola's relationship with Pope Alexander VI deteriorated, he was eventually excommunicated. To reinforce his position, he received symbolic tribute during the Lent of 1497 when citizens burned such personal vanities as jewelry, lewd pictures, and cards and gambling tables. A government controlled by the *Arrabbiati* stopped him from preaching and incited a riot against him on Ascension Day. Later that year Savonarola was burnt at the stake on a spot that is still marked in Florence's Piazza della Signoria.

The selections from Savonarola's writings presented here are from his *Rime* (Poems). Although well educated and extremely intelligent, one might say of Savonarola that he understood the Renaissance, but did not particularly like it. Even though he did intervene to save the Medici library from being dispersed, his ethos is nowhere more emblematic than in the repentant figure of his friend Botticelli who could no longer paint, having lost that creative spark somewhere on his way to church. This puritanism is evident in Savonarola's verse. Eschewing the usual refinement associated with Petrarchism, Savonarola developed clear, simple and forceful poems about the basic tenets of Christianity: sin, humanity's corruption and its need for redemption through Christ. In a very real sense, it is with him that the Renaissance of Medicean in Florence is over.

## Girolamo Savonarola

*De ruina mundi*

Se non che pur è vero e così credo,
rettor del mondo, che infinita sia
toa providenzia; né già mai potria
creder contra, perché ab experto el vedo;
talor serìa via più che neve fredo,
vedendo sottosopra volto el mondo
ed esser spenta al fondo
ogne virtute e ogne bel costume:
non trovo un vivo lume,
né pur chi de' soi vizi se vergogni;
chi te nega, chi dice che tu sogni.

Ma credo che ritardi, o Re superno,
a maggior pena de' soi gran difetti
on pur ch'è forsi appresso, e tu l'aspetti,
l'estremo dì che fa tremar l'inferno.
A noi virtù non tornarà in eterno:
quivi se estima chi è de Dio nemico;
Catone va mendico;
ne le man di pirata è gionto il scetro;
a terra va San Pietro;
quivi lussuria ed ogne preda abunda,
che non so come il ciel non si confunda.

Non vedi tu il satirico mattone
quanto è superbo ed è di vizi un fiume,
che di gran sdegno il cor mi se consume?
Deh! mira quel cinedo e quel lenone
di porpora vestito, un istrione
che 'l vulgo segue e il cieco mondo adora!
Non ti ven sdegno ancora
che quel lussurioso porco gode,
e le toe alte lode
usurpa, [ha] assentatori e parasciti,
e i toi di terra in terra son banditi?

# Girolamo Savonarola

*On the Ruin of the World*

But even it is true and I believe so,
Prior of the World, whose providence
is infinite, never could I believe
the contrary, for I see it from experience;
sometimes the serious path is colder than snow,
seeing the world turned upside down
and every virtue and all good behavior
extinguished in the depths:
I find no light alive,
not even those ashamed of their vices—
whoever denies it, I'd say you were dreaming.

But I believe that you delay, o Eternal King,
the major punishment of his great sinners
or even that it is perhaps near—and you wait—
the ultimate day that makes Hell tremble.
Virtue will never return to us:
at that time one will judge who is an enemy of God;
Cato wanders a poor man;
the scepter has reached the hands of a pirate;
St. Peter comes to earth;
at that moment luxury and every vice abound,
so I don't know how Heaven isn't confused.

Don't you see how the mocking bore
is a river of pride and vice,
that his heart consumes me with great wrath?
Alas! look at that pederast and that pimp
dressed in purple, a ham who
the vulgar follow and the world adores!
Doesn't wrath come to you
when such a luxurious pig enjoys
and then steals your high
praises—he has flatterers and parasites—
and yours followers are banished throughout the world?

Felice or mai chi vive di rapina,
e chi de l'altrui sangue più se pasce,
che vedoe spoglia e soi pupilli in fasce
e chi di porvi corre a la ruina!
Quella anima è gentil e peregrina,
che per fraude o per forza fa più acquisto.
Chi spreza il ciel cum Cristo
e sempre pensa altrui cacciar al fondo:
colui onora el mondo,
che ha pien di latrocinii libri e carte
e chi d'ogne mal far se meglio l'arte.
La terra è sì oppressa da ogne vizio,
che mai da sé non levarà la soma:
a terra se ne va il suo capo, Roma,
per mai più non tornar al grande offizio.
Oh! quanta doglia hai, Bruto, e tu, Farizio,
se hai intesa questa altra gran ruina!
Non basta Catilina,
non Silla, Mario, Cesaro o Nerone,
ma quivi òmini e done,
ogn'om si sforza dargli qualche guasto:
passato è il tempo pio e il tempo casto.

—Virtù mendica, mai non alzi l'ale—
grida il vulgo a la ciecca gente ria;
lusura si chiama or filosofia;
al far bene ogn'om volta pur le spale;
non è chi vada or mai per dritto cale:
tal che 'l valor se agiaza che me avanzia;
se non che una speranzia
pur al tutto nol lassa far partita,
ch'io scio che in l'altra vita
ben si vedrà qual alma fo gentil
e chi alziò l'ale a più legiadro stile.

Canzion, fa' che sia acorta,
che a purpureo color tu non te apogie;
fugi palazi e logie
e fa' che toa ragion a pochi dica,
ché a tuto el mondo tu serai nemica.

Happy forever one who now lives on robbery
and nourishes himself on the blood of others,
who marries widows with babies
and brings them to ruin!
That soul is gently noble and rare,
who by fraud or force does some shopping,
who scorns the Heavens with Christ
and always thinks others are chased into the depths;
he honors the world
who has his fill of larcenous books and cards,
and who knows how to do every vice better.

The earth is so oppressed by every vice
that it will never recover from their totality by itself:
its leader, Rome, disappears on earth,
never to return to its greatness.
Oh! You've has so much suffering Brutus, and you, Fabian,
if you intended this great ruin!
Not enough Catiline,
not Scylla, Marius, Cesare or Nero—
but here men and women,
every man strives to desolate them—
the pious and chaste time is passed.

"Begging virtue, may you never raise your wings,"
scream the rotten and blind vulgar masses;
Luxury now calls itself Philosophy;
every man turns his back on doing good;
successful people don't care about the law:
so that the courage is suiting that advances me;
otherwise a hope
doesn't even let me play the game with everyone—
for I know that in the next life
you'll see that I will be that gently noble soul
who raised his wings to that graceful style.

Canzone, see that you're alert,
that you don't rely on the purple;
avoid palaces and lodges,
and be sure your reason reaches few,
for you will be an enemy to the whole world.

*De ruina ecclesiae*

 —Vergene casta, ben indegno figlio,
pur son di membri de l'eterno Sposo:
però mi duol asai che l'amoroso
antiquo tempo e il dolce suo periglio
or mai sia perso, e non par più consiglio
che ristorar il possa on forsi ardisca;
l'ardente voce prisca
più non cognosce i Greci né ' Romani;
el lume de' primi ani
è ritornato in ciel cum la Regina
ed a noi, lasso me! più non se inchina.

 U' son, oimè! le gemme e i fin diamanti?
U' son le le lampe ardente e i bei xafiri?
O gran pietade, o lacrime, o sospiri!
U' son le bianche stole e i dolci canti?
U' son or mai le corna e gli occhi santi,
le zone d'oro e i candidi destrieri,
tri, quattro e cinque altieri,
e le grande ale, l'aquila e 'l leone?
A pena che 'l carbone
si trova caldo fra lo ignito incostro!
Mostratime, vi prego, il pianto vostro!—

 Così dissi io a la pia Madre antica
per gran desio ch'io ho di pianger sempre;
e Lei, che par che gli ochi mai non tempre,
col viso chino e l'anima pudica
la man mi prese ed a la soa mendica
spelonca mi condusse lacrimando;
e quivi disse: —Quando
io vidi Roma intrar quella superba,
che va tra' fiori e l'erba
securamente, mi ristrinsi alquanto
ove io conduco la mia vita in pianto.—

*On the Ruin of the Church*

    "Chaste Virgin, rather than an unworthy son,
I am of the limbs of the eternal Bridegroom:
but I grieve so much because that the loving
ancient time and the his sweet sacrifice
are now lost, and it doesn't appear that more counsel
could or would venture to restore it;
the burning urgent voice
no longer knows the Greeks and Romans;
the light of the early years
has returned to Heaven with the Queen
and no longer—weary me!—bows to us.

    "Where are—Alas!—the gems and fine diamonds?
Where are the burning splendors and beautiful sapphires?
Oh great mercy, oh tears, oh sighs!
Where are the white robes and sweet songs?
Where, by now, are the trumpets and the reverent glances,
the golden girdles and white horses,
three, four and five proud ones,
and the great wings, the eagle and the lion?
    One hardly finds hot coals
flaming among them!"
Show me, I beg you, your plan!—

    So I spoke to the pure ancient Mother
of the great desire I has to always cry;
and She—whose eyes appeared not to soften—
with head bowed and soul modest
took my hand and, crying, led
me to her humble cavern;
saying there, "When
I saw Rome become proud,
when she went confidently among the flowers
and fields, I shrunk to the point
where my life came to tears."

Poi: —Mira,—disse—figlio, crudeltade!—
E qui scoperse da far pianger sassi.
Iacinti ivi io non vidi o crisopassi,
né pur un vetro mondo. Oh! che pietade!
O Silla, o Mario! U' son le vostre spade?
Perché non sorge, dissi, Neron felo?
La terra, l'aria e 'l cielo
vendetta grida del suo sangue iusto:
el latte io vedo esuto
e lacerato in mille parte il petto,
fuor de l'umil suo primo santo aspetto.

Povra va con le membra discoperte,
i capei sparsi e rotte le girlande;
ape non trova, ma a le antique giande
avidamente, lasso! si converte.
Scorpio la punge e l'angue la perverte
e le locuste le radice afferra;
e così va per terra
la coronata e le soe sante mani,
biastemata da' cani,
che van truffando sabbati e calende.
Altri non pono e altri non intende.

Piangete or quatro sei canute crine,
quatro animali e sette tube sante;
or piangi, stabulario mio zelante,
piangete, sanguigne aque pelegrine;
o pietre vive, altissime e divine,
or pianga ogne pianeta ed ogne stella.
Se gionta è la novella
là su, dove è ciascun di voi felice,
ben credo (se dir lice)
che avete doglia assai di tanto guasto:
prostrato è il tempio e lo edificio casto.

Dopoi: —Madonna,—dissi—s'el ve piace,
di pianger con voi l'alma contenta.
Qual forza ve ha così del regno spenta?
Qual arrogante rompe vostra pace?
Rispose sospirando:  —Una fallace,
supeba meretrice, Babilona.—
E io: —Deh! per Dio, Dona,
se romper se potria quelle grande ale?—
E Lei: —Ligua mortale
non pò, né lice, non che mover l'arme.
Tu piangi e taci, e questo meglio parme.

Then: "Look," she said, "son—What cruelty!"
And here she learned how to weep stones
I saw there neither hyacinths nor chrysanthemums,
nor even a polished glass. "Oh, what a pity!!
Oh, Sulla—oh, Marius! Where are your swords?
Why don't you arise," she said, "wicked Nero?"
The earth, air and sky
scream revenge against your just blood:
I see your milk burnt
and your breast cut into a thousand pieces—
beyond the humility of your earlier saintly demeanor.

The poor one went with her limbs bare,
hair disheveled and virginity broken;
the bee doesn't look, but at the old flowers—
Alas!—is eagerly converted.
A scorpion stings her, the serpent corrupts her
and the locusts devour the roots;
and so goes the crowned one with
holy hands across the earth,
blasphemed by dogs,
who cheat on Sabbaths and the first day of each month.
I assert and mean nothing less.

Now cry four Fathers,
four animals and seven holy trumpets;
now cry, my zealous stable-boy,
cry, bloody pilgrim's water;
oh alive stones, most lofty and divine,
now cry every planet and every star.
If the news has arrived
there above—where everyone of you is happy—
I well believe (if to say there)
that you have enough suffering from so much hate:
the temple and chaste house is prostrate.

Afterwards: "My Lady," I said, "if you like,
I will cry with your soul.
What force is extinguished in your kingdom?
What arrogant soul disturbs your peace?"
She responded moaning: "A false,
proud prostitute, Babylon."
And I: "Alas! For God's sake, my Lady,
could we break those great wings?"
And she: "Mortal tongue,
I can't, not there, let alone raise an army.
You cry and keep silent—this seems better to me."

Canzione, io non fo stima
di scorpio ponto. Non pigliar impresa;
se non serai intesa,
forsi è meglio; sta' pur contenta al quia.
Dopoi che fa mestier che così sia.

Canzone, I can't estimate
the reach of the scorpion. Don't undertake the venture;
if you will not be understood.
Perhaps it's better; be happy with the reason.
After, make what you will of what happens.

*Ad Virginem*

Salve, Regina, virgo gloriosa,
ne la cui fronte el Sol soa luce prende,
Madre di Quel a cui l'onor si rende,
e del suo Padre dolce figlia e sposa;

nel ciel trionfo, lampa valorosa,
che al mondo e ne lo abisso ancor risplende,
alto valor, ch'el secol non comprende,
celeste orïental gemma preziosa;

Vergene, in me, deh! volgi i toi bei ochi,
    se mai a te fo grato quel primo Ave,
che dal ciel venne in questi bassi lochi;

non risguardar al mio fallir, ch'è grave:
la via mi mostra dove vanno i pochi,
ché del mio cor mai ti do la chiave.

*To the Virgin*

Hail, Queen, glorious Virgin,
from whose face the Sun takes its light,
Mother of That One to whom we pay homage,
and sweet daughter and bride of his Father;

in whose triumphant heaven, a powerful light
still shines in the world and down the abyss—
lofty power that the ages don't understand—
heavenly, precious Eastern gem;

Virgin, look inside me—Alas!—with your beautiful eyes,
if I ever make that first Ave to please you,
who came from heaven to these lowly places;

don't examine my sins, which are serious:
show me the road few have taken,
for now I ever give you the key to my heart.

# Leonardo da Vinci
# (1452–1519)

Artist, scientist, inventor, engineer, botanist, biologist, stage designer, theatrical producer and liberator of captive birds, Leonardo da Vinci was born in the Tuscan town of Vinci the illegitimate son of Ser Piero da Vinci, a notary and nobleman of minor rank, and a woman of whom little is known other than her name was Caterina. Young Leonardo received a grammar school education in the village ambiance of Vinci, passing most of the time with his paternal grandparents and some of his cousins. He spent less of his time with his father who was off attempting build a career in Florence and only a few occasions with his mother. As a child, Leonardo wandered the fields surrounding Vinci, possessing a keen eye for observing the physical features and interrelationships of all natural phenomena. Apprenticed at an early age to the bottega of the noted Florentine artist Andrea del Verrocchio (1435-1488), Leonardo eventually surpassed his master by gaining some amount of fame after painting one of the periphery angels in Verrocchio's *Baptism of Christ* (c.1470). One of the first people in history to dissect corpses and make reasonably correct anatomical drawings of the human body, Leonardo also pushed the Renaissance concept of painting to new limits. Among his pictorial innovations are such things as: 1. The creation of visual form, not by coloring in an outline, but by building up layer upon layer of glazes in order to construct the nuanced color, light and shading of an actual object and its three dimensional space. 2. The creation of tonal unity in a painting through the use of the new medium of oil painting by toning down brights such as yellow with a darker tone and bringing up darks such as blue with yellow and whites. 3. The creation of realistic action and movement in a painting by making one figure appear to flow, via implied lines, into another. 4. The use of sharp contrasts of light and shade (chiaroscuro) to heighten the effect of three-dimensionality in both figures and the space they inhabit. 5. The presention of the theme (istoria) in a non-stereotypical way, avoiding the formulaic in everything from the folds in the garments, to the positioning of hands and fingers, to the subtle relationship of all the parts in revealing the theme. 6. The invention of bold, striking compositions that immediately grasp the eye and never let go. All of this comes to fruition in his unfinished *Adoration of the Magi* (begun 1481), a work that contains all the pictorial implications for painting for the next two centuries, with its repoussoir figures, climactic movement in the groupings in the background and almost caricatured naturalism of the figures surrounding the Virgin.

Leonardo, proud of the fact that he was not formally schooled in Latin, the writers of Antiquity and such relatively recent poets Dante and Petrarch, described himself as "omo sanza lettere" ("a man without a literary education"). He felt that the litterati only wrote about what doers, such as he, actually went out and did. This is not to say that Leonardo was not a writer. He did make copious annotations on his hundreds of drawings and also planned, but never completed, treatises on several subjects. Although we possess only a few lines of poetry by Leonardo, his prose style, whether in his annotations or his planned manuscripts, was highly original. Using the Florentine dialect to its maximum resonance, he asked profound questions, expressed deep thoughts and made keen observations about a wide variety of subject matter. His prose, direct in description and vivid in detail, bears a marked resemblance to the economic English prose style associated with the incipient age of science and mature age of exploration in the later 16th century and beyond. However, there is one key difference. Few writers in any age possess the imagination revealed in the prose passages selected for this volume, an imagination that transforms any writing into pure poetry.

# Leonardo da Vinci

*Da Scritti scelti*

*Paura e desidèro*

Non fa sì gran muglia il tempestoso mare, quando il settantrionale aquilone lo ripercuote, colle schiumose onde fra Silla e Cariddi, né Stromboli o Mongibello quando le zolfuree fiamme, essendo rinchiuse, per forza rompendo e aprendo il gran monte, fulminando per l'aria pietra, terra, insiem coll'uscita e vomitata fiamma; né quando le 'nfocate caverne di Mongibello rendan il male tenuto elemento, rivomitandolo e spigniendolo all sua regione con furia, cacciando innanzi qualche ostacolo s'interpone all sua impetuosa furia.

E tirato dalla mia bramosa voglia, vago di vedere la gran copia delle varie e strane forme fatte dalla artifiziosa natura, raggiratomi alquanto infra gli ombrosi scogli, pervenni all'entrata d'una gran caverna, dinanzi alla quale, restato alquanto stupefatto e ignorante di tal cosa, piegato le mie reni in arco, e ferma la stanca mano sopra il ginocchio, e cola destra mi feci tenebre alle abbassate e chiuse ciglia, e spesso piegandomi in qua e in là per vedere dentro vi discernessi alcuna cosa, e questo vietatomi per la grande oscurità che là entro era. E stato alquanto, subito salsero in me due cose: paura e desidèro; paura per la minacciante e scura spilonca, desidèro per vedere se là entro fusse alcuna miracolosa cosa.

*Nessun ombra*

Il sole non vide mai nessuna ombra.

*Essenzia della luna*

La luna, densa e grave, densa e grave, come sta, la luna?

*Guarda il lume*

Guarda il lume e considera la sua bellezza. Batti l'occhio e riguardalo: ciò che di lui tu vedi prima non era e ciò che di lui era più non è.

Chi è quel che lo rifà se 'l fattore al continuo more?

# Leonardo da Vinci

*From the Selected Writings*

*Fear and Desire*

The stormy sea doesn't howl so much when the northern wind beats it back, with foaming waves between Silla and Cariddi, nor Stromboli or Mongibello when the sulphur flames—being closed—with force breaking and opening the great mountain, exploding stone and earth in the air, together with escaping and vomited flames—nor when the burning caverns of Mongibello emit the poorly kept element, revomiting and spewing it with fury all around, pushing overwhelming any obstacle in the way of its vehement fury.

Then pulled by my eager will, I wander to see the great number of various and strange forms made by creative nature, enticing me somewhat into the dark rocks, having reached the entrance of a great cavern, in front of which, standing somewhat stupefied and ignorant of such a thing, bending forward—one hand on my knee, the right one covering my eyes—often bending forward here and there to see if I can discern something—with the great darkness inside hindering me. Then, frozen a little, two things suddenly rose up in me: fear and desire—fear of the threatening and dark cave—desire to see if some miraculous thing was there inside.

*No Shade*

The sun never sees any shade.

*Essence of the Moon*

The moon, dense and solemn, dense and solemn, how does it endure, the moon?

*Look at the Light*

Look at the light and consider its beauty. Blink your eye and look again: what you first see of it wasn't—and that of it that was is no more.

Who is it who restores it if the maker of the continuity dies?

## Mischie di pioggia e di venti

Vedesi l'aria tinta d'oscura nuvolosità nelli apparecchi delle procelle overo fortune del mare (le quali sono mischie di pioggia e di venti),con serpeggiamenti delli tortuosi corsi delle minaccianti folgori celesti, e le piante piegate a terra co' le aroversiate foglie sopra li declinanti rami, le quali pare voler fuggire dalli loro siti, come spaventate dalle percussioni delli orribili e spaventosi voli de' venti, fra li quali s'infonde li revertiginosi corsi della turbulenta polvere e arena delli liti marini; l'oscuro del cielo si fa campo di fumolenti nuvoli, li quali percossi dalli solari razzi, pentrati per le opposite rotture de' nuvoli, percotano la terra....

## L'isola di Cipro

Dalli meridionali lidi di Cilizia si vede per australe la bell'isola di Cipri, la qual fu regnio della dea Venere, e molti, incitati dalla sua bellezza, hanno rotte lor navili e sarte infra li scogli....Oh! quante navi quivi già son sommerse! quanti navi rotti negli scogli! Quivi si potrebbero vedere innumerabili navili, chi è rotto e mezzo coperto dall'arena, chi si mostra da poppa e chi da prua, chi da carena e chi da costa,—e parrà a similitudine d'un Giudizio che voglia risuscitare navili morti, tant'è la somma di quelli che copre tutto il lito settentrionale. Quivi i venti d'aquilone, resonando, fan varî e paurosi soniti.

## Signoria

Dov'è libertà non è regola.

## La vita

Quando io credevo imparare a vivere, e io imparerò a morire.

## Rigore

Dov'è più sentimento lì è più, ne' martiri, gran martiri.

Il voto nasce quando la speranza more.

## Così il tempo presente

L'acqua che tocchi de' fiumi è l'ultima di quella che andò, e la prima di quella che viene: così il tempo presente.

## The Struggle between the Rain and Wind

You see the air tinted with dark clouds in the array of storms or else storms of the sea (which is a struggle between the rain and the wind), with meanders of winding runs of threatening celestial thunderbolts—and the plants bent to the ground with turned over leaves above the lowered branches, which themselves appear to want to flee from their lodgings, as if terrorized by the blows of the horrible and frightening gusts of wind, within which the whirling gusts of turbulent dust and ocean sand infuse themselves—the darkness of the sky becomes a battleground of smoldering clouds, which are stricken by the solar rays, penetrated by the contrary rupture of clouds, striking the earth....

## The Island of Cyprus

Looking south from the southern shores of Cilicia you see the beautiful island of Cyprus, which was the realm of the goddess Venus, and many, provoked by her beauty, wrecked their ships and shrouds on its reefs....Oh! how many ships have already sunk here! How many ships broken on the rocks! Here you might see innumerable ships, broken and half covered by the sand, prows and decks sticking out, keels and ribs—it seems similar to a Judgment that wants to revive dead ships, such is the number that cover the entire northern coast. Here monsoon winds, echoing, make various frightful sounds.

## Power

Where there is liberty, there is no rule.

## Life

When I think I've learned to live, then I will learn to die.

## Severity

Where strong feeling is even stronger—in suffering, great suffering.

Emptiness is born when hope dies.

## And So the Present Time

The water that moves upon the rivers is the last of what went and the first of what comes: and so the present time.

# Raffaello Sanzio
## (1483–1520)

Leonardo, Michelangelo and Raphael were considered by their contemporaries as the culmination of perfection in the visual arts. Contemporary accounts labeled Leonardo as the marvelous, Michelangelo as the divine and Raphael as the princely. Raphael was born in Urbino to Giovanni Sanzio, a painter of minor importance, and Magia di Battista di Nicola Ciarla. Although a small city, Urbino had developed a first rate artistic culture under its ruler Duke Federigo da Montefeltro. Piero della Francesco painted there in the 1460s and 1470s. The noted architect Donato Bramante came from Urbino, as did the famous humanist Baldassare Castiglione, author of *The Book of Courtier*. Raphael's mother died in 1491 and his father in 1494. Although the earliest works from his Florentine period date from 1504, there is evidence to suggest that he may have become a part of Pietro Perugino's Florentine workshop soon after his father's death. Whatever the case may be, Raphael demonstrated time after time in his brief life that he was capable of absorbing and transforming the latest developments in painting into his own original expressions. If Leonardo's painting was an investigation of the natural world and Michelangelo's art was an exploration of the expressive possibilities of the human form, Raphael's was a search for new ways create human narratives in three-dimensional space. From his numerous themes and variations on the Madonna and Child and Holy Family subjects to his masterful fresco cycles in the Vatican, Raphael imbued his figures with nuances of personality that require reinvestigation time and time again.

Raphael's literary output was rather meager. Depending on the viewpoint, he wrote either five or six sonnets. None of these sonnets is in polished form. Of the first five, four of them appear on folios containing drawings for *The Disputation of the Sacrament*, one of the frescoes in the Stanza della Segnatura, his first Vatican fresco cycle (1509-1511). The sixth, which many consider apocryphal, supposedly contains a drawing of his girlfriend, the so-called Fornarina, or Baker's Daughter. One can judge these sonnets in two plausible ways. On the one hand, it is clear that Raphael possessed the intelligence and wit to absorb and participate, in a somewhat abbreviated way, in the sophisticated literary culture of Julius II's pontificate. In particular, the Petrarchan theme of questing for an ideal love intellectually melds with the themes of the Segnatura cycle, with its respective frescos about the ideals of secular knowledge, divine revelation, artistic and poetic creativity, and justice. On the other hand, Raphael, whose only formal education was grammar school, attempted something that many literate Italians were capable of doing during the Cinquecento, which was to write a few highly derivative Petrarchan sonnets.

## Raffaello Sanzio

I

Amor, tu m'envesscasti con doi lumi
de doi beli ochi dov'io me strugo e [s]face,
da bianca neve e da rosa vivace,
da un bel parlar in donnessi costumi.

Tal che tanto ardo, ch[e] nè mar nè fiumi
spagnar potrian quel focho, ma non mi spiace,
poichè 'l mio ardor di ben mi face,
c'ardendo onior più d'arder me consu[mi].

Quanto fu doce el giogo e la catena
de toi candidi braci al col mio vol[ti].
che sogliendomi io sento mortal pen[a].

D'altre cose in non dicho, che fôr m[olti],
ché soperchia docenza a mo[r]te men[a],
e però tacio, a te i pensi[e]r rivolti.


II

Como non podde dir d'arcana dei
Paul, como disceso fu dal celo,
così el mio cor d'uno amoroso velo
a ricoperto tuti i penser mei.

Però quanto ch'io viddi e quanto Io fei
pel gaudio Taccio, che nel petto celo,
ma prima cangerò nel fronte el pelo,
che mai l'obligo volga in pensi[e]r rei.

E se quello altero almo basso cede,
vedrai che non fia a me, ma al mio gran focho,
qual più che gli altri in la ferventia esciede.

Ma pensa ch'el mio spirito a pocho a p[o]hho
el corpo lasarà, se tua mercede
socorso non li dia a tempo e locho.

# Raffaello Sanzio

I

Love, you clothed me with the light
of your beautiful eyes where I melt and dissolve
from the white snow and bright roses,
from a beautiful song in a woman's manner.

So do I burn that neither sea nor rivers
could quench that fire—not that I dislike it—
since my passion suits me,
forever burning brighter the more it consumes me.

How sweet was that yoke and chain
of your white arms around my neck,
raising me to feel mortal pain.

Of other things I do not speak, beyond the multitude,
for it surpasses sweetness in leading me to death—
however, I remain silent, my thoughts returning to you.

II

As Paul couldn't speak of God's mystery,
how it descended from Heaven,
so has my heart covered my
thoughts with an amorous veil.

However, no matter how much I saw and I much I did,
I keep quiet from the joy that I hide in my chest—
so first I will change my nature
that turns duty into wicked thoughts.

And if that proud soul yields to the lower,
you will see that it is not due to me, but to my great fire
that—more than the others—bursts with great passion.

But imagine that my spirit gradually
leaves my body, if your mercy
will not give it a time and a place for aid.

III

Un pensier dolce è rimembra[r]se in modo
di quello asalto, ma più gravo è il danno
del partir, ch'io restai como quei c'ano
in mar perso la stella, se 'l ver odo.

Or, lingua, di parlar disogli el nodo
a dir di questo inusitato ingano
ch'amor mi fece per mio gravo afanno,
ma lui pur (?) ne ringratio e lei ne lodo.

L'ora sesta era, che l'ocaso un sole
aveva fatto, e l'altro surse in locho
ati più da far fati che parole.

Ma io restai pur vinto al (?) mio gran focho
che mi tormenta, ché dove l'on sole
disiar di parlar, più riman fiocho.

III

A sweet thought calls to mind the manner
of that attack, but more serious is the damage
from parting—so I remained as one who's
lost his star at sea, if I remember correctly.

Now, my tongue, loosen the knot
to speak of the uncommon ploy
love used to cause me great anguish—
still, for it I thank him and praise her.

It was six o'clock when the western sun
set and the other raised in its place
actions that did more deeds than words.

But still, I am defeated by the great fire
that torments me, because when a man is used
to speaking of desire, the more mute he becomes.

# Michelangelo Buonarotti
## (1475–1564)

If any one figure typified the Renaissance in all its moral complexity, that figure was Michelangelo. On the one hand, devoutly Christian – on the other, egotistic, needing gratification by single-handedly completing large public projects. A soul that often sought the quiet of meditative solitude – by contrast, a personality capable of expressing anger and rage in an unbridled way. Above all, one aware of the contradiction between the celestial aspirations of the soul and the worldly desires of the body.

Michelangelo Buonarroti was born to Ludovico and Francesca Buonarroti in Caprese, a small town near Arezzo. Soon after his birth, his family moved back to Florence, living near Santa Croce. Michelangelo was the second of five sons that Francesca would bear before she would die when Michelangelo was six. Although previous generations of the Buonarroti family had been successful as moneylenders, Michelangelo's was not, with his grandfather losing money at the family business. Ludovico did not improve the family's financial situation, either not wanting or understanding how to work. Even though he would come to write beautiful poetry in an exquisite hand, Michelangelo had a nominal education. He was sent to grammar school at ten, under his father's wish that he have a literary career. Michelangelo, however, had different ideas, wanting to be an artist. Surviving a round of paternal beatings, Michelangelo got his way and was apprenticed at thirteen to Domenico Ghirlandaio's studio. By 1489 he was regularly studying the Medici collection of ancient sculpture kept in a house and garden near San Marco. Michelangelo was noticed and then regularly instructed by the collection's curator, Bertoldo di Giovanni, an aging pupil of Donatello. Soon after, Lorenzo de' Medici took him into his household, affording the budding sculptor all the cultural advantages the Medici circle had to offer.

Needless to say, Michelangelo proceeded to have a wonderful career as an artist. In addition, he wrote a large number of occasional poems, most of them sonnets. Among his verse was a book of poetry that was never published. If Michelangelo's verse can be summarized in a few brief observations, perhaps the central element to understanding his verse is not its apparent Petrarchism, but its underlying Neoplatonism. Especially crucial for Michelangelo is the concept of wanting to reunite with God and feeling extreme angst over the fact that such a reunion cannot be immediately realized since the soul is trapped within the body.

# Michelangelo Buonaroti

### 1

Davide colla fromba
e io coll'arco.

Michelangolo.

Rott'è l'alta colonna.


### 2

Colui che 'l tutto fe', fece ogni parte
e poi del tutto la più bella scelse,
per mostrar quivi le sue cose eccelse,
com'ha fatto or colla sua divin'arte.


### 3

El Dì e la Notte parlano e dicono:
—Noi abbiam col nostro veloce corso condotto alla morte
    el duca Giuliano;
è ben giusto, che e' ne faccia vendetta come fa.
E la vendetta è questa:
che, avendo noi morto lui,
    lui così morto ha tolta la luce a noi, e cogli occhi chiusi ha
serrato e' nostri, che non risplendon più sopra la terra.
Che avrebbe di noi, dunque, fatto, mentre vivea?—


### 4

Dentr'a me giunge al cor, già fatto tale.


### 5

D'un oggetto leggiadro e pellegrino,
d'un fonte di pietà nasce 'l mio male.

# Michelangelo Buonaroti

1

David with his sling
and I with my bow.

Michelangelo.

The high column is broken.

2

He who made everything, made every part
and then chose the most beautiful of all
to show here his sublime things,
how he's now composed with his divine art.

3

Day and Night speak and say:
"With our swift course, we have led Duke
Giuliano to death—
and rightly so, for he would've made a vendetta of it as he does.
And the vendetta is this:
that, we having killed him,
he, even dead, took the light from us and with closed eyes
sealed ours, so they no longer shines on the earth.
What, then, would he have done with us while he lived?

4

It reaches inside to my heart, already finishing such.

5

From an elegant and exquisite object,
from a source of mercy my trouble is born.

6

Sol io, ardendo, all'ombra mi rimango,
quand'el sol de suo' raggi el mondo spoglia;
ogni altro per piacere, e io per doglia,
prostrato in terra, mi lamento e piango.


7

Ogn'ira, ogni miseria e ogni forza
chi d'amor s'arma vince, ogni fortuna.


8

Che mal si può amar ben chi non si vede.


9

Non posso or non veder dentr'a chi muore
tua luce eterna senza gran desio.


10

Spirito ben nato, in cu' si specchia e vede
nelle tue belle membra oneste e care
quanto natura e 'l ciel tra no' può fare,
quand'a null'altra suo bell'opra cede:

spirito leggiadro, in cu' si spera e crede
dentro, come di fuor nel viso appare,
amor, pietà, mercé, cose sì rare,
che ma' furn' in beltà con tanta fede:

l'amor mi prende e beltà mi lega;
la pietà, la mercé con dolci sguardi
ferma speranz'al cor par che ne doni.

Qual uso o qual governo al mondo nega,
qual crudeltà per tempo o qual più tardi,
ch'a sì bell'opra morte non perdoni?

6

Only I, burning, remain in the shade,
when the world strips the sun of its rays—
every other for pleasure and I in suffering,
prostrate on the ground, I moan and cry.

7

Every wrath, every misery, every force—
whoever arms themself with love overcomes—even every fortune.

8

What evil you can love if you don't see.

9

Now I can't not see inside someone who dies
your eternal light without great desire.

10

Well born spirit on whom we model ourselves and
see in your honest and dear members
how much nature and heaven can do among us,
when its beautiful work cedes to no other:

beautiful spirit in whom we hope and believe
that inside—as appears outside on your face—
love, pity, mercy, things so rare,
that never were they in beauty with such faith:

love takes me and beauty binds me—
with sweet glances, pity, mercy
appear to give solid hope to my heart.

What custom, what government, what cruelty
or what else delays the time
that death doesn't save such a beautiful work?

11

In me la morte, in te la vita mia.
Tu distingui e concedi e parti el tempo;
quanto vuo', breve e lungo è 'l viver mio.

Felice son nella tua cortesia.
Beata l'alma, ove non corre tempo,
per te s'è fatta a contemplare Dio.


12

Non posso altra figura immaginarmi
o di nud'ombra o di terrestre spoglia,
col più alto pensier, tal che mia voglia
contra la tua beltà di quella s'armi.

Che da te mosse, tanto scender parmi,
ch'amor d'ogni valor mi priva e spoglia,
ond'a pensar di minuir mia doglia
duplicando la morte viene a darmi.

Però non val che più sproni mia fuga,
doppiando 'l corso alla beltà nemica,
ché 'l men dal più veloce non si scosta.

Amor con le sue man gli occhi m'asciuga,
promettendomi cara ogni fatica;
ché vile esser non può chi tanto costa.


13

O notte, o dolce tempo, benché nero,
con pace ogn' opra sempr'al fin assalta;
ben vede e ben intende chi t'esalta,
e chi t'onora, ha l'intelletto intero.

Tu mozzi e tronchi ogni stanco pensiero
che l'umida ombra e ogni quiete appalta;
e dall'infima parte alla più alta
in sogno spesso porti, ov'ire spero.

11

In me death, in you my life.
You distinguish, concede and leave time—
as you want, the brevity or length of my life.

Happy am I in your courtesy.
Blessed soul, where time no longer runs,
For you are made to contemplate God.


12

I can't imagine another figure
or nude shade or earthly body,
with loftier thought, such that my desire
could arm itself with it against your beauty.

That removed from you, appeared to me so much descent,
that love deprives and strips me of all power,
whence thinking of lowering my suffering,
doubling itself, it brings me death.

However, more won't help me escape,
doubling the race to my enemy beauty,
for the slower can't escape the faster.

Love dries my eyes with his hands,
promising me dear every hardship—
for something costing so much can't be vile.


13

O night! O sweet time!! Although dark,
with peace you assault every work to the end.
Who exalts you sees and knows well,
for whoever honors you has a complete mind.

You cut off every tired thought
that beckons your dense darkness and total quiet—
and from the lowest to highest place
you carry the constant dream of where I hope to go.

O ombra del morir, per cui si ferma
ogni miseria, a l'alma, al cor nemica,
ultimo degli afflitti e buon rimedio;

tu rendi sana nostra carne inferma,
rasciughi i pianti, e posi ogni fatica,
e furi a chi ben vive ogni ira e tedio.

14

Sol d'una pietra viva
l'arte vuol che qui viva
al par degli anni il volto di costei;
che dovria il ciel di lei,
sendo mia questa, e quella sua fattura,
non già mortal, ma diva,
non solo agli occhi miei?
E pur si parte e picciol tempo dura.
Da lato destro è zoppa sua ventura,
s'un sasso resta e pur lei morte affretta.
Chi ne farà vendetta?
Natura sol, se de' suo' nati sola
l'opra qui dura, e la sua 'l tempo invola.

15

Per ritornar là, donde venne fora
l'immortal forma al tuo carcer terreno
venne com'angel, di pietà si pieno,
che sana ogn'intelletto e 'l mondo onora.

Questo sol m'arde e questo m'innamora,
non pur di fuora il tuo volto sereno:
ch'amor non già di cosa, che vien meno.
Tien ferma speme, in cui virtù dimora.

Né altro avvien di cose altere e nove,
in cui si preme la natura; e'l cielo
è, ch'a lor parto, largo s'apparecchia.

Né Dio, sua grazia, mi si mostra altrove
più che 'n alcun leggiadro e mortal velo;
e quel sol, amo perch'in lui si specchia.

O darkness of death! For which every
misery stops, enemy to my heart and soul,
last of the sicknesses and cures—

you heal our sick flesh,
dry our tears, ease every strain and
take away every anger and tedium from who lives well.


## 14

Only from a live stone,
art wants her face
that lives forever—
What should Heaven do with her,
this being mine, that his making,
no longer mortal, but divine—
not only to my eyes?
And even it crumbles, lasting little time.
From the right side his work is defective,
if a stone remains and death hurries to her.
Who will make amends?
Only nature, if from her offspring alone
does the work live on and rob time.


## 15

To return there from whence comes
immortal form to its earthly prison,
she came like an angel, so full of mercy
that heals every mind and the world esteems.

This alone inflames me and this captivates me,
not only the appearance of her serene face:
for love is certainly not of things that fade away.
It holds strong hope in which virtue lives.

Nor do other things happen, lofty and new,
which nature impels—and Heaven,
for its offspring, generously provides.

Nor does God, his grace, show me anything
more than in this graceful and mortal covering—
and that alone I love, for in it he is mirrored.

16

Giunto è già 'l corso della vita mia
con tempestoso mar, per fragil barca
al comun porto, ov'a render si varca
conto e ragion d'ogni opra trista e pia.

Onde l'affettüosa fantasia,
che l'arte mi fece idolo e monarca,
conosco or ben com'era d'error carca,
e quel ch'a mal suo grado ogni uom desia.

Gli amorosi pensier, già vani e lieti,
che fian or, s'a due morti m'avvicino?
D'una so 'l certo, e l'altra mi minaccia.

Né pinger né scolpir fia più che quieti
l'anima volta a quell'amor divino,
ch'aperse a prender noi 'n croce le braccia.


17

...o e stanco anelo
...o el tempo rio
...luce al gioir mio
...in tenebre e gelo

...ombra discaccia
...e l'altra penna
...ter no porta

...el ciel conforta.

16

Already past is the course of my life,
with stormy seas in a fragile boat
to everyone's port, where one crosses over
to account for every good and evil act.

Whence the artificial fantasy
that my art made its idol and king,
I well know now how it was loaded with error,
and that which every man desires, to his ill.

Amorous thoughts, vain and happy,
now become what while I near two deaths?
Of one I know for sure and the other threatens me.

Neither painting nor sculpture can quiet
the soul turned toward divine love,
that opens its arms in a cross to take us.

17

...o then the link tires
....o then time ruins
....light to my joy
....in darkness and cold

....darkness dismisses
....and the other suffers
....eternity endures

....Heaven comforts

# Pietro Bembo
## (1470–1547)

Pietro Bembo, humanist and cardinal, was born in Venice. His father, Bernardo Bembo, a powerful man in the Venetian Republic, educated him, introducing him to Lorenzo de' Medici's Florence. Pietro went to Rome with Giulio de' Medici and became the papal secretary to Giulio's cousin Giovanni, when Giovanni became Pope Leo X. After Leo's death in 1521, Pietro retired to Padua. In 1529 he became Venice's historiographer and soon after became the librarian of St. Mark's. In 1539 he was appointed cardinal, going to Rome where he steeped himself in theology and classical history. For his service he received both Bergamo and Gubbio as bishoprics. Bembo died in Rome.

Bembo had an interesting literary career. His Latin letters as papal secretary were, and still are, considered models of Ciceronian Latin, with their blend of precision and eloquence. He also wrote a history of Venice from 1487 to 1539. Among his numerous dialogues in Italian, his *Gli asolani* from 1505 discusses the virtue of Platonic love. In 1525 he wrote *Prose della volgar lingua* (Prose in the Vernaculars), which defends regional dialects as opposed to what had become the literary vernacular of Italy, the Florentine dialect. Selections from his work in this volume are from his *Rime*, which Bembo modeled after Petrarch, who he considered, along with Cicero, a master of a perfect style. Although any general reader could be moved by Bembo's renderings of poetic solitude, the caveat on Petrarchism earlier in this volume should give one pause, as originality in the arts was a central Renaissance idea.

## Pietro Bembo

1
Viva mia neve e caro e dolce foco,
vedete com'io agghiaccio e com'io avampo,
mentre, qual cera, ad or ad or mi stampo
del vostro segno, e voi di ciò cal poco.

Se gite disdegnosa, tremo e loco
non trovo che m'asconda, e non ho scampo
dal gelo interno; se benigno lampo
degli occhi vostri ha seco pace e gioco,

surge la speme, e per le vene un caldo
mi corre al cor e sì forte l'infiamma,
come s'ei fosse pur di solfo e d'esca.

Né per questi contrarî una sol dramma
scema del penser mio tenace e saldo,
c'ha ben poi tanto, onde s'avanzi e cresca.


2
Già vago, or sovr'ogni altro orrido colle,
Poi che 'l bel viso, in cui volse mostrarsi
Quanto ben qui fra noi potea trovarsi,
Luce ad altro paese, a te si tolle;

Dura quell'acqua e questa selce molle
Fia, prima ch'io non senta al cor girarsi
La memoria del dì, quando alsi et arsi
Nel bel soggiorno tuo, come 'l ciel volle.

Por si pò ben nemica e dura sorte
Fra noi talora e 'l nostro vital lume,
Romper no a l'alma il pensier vivo e forte;

Che, speri o tema o goda o si consume,
Torna sempre a quel giorno, e le sue scorte
Sono due stelle e gran desio le piume.

## Pietro Bembo

1

My deep snow and sweet, dear fire,
you see how I freeze and how I burn
while—that face—I now imprint myself
with your sign...and you care little.

If you wander angry, I shiver and don't
find a place to hide...and I don't find refuge
from that inner cold—for, if that benign flash
from your eyes brings peace and happiness,

hope rises and a warmth runs
in my veins to my heart and strongly inflames it,
as if it were even of sulphur and tinder.

Nor by these opposites does a single dram
of my tenacious and solid thought lessen,
for it has so much, whence it overflows and grows.


2

Now I wander over rugged hills,
since the open visage, with which he showed
how much good there was between us,
took its light to you in another land—

hard that water making this stone weak,
even before I felt my heart reveal
the memory of the day when I awoke and burned
in your beautiful presence like the heavens wanted—

sometimes one can plant a strong enemy and hard luck
between us and our vital light,
unable to break my soul's live and strong thought

that—may it hope or fear or enjoy or waste away—
returns to that day when its escorts
are two stars and great desire its prize.

3

Ov'è mia bella e cara e fida scorta,
l'usata tua pietà, che sol mi lassi
al camin duro, ai perigliosi passi,
da me cotanto dilungata e torta?

Vedi l'alma, che trema e si sconforta
per lo tuo dipartire, e 'n prova stassi,
d'abandonarmi e sfida i membri lassi,
    per seguir te, qual viva, or così morta.

Ben le dice mio cor: —Chi t'assecura?
E forse a lei sua pace turberai,
che di nostra salute in cielo ha cura.—

Ella: —Che fo più qui? —risonde— mai
sostengo tale e ben tanto e ventura
perdé null'altra, e tu misero il sai.

3
Where is—my beautiful and dear and faithful escort—
your usual mercy that left me alone
on that hard road, on those dangerous passages,
so removed and twisted from me?

You see the soul—that trembles and suffers
over your parting and continues to look
by abandoning me and defying weary bones
in order to follow you—that lives, now dead.

My heart sharply asks it: "Who gives you courage?
Then perhaps you will disturb her peace,
she who cares for our health in heaven."

My soul asks: "What more can I do here?" The heart responds,
"Never will I defend such, I will lose
no other venture—and you, wretch, know it."

# Barbara Torelli
# (1475–1533)

Born in Ferrara in 1475, Barbara Torelli was the daughter of Marsiglio Count of Montechiarugolo. In 1491, she married Ercole Bentivoglio, who she subsequently left, after having fallen in love with Ercole Strozzi, a poet of elegant Latin elegies. She married Strozzi in 1508 and, tragically, he was assassinated. There is evidence to suggest one of three possibilities as to why: under the orders of Alfonso d'Este who was jealous of him; at the charge of Galeazzo Sforza of Pesaro; or, as a vendetta by her first husband. Barbara died in Bologna in 1533. *Spenta è Amor la face* is a sonnet that sincerely and beautifully laments Strozzi's death.

## Barbara Torelli

Spenta è d'Amor la face, il dardo è rotto,
e l'arco e la faretra e ogni sua possa,
poin che ha Morte credel la pianta scossa,
a la cui ombra cheta io dormia sotto.

Deh, perché non poss'io la breve fossa
seco entrar, dove l' ha il destin condotto,
colui che appena cinque giorni e otto
Amor Legò pria de la gran percossa?

Vorrei col foco mio quel freddo ghiaccio
intepidire, e rimpastar col pianto
la polve, e ravvivarla a nuova vita:

e vorrei poscia, baldanzosa e ardita,
    mostrarlo a lui, che ruppe il caro laccio,
e dirgli: —Amor, mostro crudel, può tanto!

## Barbara Torelli

Love's torch is dead, his dart broken,
as are his bow, quiver, and every other power,
since cruel Death has shaken the plant
under whose quiet shadow I used to sleep.

Alas, why can't I enter the shallow
grave with him, where destiny has taken him,
he who thirteen days ago
was bound by love just before the fateful blow?

I would like to warm that ice with my great
fire, reform his dust with
tears and create a new life:

and after I'd like, boldly and openly,
to show him to the one who set the dear snare,
telling him, "Love, you cruel monster, can overcome!"

# Ludovico Ariosto
## (1474–1533)

Ludovico Ariosto, the first of ten children, was born September 18, 1474 in Reggio Emilia to Daria Malaguzzi and Count Niccolò Ariosto. His father was Governor, with the title Capitano della Rocca, of the city of Reggio under the Este family. In 1484 his father, again under the Este, was charged with administering Ferrara. Early on, Ludovico showed an interest in literature, but was, at the behest of his family and its political position, pushed to study law. His father finally relented and young Ludovico began composing poems in Latin and Italian. In 1500, his father died and Ludovico had to care for his mother and 9 siblings. From 1500-03, he served the Este as Governor of Canossa. After 1503, he serves Cardinal Ippolito d'Este, the brother of Duke Alfonso, ruler of Ferrara. In addition, he takes minor religious orders in order to receive ecclesiastical benefices. Not particularly happy with his charges by the Cardinal, some of which entailed extensive travel and diplomatic work, Ludovico, nonetheless, continued to support his family and write. A multitalented individual in statecraft, politics, literature and family care, Ariosto clearly thought for himself and had a very accurate picture of the state of affairs for an individual with talent but limited power when he wrote:

> Pazzo chi al suo signor contradir vole,
> se ben dicesse c'ha veduto il giorno
> pieno di stelle e a mezzanotte il sole.
> *Satire*, I, 10-12

As Ferrarese envoy to Leo X's curia in 1513, Ludovico garned praise for his writing from the Pope. After refusing to follow the Cardinal to his new appointment as Bishop of Buda in Hungary in 1517, Arisoto served Duke Alfonso, who, at least initially, allowed him time to write. In 1522, Ludovico accepted the difficult task of governing Garfagnana. Far from home and his poetic interests, he was an able and honest man who governed fairly. Interestingly, in 1513, when in Florence after returning from Rome he met and fell in love with Alessandra Benucci, herself married to a gentleman from Ferrara, who died two years later. They married in 1527, keeping it a secret so she would not lose her inheritance from her late husband to her children. Ariosto was given the title poet laureate by Emperor Charles V in 1533.

Ariosto began his *Orlando furioso* in 1505, publishing it in Ferrara on April 21, 1516, with a dedication to Cardinal Ippolito. He issued a corrected and expanded 2nd edition in 1532, in which, Ludovico sided with Bembo and the Tuscan purists by eliminating elements of the Emilian and other dialects in favor of a purified Tuscan. Between 1517 and 1531, Ludovico wrote in *terza rima* seven *Satire* that give us an indication of his life, thoughts and Cinquecentesque human condition. He also wrote comedies for the stage.

The *Orlando furioso* – a genuine adventure, fantasy and insight into human nature – is a masterpiece of Renaissance literature and, with doubt, ranks Ludovico along side, if not above, Dante. In part, in the tradition of the French chanson de geste, and in part, the completion of the unfinished story by Boiardo, the *Orlando innamorato*, Ariosto's epic towers above the rest of Cinquecento poetry. In his epic, Ariosto intertwines three main themes: 1. The siege of Paris by the Saracens, a theme taken from Boiardo. 2. The love of Orlando for Angelica, princess of the eastern realm of Catai. 3. The love between Bradamante, sister of Rinaldo, and Ruggiero, the head of the Este family. As Enrico Galavotti writes, we can see these three themes, respectively, as epic, with the war between Christian and Moslems; erotic, with Orlando's passion for Angelica; and, encomiastic, as the founding of the House of Este by Bradamante and Ruggiero. Even though themes from the story relate to such classics as *The Iliad* and *The Aeneid* – with the central theme, beginning in the middle of the poem, of Orlando's madness owing to the wrath of Achilles in Homer's *Iliad* – the poem is fully original, one that comes down heavily on the *invenzione* side of the *invenzione/imitazione* duality.

Ariosto's narrative and poetic techniques, which could reasonably be seen as an embodiment of the the seemingly complex courtly (or pseudo-courtly) aesthetic of Mannerism, are, if taken from point of view of the "systems theory" of Stephen Wolfram's *A New Kind of Science*, deceptively simple. Ariosto starts with one of his three themes, then changes to another of them as soon as he emotionally and dramatically hooks the reader. As he develops each theme, he imaginatively uses plot twists and characters who are, indeed, genuine surprises. All this is told in a Tuscanized Italian that is poetic in sound, in the visual impressions it generates and in the conceptual linguistic periods it embraces. Although exclusively using the by then well-known octavo with its *ababab cc* rhyme scheme throughout the forty-six cantos of his poem, Ariosto is subtle, never allowing his rhyme to dominate the poetic image at hand. This is the stuff of Ruth at bat for the Bronx Bombers or Feynman pondering quantum electrodynamics

The selected passages in this tome deal with a part of the story of Bradamante's love for Ruggiero. Bradamante is wonderfully strong female character, one who calls to mind the Caryatids on the south porch of the Erectheum on the Acropolis or Sophocles' *Antigone*, while anticipating Cervantes' Micaela in *Don Quixote* or contextualizing such popular contemporary TV heroines as *Xena, Warrior Princess* or *Buffy the Vampire Slayer*.

# Orlando furioso

*Canto 1*

60
Ecco pel bosco un cavallier venire,
il cui sembiante è d'uom gagliardo e fiero:
candido come nieve è il suo vestire,
un bianco pennoncello ha per cimiero.
Re Sacripante, che non può patire
che quel con l'importuno suo sentiero
gli abbia interrotto il gran piacer ch'avea,
con vista il guarda disdegnosa e rea.

61
Come è più appresso, lo sfida a battaglia;
che crede ben fargli votar l'arcione.
Quel che di lui non stimo già che vaglia
un grano meno, e ne fa paragone,
l'orgogliose minacce a mezzo taglia,
prona a un tempo, e la lancia in resta pone.
Sacripante ritorna con tempesta,
e corronsi a ferir testa per testa.

62
Non si vanno i leoni o i tori in salto
a dar di petto, ad accozzar sì crudi,
sì come i duo guerrieri al fiero assalto,
che parimente si passar li scudi.
Fe' lo scontro tremar dal basso all'alto
l'erbose valli insino ai poggi ignudi;
e ben giovò che fur buoni e perfetti
gli osberghi sì, che lor salvaro i petti.

63
Già non fero i cavalli un correr torto,
anzi cozzaro a guisa di montoni:
quel del guerrier pagan morì di corto,
ch'era vivendo in numero de' buoni:
quell'altro cadde ancor, ma fu risorto
tosto ch'al fianco si sentì gli sproni.
Quel del re saracin restò disteso
adosso al suo signor con tutto il peso.

# Orlando furioso

*Canto 1*

60

Into the forest comes a warrior
who seems like a powerful and fierce man:
dressed in white like the snow,
a white plume for a crest.
King Sacripante, who can't endure
this pest whose path
interrupted his pleasure,
looked at the guilty one with disdain.

61

As he drew nearer, he challenges him to battle—
and really thinks he makes him lose his saddle.
I can't say of him other than he's worth
a grain less, and he'll prove his equal,
he threatens boldly to cut him in half,
goading him in a beat, with his lance ready.
Sacripante returns with a storm,
then they run head to head.

62

Neither lions nor bulls go to the field
confronting each other in such a raw mix
as two warriors in fierce battle
who likewise cross shields.
This collision shakes the lush valleys
and bare heights from bottom to top—
and well and perfect was
the armor that saved their breasts.

63

The horses didn't run a crooked path,
but ran like rams:
that of the pagan warrior died suddenly,
among the best horses while alive:
the other's fell again, but got up,
feeling spurs in his side.
That of the Saracen remained down
on top of his master with all his weight.

64

L'incognito campion che restò ritto,
e vide l'altro col cavallo in terra,
stimando avere assai di quel conflitto,
non si curò di rinovar la guerra;
ma dove per la selva è il camin dritto,
correndo a tutta briglia si disserra;
e prima che di briga esca il pagano,
un miglio o poco meno è già lontano.

70

Ella è gagliarda ed è più bella molto;
né il suo famoso nome anco t'ascondo:
fu Bradamante quella che t'ha tolto
quanto onor mai tu guadagnasti al mondo. –
Poi ch'ebbe così detto, a freno sciolto
il Saracin lasciò poco giocondo,
che non sa che si dica o che si faccia,
tutto avvampato di vergogna in faccia.

71

Poi che gran pezzo al caso intervenuto
ebbe pensato invano, e finalmente
si trovò da una femina abbattuto,
che pensandovi più, più dolor sente;
montò l'altro destrier, tacito e muto:
e senza far parola, chetamente
tolse Angelica in groppa, e differilla
a più lieto uso, a stanza più tranquilla.

64

The unknown champion, who stayed upright,
And saw the other on the ground with his horse,
judging to have had enough of that conflict,
didn't care to renew the fight—
but directly headed into the woods,
running full speed he disappears—
and before new trouble avoids the pagan,
a mile or less and he's long gone.

70

She is very powerful and more beautiful,
Nor does her famous name still conceal from you:
She was Bradamante who took away
all the honor you ever earned in the world. –
Since that was said, with the reins free,
The Saracen was little cheered,
because he didn't know what to say or do,
his face enflamed with shame.

71

When he thought vainly of a great part
of what happened and he finally
concluded he was bested by a woman—
for the more he thought, the more pain he felt—
he mounted the other horse, quite and mute:
and without saying a word, he quietly
took Angelica on horseback and carried her
to a happier end, to a quieter room.

*Canto 2*

31
Io parlo di quella inclita donzella,
per cui re Sacripante in terra giacque,
che di questo signor degna sorella,
    del duca Amone e di Beatrice nacque.
    La gran possanza e il molto ardir di quella
non meno a Carlo e a tutta Francia piacque
(che più d'un paragon ne vide saldo),
che 'l lodato valor del buon Rinaldo.

32
La donna amata fu da un cavalliero
che d'Africa passò col re Agramante,
che partorì del seme di Ruggiero
la disperata figlia di Agolante:
e costei, che né d'orso né di fiero
leone uscì, non sdegnò tal amante;
ben che concesso, fuor che vedersi una
volta e parlarsi, non ha lor Fortuna.

33
Quindi cercando Bradamante già
l'amante suo, ch'avea nome dal padre,
così sicura senza compagnia,
come avesse in sua guardia mille squadre:
e fatto ch'ebbe al re di Circassia
battere il volto dell'antiqua madre,
traversò un bosco, e dopo il bosco un monte,
tanto che giunse ad una bella fonte.

34
La fonte discorrea per mezzo un prato,
d'arbori antiqui e di bell'ombre adorno,
Ch'i viandanti col mormorio grato
a ber invita e a far seco soggiorno:
un culto monticel dal manco lato
le difende il calor del mezzo giorno.
Quivi, come i begli occhi prima torse,
d'un cavallier la giovane s'accorse;

Canto 2

31
I speak of that celebrated young woman,
from whom King Sacripante lay on the ground,
the worthy sister of this lord,
born of Duke Amone and Beatrice.
Her great power and passion
pleased no less than Charles and all France
(who saw in her more than an equal),
than the praised bravery of the good Rinaldo.

32
The woman was loved by a cavalier
who came from Africa with King Agramante,
who came from the seed of Ruggiero
and the hopeless daughter of Agolante:
and she, who came from neither bear
nor lion, did not scorn such a lover—
good that she conceded, beyond seeing each other
one time and speaking, they had no luck.

33
So Bradamante was searching
for her lover, who had the name of his father,
so secure without company,
as if guarded by a thousand squadrons:
and she who made the king of Circassia
bow his face to old mother earth,
crossed a forest, and after the forest a mountain,
until she reached a beautiful fountain.

34
The fountain flowed from the middle of a field,
by ancient trees and beautiful shades adorned,
and passersby with pleasant murmuring
invites to pass the time with her:
a cultivated hill on the left side
defends the heat of the midday sun.
Here, as her beautiful eyes turn,
the young girl is aware of a cavalier—

35

d'un cavallier, ch'all'ombra d'un boschetto,
nel margin verde e bianco e rosso e giallo
sedea pensoso, tacito e soletto
sopra quel chiaro e liquido cristallo.
Lo scudo non lontan pende e l'elmetto
dal faggio, ove legato era il cavallo;
ed avea gli occhi molli e 'l viso basso,
e si mostrava addolorato e lasso.

36

Questo disir, ch'a tutti sta nel core,
de' fatti altrui sempre cercar novella,
fece a quel cavallier del suo dolore
la cagion domandar da la donzella.
Egli l'aperse e tutta mostrò fuore,
dal cortese parlar mosso di quella,
e dal sembiante altier, ch'al primo sguardo
gli sembrò di guerrier molto gagliardo.

*Canto 22*

31

Ma mi bisogna, s'io vo' dirvi il resto,
ch'io trovi Ruggier prima e Bradamante.
Poi che si tacque il corno, e che da questo
loco la bella coppia fu distante,
guardò Ruggiero, e fu a conoscer presto
quel che fin qui gli avea nascoso Atlante:
fatto avea Atlante che fin a quell'ora
tra lor non s'eran conosciuti ancora.

32

Ruggier riguarda Bradamante, ed ella
riguarda lui con alta maraviglia,
che tanti dì l'abbia offuscato quella
illusion sì l'animo e le ciglia.
Ruggiero abbraccia la sua donna bella,
che più che rosa ne divien vermiglia;
e poi di su la bocca i primi fiori
cogliendo vien dei suoi beati amori.

35

of a cavalier, who in the shade of the wood,
on the edge green, white, red and yellow
was seated thoughtful, quiet and quite alone
above that clear and crystal liquid.
His shield hanging not far away and his helmet
from the beech, where he tied his horse—
with soaked eyes and head low,
he seemed tired and to suffer.

36

This desire, that is in everyone's heart,
of always wanting to know everyone else's business,
made the maiden ask of
the cavalier's suffering.
He opened up and revealed everything,
moved by her courteous speech,
and lofty demeanor, who at first glance,
seemed to him that of a powerful warrior.

*Canto 22*

31

But it's necessary for me to tell you the rest,
that I found Ruggiero and Bradamante.
After the horn quieted and the
beautiful couple was far from this place,
Ruggiero looked and was to know
that which until then Atlante concealed from him:
until that moment Atlante determined
hat they shouldn't know each other again.

32

Ruggiero looked at Bradamante and she
looked at him with wonder,
because for many days that deception had
so obscured mind and eyes.
Ruggiero embraced his beautiful lady,
who more than a rose blushed deeper—
and then from her mouth gathers
the first flowers of their blessed affections.

33
Tornaro ad iterar gli abbracciamenti
mille fiate, ed a tenersi stretti
i duo felici amanti, e sì contenti,
ch'a pena i gaudi lor capiano i petti.
Molto lor duol che per incantamenti,
mentre che fur negli errabondi tetti,
tra lor non s'eran mai riconosciuti,
e tanti lieti giorni eran perduti.

34
Bradamante, disposta di far tutti
i piaceri che far vergine saggia
debbia ad un suo amator, sì che di lutti,
senza il suo onore offendere, il sottraggia;
dice a Ruggier, se a dar gli ultimi frutti
lei non vuol sempre aver dura e selvaggia,
la faccia domandar per buoni mezzi
al padre Amon: ma prima si battezzi.

35
Ruggier, che tolto avria non solamente
viver cristiano per amor di questa,
com'era stato il padre, e antiquamente
l'avolo e tutta la sua stirpe onesta;
ma, per farle piacere, immantinente
data le avria la vita che gli resta:
– Non che ne l'acqua (disse), ma nel fuoco
per tuo amor porre il capo mi fia poco. –

33
They returned to their embrace
a thousand times, and held each other tightly,
the two happy lovers, and so content,
that their breasts barely held their joy.
But their suffering, the result of witchcraft,
while they were under the wrong roof,
they couldn't recognize one another
and lost many happy days.

34
Bradamante—disposed to give all
the pleasures a knowing virgin
would owe to her lover, ridding
his suffering without offending her honor—
says to Ruggiero, if he wants the ultimate fruits,
she doesn't want to always be hard and distant,
with good heart he could ask
her father: but first he must get baptized.

35
Ruggiero, who would have not only taken away
the Christian life for the love of her,
as had his father, and further back,
his grandfather and all his noble family line—
but to please her, immediately
would give what life he had:
"Not only in water," he said, "but in fire
would I put my little head for your love."

*Canto 32*

13
Di qua di là va le noiose piume
tutte premendo, e mai non si riposa.
Spesso aprir la finestra ha per costume,
per veder s'anco di Titon la sposa
sparge dinanzi al matutino lume
il bianco giglio e la vermiglia rosa:
non meno ancor, poi che nasciuto è 'l giorno,
brama vedere il ciel di stelle adorno.

14
Poi che fu quattro o cinque giorni appresso
il termine a finir, piena di spene
stava aspettando d'ora in ora il messo
che le apportasse: - Ecco Ruggier che viene. -
Montava sopra un'alta torre spesso,
ch'i folti boschi e le campagne amene
scopria d'intorno, e parte de la via
onde di Francia a Montalban si gìa.

15
Se di lontano o splendor d'arme vede,
o cosa tal ch'a cavallier simiglia,
che sia il suo disiato Ruggier crede,
e rasserena i begli occhi e le ciglia;
se disarmato o viandante a piede,
che sia messo di lui speranza piglia:
e se ben poi fallace la ritrova,
pigliar non cessa una ed un'altra nuova.

16
Credendolo incontrar, talora armossi,
scese dal monte e giù calò nel piano;
né lo trovando, si sperò che fossi
per altra strada giunto a Montalbano:
e col disir con ch'avea i piedi mossi
fuor del castel, ritornò dentro invano.
Né qua né là trovollo; e passò intanto
il termine aspettato da lei tanto.

*Canto 32*

13

Here and there rolling in
her feather bed with no rest,
often opening the window,
as was her way, to see if Tithon's spouse
lays before the morning light
the white lily and red rose:
no less still when the day is born,
she wants to see the sky adorned with stars.

14

After the next four or five days
came to pass, full of hope,
she waited each moment for the messenger
who would bring to her: "It's Ruggiero who comes."
Often she climbed a high tower
scouring the thick woods and pleasant fields
all around—and the part of the road
that lies on the way to Montalban in France.

15

If from afar she sees the flashing of armor
or something that resembles a knight,
she believes it's her desired Ruggiero,
and she clears her beautiful eyes and lashes—
if unarmed and on foot
the messenger would take hope away:
and if she finds him again false,
she doesn't stop looking at each new one.

16

Believing to have seen him, sometimes armed,
she descended from on high down into the valley—
and not finding him, she hoped he would be
arriving on another road from Montalbano:
and from the desire that made her move her feet
outside the castle, she returned in vain.
Neither here nor there did she find him—meanwhile that season
passed so anticipated by her.

17
Il termine passò d'uno, di dui,
di tre giorni, di sei, d'otto e di venti;
né vedendo il suo sposo, né di lui
sentendo nuova, incominciò lamenti
ch'avrian mosso a pietà nei regni bui
quelle Furie crinite di serpenti;
e fece oltraggio a' begli occhi divini,
al bianco petto, all'aurei crespi crini.

30
Ma come poi soggiunse, una donzella
esser nel campo, nomata Marfisa,
che men non era che gagliarda, bella,
né meno esperta d'arme in ogni guisa;
che lei Ruggiero amava e Ruggiero ella,
ch'egli da lei, ch'ella da lui divisa
si vedea raro, e ch'ivi ognuno crede
che s'abbiano tra lor data la fede;

31
e che come Ruggier si faccia sano,
il matrimonio publicar si deve;
e ch'ogni re, ogni principe pagano
gran piacere e letizia ne riceve,
    che de l'uno e de l'altro sopraumano
conoscendo il valor, sperano in breve
far una razza d'uomini da guerra
la più gagliarda che mai fosse in terra;

32
credea il Guascon quel che dicea, non senza
cagion; che ne l'esercito de' Mori
openione e universal credenza,
e publico parlar n'era di fuori.
I molti segni di benivolenza
stati tra lor facean questi romori;
che tosto o buona o ria che la fama esce
fuor d'una bocca, in infinito cresce.

17

The time passed one, two,
three days, six, eight and twenty—
she didn't see her spouse, nor hearing
news from him, she began a lament
that would have moved in the dark realm
those Furies who had hair of snakes—
and made outrage to those beautiful divine eyes,
to that white breast and golden tresses.

30

Then someone remarked, a young lady,
named Marfisa, came to the camp,
who wasn't less beautiful than powerful,
nor less expert in every type of arms—
that she loved Ruggiero and Ruggiero her,
that he from her and she from him
rarely apart, that there everyone believes
they have pledged to one another—

31

and that since she has made Ruggiero healthy,
their marriage will have to happen—
and that every king and pagan prince
will receive great pleasure and happiness from it—
because knowing the power of one and
of the other, they hope quickly
to make a race of warriors
more powerful than were ever on earth—

32

she believed what the Gascon said, without
doubt—a universal belief and opinion
throughout the Moorish army,
and public discussion was out and about.
The many signs of happiness
between them created these rumors—
that bold or good or bad, the renown that comes
from such a voice, is believed by all.

33

L'esser venuta a' Mori ella in aita
con lui, né senza lui comparir mai,
avea questa credenza stabilita;
ma poi l'avea accresciuta pur assai,
ch'essendosi del campo già partita
portandone Brunel (come io contai),
senza esservi d'alcuno richiamata,
sol per veder Ruggier v'era tornata.

34

Sol per lui visitar, che gravemente
languia ferito, in campo venuta era,
non una sola volta, ma sovente;
vi stava il giorno e si partia la sera:
e molto più da dir dava alla gente,
ch'essendo conosciuta così altiera,
che tutto 'l mondo a sé le parea vile,
solo a Ruggier fosse benigna e umile;

35

come il Guascon questo affermò per vero,
fu Bradamante da cotanta pena,
da cordoglio assalita così fiero,
che di quivi cader si tenne a pena.
Voltò, senza far motto, il suo destriero,
di gelosia, d'ira e di rabbia piena;
e da sé discacciata ogni speranza,
ritornò furibonda alla sua stanza.

49

Senza scudiero e senza compagnia
scese dal monte, e si pose in camino
verso Parigi alla più dritta via,
ove era dianzi il campo saracino;
che la novella ancora non s'udia,
che l'avesse Rinaldo paladino,
aiutandolo Carlo e Malagigi,
fatto tor da l'assedio di Parigi.

33

She brought the Moors aid
with him, and never appeared without him—
this was always known—
but then it grew even more,
that being gone from the camp and
returning Brunel, as I relate,
without being told by anyone,
only to see Ruggiero return.

34

She came to camp only to see him,
who seriously lay wounded,
not just once, but often—
she stayed the day and left at night:
and gave people a lot to talk about,
for being known as so proud,
that all the world seemed vile to her,
that only Ruggiero was gentle and humble—

35

as the Gascon affirmed this to be true,
Bradamante was in such pain,
assailed by such fierce grief,
she struggled to keep from falling.
She turned her horse, without moving a muscle,
full of jealousy, anger and rage—
any hope dispelled from her,
returning furious to her room.

49

Without shield and without company,
She descended the mountain and put herself
On the shortest route to Paris,
where the Saracen camp was—
because she had yet to hear
that paladin Rinaldo,
helping Charles and Malagigi,
had twisted Paris from the siege.

# Veronica Gambara
## (1485–1550)

Born in 1485 in Pratalboino near Brescia, Veronica was a refined, cultured and lofty intellect who befriended with the likes of B. Tasso, Pietro Aretino and Il Bandello. In 1509, she married Gilberto X, Lord of Correggio. She loved him and lamented his death in 1518. Picking up her husband's mantle of leadership, Veronica ruled wisely in a region in which courage, a sharp mind and subtle international relations were required. She led Correggio to military victory in thwarting the attack of Galeotto Pico della Mirandola in 1538. She died in Correggio in 1550. Her verse is characterized by a certain restraint resulting from a very intelligent, sensitive mind that embodies that Renaissance ideal of *festina lente*. Literally, "make haste slowly," understood to mean "don't act without thinking," a balance between the *vita activa* and *vita contemplativa*. *Occhi lucenti e belli* is a madrigal. *Sulla caducità dei beni tereni* is a poem of twenty-seven *ottave*, much in the tradition of the *momenti mori*, a reminder of the fleeting nature of both life and earthly pleasures.

## Veronica Gambara

1
Occhi lucenti e belli,
com'esser può che in medesmo istante
nascan da voi sí nove forme e tante?

Lieti, mesti, superbi, umili, alteri
vi mostrate in un punto, onde di speme
e di timor m'empiete,
e tanti effetti dolci, acerbi e fieri
nel core arso per voi vengono insieme
ad ognor che volete.
Or, poi che voi mia vita e morte sète,
occhi felici, occhi beati e cari,
siate sempre sereni, allegri e chiari.

*Stanze da Sulla caducità dei beni tereni*

1
Quando miro la terra ornata e bella
di mille vaghi ed odorati fiori,
e che, come nel ciel luce ogni stella,
cosí splendono in lei vari colori,
ed ogni fiera solitaria e snella,
mossa da naturale istinto, fuori
de' boschi uscendo e de l'antiche grotte,
va cercando il compagno e giorno e notte;

2
e quando miro le vestite piante
pur di bei fiori e di novelle fronde,
e de gli augelli le diverse e tante
odo voci cantar dolci e gioconde,
e con grato rumore ogni sonante
fiume bagnar le sue fiorite sponde,
tal che ci sè invaghita la natura
gode in mirar la bella sua fattura,

# Veronica Gambara

### 1

Eyes bright and beautiful,
how can it be that in this very moment
so many new forms come out of you?

Joyous, sad, arrogant, humble, proud
you show yourself all at once, giving me
hope and fear,
and other feelings sweet, bitter and fiery
from you who enters my burnt heart
any time you want.
Now, since you're my life and death,
happy eyes, eyes blessed and dear,
may you always be calm, cheery and clear.

*Lines from On the Transience of Earthly Goods*

### 1

When I see the earth adorned and beautiful
from thousands of wonderful and fragrant flowers,
and as light in every star of heaven
so splendid in its many colors,
with every beast sturdy and nimble,
moved by natural instinct, coming
out of the woods and ancient caves,
seeking a mate day and night,

### 2

and when I see the planted
dressed in beautiful blossoms and new greenery,
and many and diverse birds,
I hear sweet and happy voices singing,
and with every pleasant sound
the flowered river banks,
so that you fall in love with nature,
enjoying the beauty of her creation,

3
dico, fra me pensando: Ahi quanto è breve
questa nostra mortal misera vita!
Pur dianzi tutta piena era di neve
questa piaggia, or sì verde e sì fiorita;
e da un aer turbato, oscuro e greve
la bellezza del cielo era impedita;
e queste fiere vaghe ed amorose
stavan sole fra monti e boschi ascose.

. . . . . . . . . . . . . . . .

23
Di così bel desio l'anima accende
questa felice e gloriosa scorta,
che a le cose celesti spesso ascende,
e l'intelletto nostro seco porta;
tal che del cielo e di natura intende
gli alti secreti; onde poi, fatta accorta
quant'ogn'altro piacer men bello sia,
sol segue quella, e tutti gli altri oblia.

24
Quanti principi grandi, amati e cari
insieme con la vita han perso il nome!
Quanti poi vivon gloriosi e chiari,
poveri nati, sol perché le chiome
di sacri lauri, alteri doni e rari,
s'adornaro felici, ed ora come
chiare stelle fra noi spendon beati,
mentre 'l mondo sarà, sempre onorati!

. . . . . . . . . . . . . . . .

27
Dietro a l'orme di voi dunque, venendo,
ogni basso pensier posto in oblio,
seguirò la virtù, sempre credendo
esser, se non quest'un dolce desio,
fallace ogn'altro; e così non temendo
o nemica fortuna o destin rio,
starò con questa, ogn'altro ben lasciando,
l'anima e lei, mentre ch'io viva, amando.

3

I think to myself: Goodness, how brief
is our miserable mortal life!
Yet earlier this shore was covered
with snow, now so green and flowered—
and from strong winds, dark and heavy,
the beauty of the sky was hidden—
and these beautiful and lustful beasts
were hidden in the mountains and woods.

. . . . . . . . . . . . . . . .

23

With this beautiful desire the soul ignites
This happy and glorious escort, virtue,
often ascends to heavenly things
and takes our minds with it—
because it understands the other secrets
of heaven and nature—whence made aware
how every other pleasure is less beautiful,
it follow only that on, forgetting the others.

24

How many great princes, loved and dear
in this life are now forgotten!
how many lived glorious and pure lives,
born poor, only because the leaves
the sacred laurel, proud and rare gifts,
adorned the happy—and how
clear stars spread blessing among us,
while the world is always honored so!

. . . . . . . . . . . . . . . .

27

In your footsteps I will walk,
forgetting every base thought,
I will follow virtue, always believing
this sweet desire and consider
others false—therefore I don't fear
bad fortune or evil destiny,
I will stay with this, leaving all other things behind,
my soul and virtue, while I am alive, loving.

# Vittoria Colonna
## (1492–1547)

The woman Michelangelo would call "Un uomo in una donna, anzi un dio" in one of his poems was born in the Castle of Marino on the Alban hills outside Rome. Daughter of Fabrizio Colonna, a prince and famous military man, and Agnese di Montefeltro, Vittoria married Ferrante Francesco d'Avalos, Marquis of Pescara, who also militarily served Holy Roman Emperor Charles V. Because Charles V was at war with Francis I of France, Ferrante was frequently away from home on military campaigns. The time they did spend together was quite happy, but short-lived, with Ferrante mortally wounded at the battle of Pavia in 1525. Childless, Vittoria passed the rest of her life engaged in dutiful and independent causes. She raised her husband's orphaned cousin, Alfonso del Vasto, as their heir. With such reformers as Valdès, Ochino and Carnesecchi, she participated an Italian evangelical movement that recognized the abuses and materialism of both Papacy and Church. She also maintained strong intellectual relationships with many of the era's most prestigious literati: Bembo, Aretino, Castiglione, Milza and Ariosto. Sometime by the mid-1530s, she developed a deep and loving relationship with Michelangelo, with whom she exchanged letters, poems and intimate conversations.

Perhaps missing the point, Muscetta and Ponchirolli diminish her verse as "a monochord and monotonous development, that, although sustained by a knowledgeable literary artifice, never succeeds in achieving a climate of true poetry, so constrained in austerity and, in the end, by suffocating thematic variations." Much closer are Stortoni and Lillie, who characterize her verse as "complex, intellectual and replete with many unusual conceits and rhetorical figures for which she was greatly admired." F.W. Bautz observes that "her lyric, whose main theme is the pain over the loss of her husband, belongs to the pearls of world literature and to the most complete expressions of Christian piety. Vittoria Colonna recognized how necessary it was that the Church be renewed from the inside, and tried to contribute to such." To appreciate this verse, a reader should bear in mind that Colonna's context was Italy ravaged by the foreign armies of Charles V and Francis I, Rome having been raped in 1527 and the Church losing half its holdings and adherents to ideas of Luther and the politics of the Reformation. In short, it was a time of loss, invasion, mass violence and retrenchment. Her verse was an attempt to transcend and make sense of these miseries. Hence, it embodies a quality produced by a high intellect, moral sincerity and aesthetic sensitivity. Our selections are from Vittoria's *Rime amorose* and also her *Rime spirituali*. *Perché del Tauro l'infiammato corno* is in the tradition of the *momento mori*, here a reminder of not only mortality, but also of the reality of the inner soul not nurtured by stereotypical "sanguine" social settings. The fist three sonnets are from her *Rime amorose*. *A quale strazio la mi vita adduce* is a bittersweet, erotic remembrance of her Ferrante. *Quando già stanco il mio dolce pensiero* deals with sweet memories and the bitter present. *Qual digiuno augellin* is from her *Rime spirituali*.

1

Perché del Tauro l'infiammato corno
mandi virtú, che con novei colori
orni la terra de' suoi vaghi fiori,
e piú bello rimeni Apollo il giorno;

e perch'io veggia fonte o prato adorno
di leggiadre alme e pargoletti amori,
o dotti spiriti a' piè de' sacri allori
con chiare note aprir l'aere d'intorno;

non s'allegra il cor tristo, o punto sgombra
della cura mortal che sempre il preme,
sí le mie pene son tenaci e sole:

ché quanta gioia lieti amanti ingombra,
e quanto qui diletta, il mio bel sole
con l'alma luce sua m'ascose insieme.


2

A quale strazio la mi vita adduce
Amor, che oscuro il chiaro sol mi rende,
e nel mio petto al suo apparire accende
maggior disio della mia vaga luce!

Tutto il bel che natura a noi produce,
che tanto aggrada a chi men vede e intende,
piú di pace mi toglie e sí m'offende,
ch'a' piú caldi sospir mi riconduce.

Se verde prato e se fior vari miro,
priva d'ogni speranza trema l'alma:
ché rinverde il pensier del suo bel frutto

che morte svelse. A lui la grave salma
tolse un dolce e brevissimo sospiro,
e a me lasciò l'amaro eterno lutto.

1

Because the inflamed horns of Taurus
send power that adorns the earth with
the new colors of their lovely flowers,
and Apollo reawakens a more beautiful day—

and because I see springs and fields adorned
with beautiful souls and childhood loves,
and gifted spirits at the foot of sacred laurels
with clear notes filling the air everywhere—

the sad heart isn't cheered, or cleansed of the question
of mortal care that always burdens it,
such are my pains tenacious and alone:

for so much joy fills happy lovers,
and how much here they delight, my beautiful sun
together with its light hides my soul.


2

To whatever torment Love leads
my life, the clear sun turns me dark,
and in my breast his appearance lights
great desire of my eager eyes!

All the beauty that nature gives us,
that pleases more who sees and hears less,
provokes and offends me more than peace,
bringing me back to the hottest desires.

If I look at green meadows and many flowers,
my soul trembles, empty of all hope:
because blooming again the thought of his beautiful fruit,

that death uprooted. The heavy burden
takes a sweet and too brief sigh from him,
and leaves me the bitter and eternal grief.

3
Quando già stanco il mio dolce pensiero
del suo felice corso giunge a riva,
dimostra il sonno poi l'immagin viva,
con altro inganno piú simile al vero.

Qual fa coi sogni bianco il giorno nero,
Questo d'oscuità la notte priva,
E se già l'aprir gli occhi mi nodriva,
Il chiuderli ora è cagion ch'io non pèro.

E se col tempo il gran martir s'avanza,
Piú salda ognor nella memoria siede
Col sonno e col pensier l'alma sembianza.

E 'l proprio ardor rinnova la mercede:
Ché se fuggi il piacere e la speranza,
Con maggior forza allor s'armò la fede.


4
Qual digiuno augellin, che vede ed ode
batter l'ali a la madre intorno quando
li reca il nudrimento, ond'egli amando
il cibo e quella si rellegra e gode,

e dentro al nido suo si strugge e rode
per desio di seguirla anch'ei volando,
e la ringrazia, in tal modo cantando
che par ch'oltra il poter la lingua snode;

tal io, qualor il caldo raggio e vivo
del divin Sole onde nudrisco il core
più de l'usato lucido lampeggia,

movo la penna, mossa da l'amore
interno, e senza ch'io stessa m'aveggia
di quell ch'io dico le Sue lodi scrivo.

3

When my sweet but now tired thoughts
of his happy life have reached the shore,
sleep shows his live image
with a deception more genuine than the real one.

What the dark day does with clear dreams,
the night takes away this confusion,
and if opening my eyes nourishes me,
closing them now is the reason that I don't die.

And if great suffering advances with time,
clearer in my sleeping and waking memory sits
the semblance of his soul.

And true passion renews mercy:
because if pleasure and hope leave,
faith then arms herself with major force.


4

That hungry little bird, who sees and bats
his wings at his mother when
she gives him food: he loves
the food and she is heartened and enjoys it.

And in the nest, he pines and gnaws
in wanting to follow her, to fly, even—
and he thanks her, singing in such a way
that it appears he persuades beyond the power of language—

such am I, provided the warm and alive rays
of the divine sun by which I nourish my heart
more than the old light of the shining lamp—

I move my pen, moved by inner
love and, without realizing
what I say, I write his praises.

# Giovanni Guidiccioni
## (1500–1541)

In his brief life Giovanni Guidiccioni, humanist and legalist, rose not only to a position of eminence within the Church, but also earned a reputation for honesty and integrity. In addition to entrusting him with high level diplomatic, administrative and political tasks, Paul III nominated him Governor of Rome and later made him the Bishop of Fossombrone. While serving as the latter, his calm caused a would-be assassin to drop to his knees and beg Guidiccione's forgiveness. His prose letters, the *Lettere di negozi,* document the political events of his time. In his *Oration to the Republic of Lucca* from 1533, Giovanni sympathizes with and laments the brutally violent response to the rebellion of the so-called *straccioni* (the Ragamuffins), common families who revolted against the Lucchese nobility because they wanted to participate in communal government. However, Guidiccioni's highest achievement is considered a handful of sonnets that he wrote between 1526 and 1530 on the pitiful state of affairs in Italy after the invasion of Charles V, the Holy Roman Emperor, and the subsequent Sack of Rome in 1527. The sonnet *Degna nutrice* laments the suffering of the people of Rome during the Sack. *Il non più udito* is a vivid description of the suffering of Rome during the Sack. *Vera fama* is an epistolary sonnet to Guidiccioni's friend Vincenzo Buonvisi, dissuading him from returning to Italy in 1528-29. He even exchanged sonnets with Vittoria Colonna. An interesting aside is that his secretary and friend was Annibale Caro, noted translator of Virgil's *Aeneid* into Italian.

## Giovanni Guidiccioni

1
Degna nutrice de le chiare genti,
ch'a' dí men foschi trïonfar del mondo;
albergo già di Dio fido e giocondo,
or di lagrime tristi e di lamenti;

come posso udir io lo tue dolenti
voci, e mirar, senza dolor profondo,
il sommo imperio tuo caduto al fondo,
tante sue pompe e tanti pregi spenti?

Tal, cosí ancella, maestà riserbi,
e sí dentro al mio cor suona il tuo nome,
che i tuoi sparsi vestigi inchino e adoro.

Che fu a vederti in tanti onor superba
seder reina e incoronata d'oro
le glorïose venerabil chiome!


2
Il non piú udito e gran pubblico danno,
le morti, l'onte e le querele sparte
d'Italia, ch'io pur piango in queste carte,
empieran di pietà quei che verrano.

Quanti, sio dritto stimo, ancor diranno:
—O nati a' peggior anni in miglior parte!—
quanti movransi a vendicarne in parte
del barbarico oltraggio e de l'inganno!

Non avrà l'ozio pigro e 'l viver molle
loco in quei saggi ch'anderan col sano
pensier al corso de gli onori eterno;

ch'assai col nostro sangue avemo il folle
error purgato di color che in mano
di sí belle contrade hanno il governo.

# Giovanni Guidiccioni

1
Worthy nurse of the beautiful people
that ruled the world in less gloomy times—
faithful and happy home of God,
now of sad tears and laments—

how can I hear your suffering
voices and look at, without deep sorrow,
your great empire fallen in the depths,
your extinguished pomp and worth?

Such—like this handmaid—discrete majesty,
for your name so rings in my heart
that I kneel and adore your scattered vestiges.

What it was to see you in such honor,
sitting as proud queen, your glorious tresses
crowned with gold!


2
The unheard cries and great public destruction,
the deaths, the disgraces and widespread tears
of Italy that I too lament in these pages,
may they fill those who succeed us with pity.

How many, if I guess right, still shout:
"O new born in the best part of the worst years!"
how many will stir to partially avenge us
against the barbaric outrage and treachery!

Laziness and the soft life will have no
place in these trials that will travel with somber
thought on the road to eternal honor,

for we have purged with enough of our blood
the stupid error of those who have the government
of such a beautiful country in their hands.

3

Vera fama fra i tuoi più cari sona
ch'al paese natio passar da quelle
quete contrade ov'or dimori e belle
(né spiar so perché) disio ti sprona.

Qui sol d'ira e di morte si ragiona,
qui l'alme son d'ogni pietà rubelle,
qui i pianti e i gridi van sovra le stelle,
e non piú al buon ch'al rio Marte perdona.

Qui vedrai campi solitari, nudi,
e sterpi e spine invece d'erbe e fiori,
e nel piú verde april canuto berno;

qui vomeri e le falci in via piú cridi
ferri converse, e pien d'ombre e d'orrori
questo di vivi doloroso inferno.

3

True news rings among your most dear
that a desire urges you to pass from that
quiet and beautiful country where you now live
(I don't know to explain why) to your fatherland.

Here we talk only of anger and death,
here souls are rebels against every mercy,
here cries and shouts reach beyond the stars,
and Mars doesn't pardon the good more than the wicked.

Here you will see deserted fields, barren,
and weeds and thorns instead of grass and flowers—
and in the ripest April, white-haired winter.

Here the plows and sickles convert to more
cruel tools—and full of shadows and horrors
this suffering inferno of life.

# Giovanni della Casa
# (1503–1556)

Giovanni della Casa, man of letters, was born in the small town of Mugello, near Florence. He studied in Bologna and in 1529 he took minor religious orders. He went to Rome in 1530. In 1544 he became the Archbishop of Benevento, but never took the position because he was sent to Venice as Papal Nuncio. During his career he worked strongly to repress heresy, perhaps hoping to gain a cardinalship for his efforts. He was nominated secretary of state by Paul IV in 1555. As a man of letters, Della Casa is noted for some youthful satirical rhymes in the style of Francesco Berni. Between 1550-55 he wrote *Galateo*, a treatise on the thoughts and manners necessary for both polite society and civilization. He named the work for his friend who suggested the undertaking to him, Bishop Galeazzo Florimonte. The selections in this volume are sonnets from Della Casa's *Rime*, considered by many to be the most original and poetic examples of Petrarchism – if that is possible – in Cinquecento Italian. These particular selections echo the melancholic sentiment of Petrarch's *Solo et pensoso*, with the poet choosing to be alone in order to meditate about feelings of self, solitude and the desire for poetic individuality.

## Giovanni della Casa

1

O sonno, o de la queta, umida, ombrosa
notte placido figlio; o de' mortali
egri conforto, oblio dolce de' mali
sì gravi, ond'è la vita aspra e noiosa;

soccorri al core omai, che langue e posa
non ave; e queste membra stanche e frali
solleva; a me ten vola, o sonno, e l'ali
tue brune sovra me distendi e posa.

Ov'è il silenzio, che 'l dì fugge e 'l lume?
E i lievi sogni, che non secure
vestigia di seguirti han per costume?

Lasso, che 'nvan te chiamo, e queste oscure
e gelide ombre invan lusingo: o piume
d'asprezza colme! o notti acerbe e dure!


2

Mendico e nudo piango, e de' miei danni
men vo la soma tardi omai contando
tra queste ombrose querce, e obliando
quel che già Roma m'insegnò molti anni.

Nè di gloria, onde par tanto s'affanni
umano studio, a me più cale, e quando
fallace il mondo veggio, a terra spando
ciascun suo dono, acciò più non m'inganni.

Quella leggiadra Colonnese e saggia
e bella e chiara, che coi raggi suoi
la luce dei Latin spenta riaccende,

nobil poeta canti e 'n guardia l'aggia;
chè l'umil cetra mia roca, che voi
udir chiedete, già dimessa pende.

# Giovanni della Casa

1
Oh, sleep, son of the quiet, dense,
dark night—oh, comfort of sick
mortals—I forget pleasure because of the
serious ills of a harsh and exhausting life—

help my heart now, so it doesn't weaken and
stop—and revive these tired, frail
members—fly with me, oh, sleep, and spread
and your sad wings over me.

Where is the silence that flees light and day?
And happy dreams with uncertain traces
that usually follow you?

Weary, in vain I call you, and in vain
I tempt these cold, dark shadows: o bed of
harshness with me! Oh, bitter, hard night!


2
Naked I wander and cry—and the worse for me—
faltering I go among these dark oaks
slowly counting the burden at length—forgetting
what Rome taught me many years ago.

Nor do I care for glory, for which it seems so much
human effort strives—and when
I see the deceitful world, I scatter the earth
with each of its gifts so I'm not deceived.

That graceful Colonna—wise,
beautiful and pure—she rekindles the extinguished
Latin light with her rays.

May the noble poet sing and be attentive,
for my humble, harsh lyre that you want
to hear hangs truly dispirited.

3

O dolce selva solitaria, amica
de' miei pensieri sbigottiti e stanchi,
mentre Borea ne' dì torbidi e manchi
d'orrido giel l'aere e la terra implica,

e la tua verde chioma ombrosa, antica,
come la mia, par d'ognintorno imbianchi;
or che 'n vece di fior vermigli e bianchi,
ha neve e ghiaccio ogni tua piaggia aprica;

a questa breve e nubilosa luce
vo ripensando, che m'avanza, e ghiaccio
gli spiriti anch'io sento e le membra farsi:

ma più di te dentro e dintorno agghiaccio;
che più crudo Euro a me mio verno adduce,
più lunga notte e dì più freddi e scarsi.


4

Questa vita mortal, che 'n una o 'n due
brevi e notturne ore trapassa, oscura
e fredda, involto avea fin qui la pura
parte di me ne l'altre nubi sue.

Or a mirar le grazie tante tue
prendo, che frutti e fior, gielo e arsura,
e sì dolce del ciel legge e misura,
eterno Dio, tuo magistero fue.

Anzi 'l dolce aer puro e questa luce
chiara, che 'l mondo a gli occhi nostri scopre,
traesti tu d'abissi oscuri e misti:

e tutto quel che 'n terra o 'n ciel riluce
di tenebre era chiuso, e tu l'apristi;
e 'l giorno e 'l sol de la tua man son opre.

3

O sweet, lonely forest, friend
of my terrified and exhausted thoughts,
while Borea in turbulent and blemished days
of horrendous freeze enmeshes the air and earth,

and your dark green leaves, ancient
like mine, are everywhere whitened;
now instead of red and white flowers,
every sunny hillside of yours has snow and ice;

I dwell on this short,
cloudy light that nears, freezing
my spirits and limbs:

Inside and out, I freeze more than you
because cruel Euro brings me winter,
a longer night—and colder, shorter days.


4

This mortal life, that in one or two
brief nocturnal hour passes, dark
and cold, has wrapped the pure
part of me in its horrible black clouds.

Now I begin to look at your
many graces: what fruits and flowers, cold and heat,
and such sweet law and measure of heaven—
Eternal God—from your mastery.

Rather the sweet pure air and this clear
light, that this world conceals from our eyes,
you pulled from the dark and mixed abyss:

and all that shines on earth and in heaven
was closed in darkness—and you opened them.
For the days and the sun are works of your hand.

# Annibale Caro
## (1507–1566)

Annibale Caro was born in Civitanova in Ancona in 1507. A student of the humanist Rodolfo Iracinto, he began his career under Giovanni Guidiccioni, bishop of Fossombrone. Later, he served an ecclesiastical position in Rome. While in Rome, Annibale was part of several literary academies, such as the Academia delle Virtù, the Academia dei Vignaiuoli, and the Academia della Nuova Poesia. Next, he became the secretary of Pier Luigi Farnese and, after Farnese became the Duke of Parma, Caro became his head of the administration of justice. During his lifetime he was friend with such notables as Benvenuto Cellini, Pietro Bembo and Bendetto Varchi. Among his literary works are his *Rime*, known for their ease and grace; *Gli Straccioni,* a comedy; translations from Aristotle and other ancient writers; letters under his own name and for the Farnese cardinals; and, his translation of Virgil's *The Aeneid* from Latin into Italian. Caro relied on the *verso sciolto*, blank verse, in rendering Virgil's epic poem about the founding of Rome by survivors of Troy into a contemporary and not archaic Italian. First Christopher Marlowe and then William Shakespeare innovated by using blank verse to tremendous advantage in their dramas. Caro's translation is still the primary text, along with the original Latin, in the Italian *liceo curriculum* for studying the *Aeneid*. The passage here is from the first few lines of the first book of *The Aeneid*. Given the invasions, the Sack of Rome in 1527, and the losses caused by the Reformation, one could see these initial lines, and in fact the entire poem, serving as a much needed *laudatores temporis acti* ("Praises of time past").

*Eneide*
*Da Libro Primo*

Quell'io che già tra selve e tra pastori
di Titiro sonai l'umil sampogna,
e che, de' boschi uscendo, a mano a mano
fei pingui e cólti i campi, e pieni i vóti
d'ogn'ingordo colono, opra che forse
agli agricoli è grata; ora di Marte
l'armi canto e 'l valor del grand'eroe
che pria da Troia, per destino, a i liti
d'Italia e di Lavinio errando venne;
e quanto errò, quanto sofferse, in quanti
e di terra e di mar perigli incorse,
come il traea l'insuperabil forza
del cielo, e di Giunon l'ira tenace;
e con che dura e sanguinosa guerra
fondò la sua cittade, e gli suoi dèi
ripose in Lazio: onde cotanto crebbe
il nome de' Latini, il regno d'Alba,
e le mura e l'imperio alto di Roma.
Musa, tu che di ciò sai le cagioni,
tu le mi detta. Qual dolor, qual onta
fece la dea ch'è pur donna e regina
de gli altri dèi, sí nequitosa ed empia
contra un sí pio? Qual suo nume l'espose
per tanti casi a tanti affanni? Ahi! tanto
possono ancor là su l'ire e gli sdegni?
Grande, antica, possente e bellicosa
colonia de' Fenici era Cartago,
posta da lunge incontr'Italia e 'ncontra
a la foce del Tebro: a Giunon cara
sí, che le fûr men care ed Argo e Samo.
Qui pose l'armi sue, qui pose il carro,
qui di porre avea già disegno e cura
(se tale era il suo fato) il maggior seggio,
e lo scettro anco universal del mondo.

*The Aeneid*
*From Book One*

That I, among the woods and shepherds,
played my humble bagpipe of Titiro,
and that, coming out of the woods, as they
made their fields rich and cultivated, and with full
marks of every well-fed farmer, work that perhaps
to the farmers is pleasant—now I sing of
the arms of Mars and the valor of the great hero,
first of Troy, by destiny, to the shores
of Italy and Lavinio were wandering—
and how he wandered, how he suffered, how many
dangers he ran into on land and sea,
as if the insurmountable force of tenacious
wrath of heaven and Juno dragged him—
and through hard and bloody wars
he founded his city, and his gods
rested in Lazio: where they created
the name of the Latins, the reign of Alba,
and the walls and lofty empire of Rome.
Muse, you who know the causes of it,
you have told me them. What suffering, what dishonor
made the goddess, who is both the lady and queen
of the other gods, so capricious and cruel
against one so pious? How did his deity expose
him so many times to so much suffering? Alas, how
could so much anger and disdain come from on high?
The great, powerful and warlike
colony of the Phoenicians was Carthage,
located along Italy and
the mouth of the Tiber: so dear to
Juno, that Argos and Samos were less dear to her.
Here were her arms, here stood her chariot,
Here she took great care to design
(if it was her doing) the great seat
and scepter still universal of the world.

# Luigi Tansillo
# (1510–1568)

Considered one of the major heirs of the Neopolitan literary tradition, Luigi Tansillo worked for most of his life in the service of the Neopolitan Vice Regent Pietro di Toledo and his son Garcia. Possessing an idyllic temperament, Tansillo wrote with an almost conversational ease developing metaphors of nature into near Baroque conceits. In addition to sonnets, Tansillo wrote other works of poetry, among which was his *Il Vendemmiatore* (The Grapepicker, 1532), which in 1559 was put on the Catholic Church's Index *Librorum Prohibitorum* (List of Forbidden Books) for its alleged obscenity. In the two sonnets presented in this anthology, Tansillo uses rather common metaphors for his own personalized expression. In the first, he develops the metaphor of flying to equate the feeling of being in love with something that is ecstatic, celestial and unattainable. In the second, nature becomes, by means of the pathetic fallacy, the timbre by which Tansillo communicates both his alienation and his resolve. The extent to which he develops a series of metaphors around one central theme is not as marked as in Baroque poetry. Readers should note that the Baroque conceit is the main idea in a work of art, music or literature built around a metaphor to which all elements, including subsidiary metaphors, contribute. In English poetry John Donne was perhaps its most famous exponent. In the 20th century, T.S. Eliot was strongly influenced by the conceitful element of Baroque (or what came to be called Metaphysical) poetry.

## Luigi Tansillo

1
Amor m'impenna l'ale, e tanto in alto
le spiega l'animoso mio pensiero,
che, ad ora ad ora sormontando, spero
a le porte del ciel far novo assalto.

Tem'io, qualor giú guardo, il vol tropp'alto,
ond'ei mi grida e mi promette altero,
che, s'al superbo vol cadendo, io pèro,
l'onor fia etterno, se mortal è il salto.

Che s'altri, cui disio simil compunse,
diè nome eterno al mar col suo morire,
ove l'ardite penne il sol disgiunse,

ancor di me le genti potran dire:
—Quet'aspirò a le stelle, e s'ei non giunse,
la vita venne men, ma non l'ardire.


2
Strane rupi, aspri monti, alte tremanti
ruine, e sassi al ciel nudi e scoperti,
ove a gran pena pòn salir tant'erti
nuvoli in questo fosco aere fumanti;

superbo orror, tacite selve, e tanti
negri antri erbosdi in rotte pietr aperti;
abbandonati, sterili deserti,
ov'han paura andar le belve erranti;

a guisa d'uom, che per soverchia pena
il cor triste ange, fuor di senno uscito,
sen va piangendo, ove il furor lo mena,

vo piangendo io tra voi: e se partito
non cangia il ciel, con voce assai piú piena
sarò di là tra le meste ombre udito.

## Luigi Tansillo

1
Love fledges my wings and high above
my courageous thought spreads them,
so, always rising higher, I expect
to make a new assault on the doors of heaven.

I fear, when I look down, of flying too high,
whence my thought shouts to me and promises me loftiness—
so, if falling from my proud flight, I perish,
the honor will be eternal, even though the fall is mortal.

If the other one [Icarus], pricked with the same desire,
gave an eternal name to the sea with his death,
where the sun dissolves daring feathers,

people will still be able to say of me:
"This one aspired to the stars, and if he did not
reach them, his life faded, but not his daring.

2
Unknown cliffs, rough mountains, high trembling
ruins—naked, bare stones in the sky,
where so many steep clouds can climb this
dark smoky wind with great pain...

Lofty dread, secret groves and so many
dark overgrown caves between the broken stones—
abandoned, barren deserts,
where wild animals are afraid to go...

Like man, whose heart aches
from excessive pain, out of his mind,
wandering in tears, where passion leads him...

...crying I wander among you: and if my will
can't change the sky, with full voice I will
be heard among the sad shades down there...

# John Milton
# (1608–1674)

At first glance seemingly beyond the scope of this volume, John Milton, one of the greatest English poets, mastered many foreign and ancient languages. Among his study and creativity in this realm, we have his translations of the *Psalms* from ancient Hebrew, *Elegies* written in Latin and even five sonnets, plus a canzone, written in Italian. Born in Cheapside in London to John and Sara Milton, young John was tutored in classical languages. He attended Cambridge, from which he was suspended for arguing with a tutor, but eventually returned, earning his M.A. In 1638 he began a European 'Grand Tour,' a significant part of which took him to Italy. While there, Milton explained that he was formulating an epic poem that he planned to write in Latin. The Italians convinced him to write in the manner that had been championed by Dante over three centuries earlier – that is, in his own vernacular. The result was a string of epic masterpieces in English: *Paradise Lost, Paradise Regained* and *Samson Agonistes*. In a sense, it is fitting to conclude this volume with a sonnet by John Milton, as it demonstrates the earlier part of the centuries of influence Italian late medieval and Renaissance poetry will have on world literature.

## John Milton

Giovane piano, e semplicetto amante,
poiché fuggir me stesso in dubbio sono,
Madonna, a voi del mio cuor l'umil dono
faró divoto; io certo a prove tante

l'ebbi fedele, intrepido, costante,
di pensieri leggiadro, accorto, e buono.
Quando rugge il gran mondo, e scocca il tuono,
s'arma di se, e d'intero diamante,

tanto del forse, e d'invidia sicuro,
di timori, e speranze al popol use,
quando d'ingegno, e d'alto valor vago,

e di cetra sonora, e delle Muse:
sol troverete in tal parte men duro
ove Amor mise l'insanabil ago.